The Other Side of the Road:
A Pool Hustler's Tale

by
Alf Taylor

Also available through Alf Taylor Productions

DVD's:

Eddie Taylor and the Legends of Pool

**Johnny Archer / Efren Reyes...Shootout in the Rockies
9 ball and 8 ball**

Please visit **www.alftaylor.com** for more information
and availability on these and other products

The Other Side of the Road: A Pool Hustler's Tale

Copyright © 2011 Alf Taylor

Proudly printed in the USA

Printed by Arizona Lithographers

ACKNOWLEDGEMENTS

"There's nothing more exhilarating than being shot at and missed."
(Anonymous)

Wow! Where do I begin? For starters, I'd like to thank all the people whose money I won over the years who let me get away with all my digits intact. It's difficult to type without thumbs.

Then there are the numerous people who assisted me, whom I haven't robbed with my cue: Some of them took the pictures so invaluable to tell my stories. Others loaned me otherwise unobtainable images of billiard history: Thank you. Bill Porter, an old pool crony of mine who went on to become a college professor, contacted me after a forty-year hiatus and helped turn my stack of stories into a book by treating me like one of his pupils. He's strict, but oh so competent. Bill also contributed a story of his own to the publication that proves he could have been a good hustler had he not escaped the dark side to nourish minds.

My main stream, more educated brother, Jay, who turned a lot of my three letter words into five or six cannot be overlooked. If you enjoy the book, we all owe him thanks. Brother Jack, whom you will read a lot about and who taught me to be a good manager and kept me from getting my head torn off multiple times during my pool period, has to be acknowledged. It's difficult to think without a head. My editor, Laura O'Bagy, has been wonderful, showing the patience of Job and relinquishing rules of proper grammar when necessary to indulge my pool room jargon.

Beverly, my wife during those years, needs to be thanked, profusely. Not only has she stayed my friend for thirty-five years after the ordeal I put her through, she even saved pictures. I can't believe I had so much hair. To all of my contemporaries in the racket, the scufflers in every town, the greats who let me travel with them and the names, no longer with us, I say thanks for the memories.

Lastly, to avoid cold breakfasts for who knows how long, I must thank, thank, and thank my wife, Judi, who has had to listen to my underworld tales so many times over the last couple of decades she could have written this book herself . . . except that she refuses to swear. Judi has supported my every idea and stayed lovingly behind me one hundred percent. I didn't know people as marvelous as Judi Taylor existed.

Table of Contents

Chapter   **Page**

Introduction 1
Oh No! They've Crippled My Horse! 8
The FBI and I 27
The Cotton Palace Years 34
The Pool Widows 58
A Glimpse of Bev's Life to Come 64
From Georgia Skin to Minnesota Fats 75
"Spook", "Break Even Bill", and Alf Beat Titanic Thompson 94
"Playing the Duck" with The Knoxville Bear 101
Too Loose in Louisiana 119
A Little Rocky in Little Rock 128
A Painful Night in Georgia 134
The West is Still Wild 137
The Sparkling Adventures of the Sun Drop Kid 147
The Other End of the Barrel 157
Six Thousand Miles to a Murder 163
See What a Dollar Can Buy 175
U. J. Puckett and the Fine Art of Bushwhacking 186
Running the Table Alfie Style 197
Thoughts of a Pool Widow 199
Not to Me, but Through Me 203
Plain Cheese, with An Angel, Please 206
My Angel Drives a Semi 210
I Stepped Out to Look Up 214
Glossary 218

INTRODUCTION

Pocket billiards: Pool

I would be remiss if I didn't lend proper perspective to a game that provided me with a couple of decades of experiences and a lifetime of memories. Pocket billiards, as a sociable game, is entertaining and engulfing and hours of playing seem to go by in minutes. Unlike most games, men, women, and children can play together, and even playing alone can be fun. But occasionally, the game will have even more meaning, as in my case. Early in my life I developed a talent for pocketing pool balls and winning people's money and with as little as I had going for me, I played the hand I was dealt. I hustled pool for a living. This "outfox the other guy" part of my life is far behind me and I haven't thought much about it in years. Now, writing about it exactly the way it happened, though fun and exciting, makes me jitterier than when I lived it. To all the people I mention in these stories, however I mention them, I mean no disrespect. These are only my recollections of events long ago.

Nobody knows the origin of pocket billiards (pool). The game of billiards has been mentioned as far back as 1607, in Shakespeare's *Antony and Cleopatra*, when the Queen of the Nile uttered the words "Let us to billiards. Come Charmain." There have been many styles of pocket billiard tables and other pool playing equipment, creating an endless variety of games. Today, more than forty million Americans play pool on a regular basis. Home game rooms are more popular than ever, and smoke-free family billiard parlors are as the name implies. Professional tournaments draw champions from Europe and Asia, and major tournaments are held all over the world. Players as young as fourteen are burning their way onto the professional scene. The 20th Century also saw the birth of the Women's Professional Billiard Association. Their televised tournaments, their talent, and the grace they lend to the sport have created interest in pocket billiards for every member of the family. *Pool & Billiard Magazine* and *Billiard Digest* are great ways to follow the game and the players who keep it exciting. OnePocket.org is another way to tune in on the action. Don't take my word for what a great game pool is: Put down the book, pick up a cue, and start having fun!

Crossroaders

That said, I want to invite you into another side of the pool playing world—a world of hustling a buck, playing the duck and business transactions that usually left one person happy and the other hungry. It's a world devoid of time constraints, social security cards, win/win situations, or handshake congratulations. It's an interesting but not pretty world, one with few exits and no sensible reason to join.

Most of us were thrust into hustling for a living in one way or another. Generally speaking, we were the under educated or under privileged. We were a subculture of our own, moving around in a world that most people never see or hear about. We traveled the road, hustling people out of their money on pool tables. We slipped around at all hours; we lived by our wits, and thought on our feet. We stayed up nights, or for days at a time, and went into places that would make a SWAT team nervous. I broke pool room color barriers throughout the South, with the attitude that bullets would either bounce off or go around me–foolish, not brave. In the small towns throughout the south, I hit the black section of town first for faster action. I played in Appalachian mountain towns where many people wore no shoes, sometimes slipping mine off to blend in. A day of that and the soles of my feet looked like retread tires; a week and it was no big deal to put out a cigarette with a toe. We lied about our names, our game, where we were from, and our reasons for being in town. We wore disguises, used poor grammar and hick accents, and repeated dumb pool expressions that we picked up along the way.

My standard country pool room hustling attire was work boots that I picked up at thrift stores and bib overalls, with multiple pockets to separate the one, five, and ten dollar bills I used to cover side bets. We lost on purpose to "salt the mine" and sometimes didn't even recover the salt. A good hustler could sniff out action and hear pool balls click from outside in the street. We avoided confusion and confrontations whenever possible and tried to stay prepared. We were a group who lived for the highways. We answered to ourselves, our bankrolls, and the next pool game. We called ourselves "Crossroaders."

Appearing in roughly chronological order, these stories will reveal that I was no champion player, rather a good one with better than average managerial skills. I didn't star in any tournaments or take down any great scores, but I did stay alert and managed myself well enough to stay in money most of the time. I treated my talent like a business asset and avoided the easy-come-easy-go weaknesses typical among those in my trade. No cards, dice, horses, booze, or women; sort of like a married monk who gambled. My pool abilities and knowledge of good action spots around the country allowed me to travel the road with some of the game's top players and hold up my end when it came to getting in, getting the money, and getting out. Other than smoking a little pot or gambling, which playing pool is technically not, I didn't break the law any more than any other jaywalker. Overall, I considered myself to be pretty honest. However, due to circumstances beyond my control and occupational hazards, I pulled more one-nighters in the slammer than Mr. Bo Jangles. Now I want to give you a chance to do a little time, without doing time.

Hialeah Beach, Florida, 1947

My earliest recollections of life came right before I died and right after I came back.

The wet sand was slipping under my feet, then my legs went out from under me altogether and I was underwater. I remember sucking both water and seaweed into my mouth and nose. I tried to gag it out but more kept coming in. I was clawing the sand and fighting with my arms and legs against an undertow, before I knew the meaning of the word. I was drowning. With all that terror going through me, the thing that concerned me most was that my two brothers, Tippy (10) and Lee (16), were going to be mad. They had told me to stay on the blanket and play while they splashed around with some girls. Death isn't a concept to a four-year old. Spankings are.

All of a sudden the struggling stopped and everything was OK. It was better than OK. The water and fear were gone and I felt the kind of calm you feel for an instant at the end of a sigh. For a moment it seemed a little dark and then it got lighter. It was strange, like I was floating through the air on my back but I could still look down. Meanwhile, back on the beach, a girl asked Lee if his brother could swim. Thinking she meant Tippy, Lee said, "Yes, he swims like a fish."

"Then why" she asked, "is he floating face down out there?" Lee swam out and brought me in and the lifeguard went to work. Ten or so minutes later when the lifeguard, with all his skills and 1940's technology gave up, Lee jumped in and pounded his fist on my back, hitting me the way big brothers all too often do, only harder. Tippy said a clump of seaweed popped out of my mouth and I made a big sucking noise. I was back. All the time this beach drama was going on, I watched the circled crowd from overhead. I remember this like it was yesterday. I wish I could do that with yesterday.

Sixty years later, a doctor had me on a treadmill but couldn't get my heart rate over 110 beats per minute. After a heart x-ray, he told me my heart had two natural pacemakers instead of one. He was scratching his temple with seeming curiosity as he said it, which I didn't find inspirational in the least. He knew nothing about the condition except to say, "We don't want the two of them to get into conflict." I agreed wholeheartedly. Today, my wife calls me the man with two hearts. Could the combination of divine intervention and one of my bro's punches have kick started number two?

My next conscious memory was lying on the sofa with my mother holding my hand and hearing her saying two things. I was so thirsty she told me I could drink all of the root beer that I wanted. I remember her telling my brothers of the grim fate that awaited them for not having watched me more closely. Mothers tend to overreact like that.

I'll never know where I really was for those moments after my soul left my body on the beach until it returned, or what force guided my journey back, but I know I wasn't alone. In my heart and soul I believe I returned with a guardian angel who never left my side and who helped me out of so many tight spots later on, as I journeyed on The Other Side of the Road.

This is for Lee and my Angel.

Dracula and I could have carpooled.

UNITED NATIONS, SEPTEMBER 1994

Little did I know when Moroccan Cultural Minister, Allal Sinaucer, asked me to bring the Taylor Moroccan textile and artifact collection to the UN, that I was venturing into uncharted territory. No items other than photographs had ever been exhibited in this Parliament of Man. King Hassan had requested and received permission from UN Secretary General Butros Butros Ghali for this one time event and Minister Sinaucer said he would intrust the mission to "none other than Mr. Taylor." I had completed enough assignments for the Moroccan Ministries of Tourism and Handicrafts that he knew of me. And I certainly knew who he was. In Morocco he was referred to as "Mustasha - High Council to the King."

When I was first summoned to Minister Sinaucer's office in Rabat, I showed up to a very formal situation wearing my usual jeans, running shoes and casual shirt. My first words to him were, "Please excuse my appearance, Mr. Minister". In a most refined manner he replied, "Mr. Taylor, I am in my work clothes and you are in yours. We have important work to do. Let us proceed". I'm certain his faith in me was due to two reasons: I'm highly competent in these matters and I never stall the process by handing Morocco a bill for my services. They, in turn, give me free run and pay me with privileges that money cannot buy, like a "White Card" from the palace stating I am a friend of the country and to not question my movements. It's an honorable exchange.

The United Nations Educational, Scientific and Cultural Organization (UNESCO) was having an exhibit of huge photographs of the medinas, old parts of the cities, of Fes and Marrakech, and the dire need for their restoration. They wanted the splendor of Moroccan hand work to draw attention to the pictures. The General Assembly was in session, so, between our conducting tours for Heads of States and the general public, my three week tour schedule was back to back. UN Under Secretary General Ambassador Joseph Verner Reed facilitated my every need to insure the exhibition's success.

My lovely wife, Judi, my crew and I filled the lobby with Moroccan textiles, costumes, pottery and silver chests full of antique silver jewelry from the Sahara. I was given a key to the side entrance and we were allowed to work through the night, elf style. The display of Moroccan treasures in this most prestigious venue was smashing, if I say so myself.

One day I was in mid-tour, posing for pictures with Mrs. Butros Ghali (scrapbook stuff, you know) when a well dressed man, as they all tended to be in this building, called me aside and asked, "You were introduced to me as Alf Taylor, but were you ever called Alfie Taylor and did you play pool?" I could tell by the way he asked, he clearly knew the truth and I answered, "Yes, why do you ask?" Before he could respond I asked, with a little contrived laugh, "And just who are you, exactly?" He said he worked in an office upstairs but in the seventies he lived in Charlotte, North Carolina and spent his lunch hours in a neighborhood pool room. He added, "To your good fortune." He went on to say how I rode up to the pool room on my bicycle and, how did he say it, "Put on quite a three or four day show." He said he was my first victim and only lost about eighty dollars but some of the better players in the place didn't get off so easy. He said it was years later before they found out who I was and what I do. By this time we were both laughing.

My newly acquired friend put his hand on my shoulder and said, in what was close to a whisper, "Tell me Alf, Alfie Taylor. How did you go from hustling in pool rooms to the United Nations? In hindsight, I could have asked him the same question. Instead I said, "Well, it went something like this.. No, exactly like this..."

OH NO! THEY'VE CRIPPLED MY HORSE!

Early '70s, North Houston, Laura Koppe Road, 1AM

They'll be coming through the door any minute. Peeking over the sink through the curtain, I can tell there are three of them, one with a handgun and another with a rifle or shotgun. A third one is carrying some kind of bag or small backpack. I hate to think of what's in it. I can hear scraping from whatever they're using to pry at the door and they're talking but I can't understand what they're saying. If I were in a regular house there would be maneuvering options, but trapped in a motor home that's disabled by two slashed tires where there's only one way in or out, all I can do is plant myself and wait. If–make that when–they get in, what do I do? I'm lying in the hallway with my .38 aimed at the door, praying I don't have to fire it. I'm a pool hustler for crying out loud, not a gunfighter. A warning shot would let them know I'm armed, but I doubt they'd leave without a like retort, and these walls are about as thick as a Japanese folding fan. It's so dark outside and there's no sign of another business or house. No street lights or cars are coming by this time of night, either. Take a breath, Alfie, think. Bruce Willis wouldn't hesitate to stay cool, lean out the window, drop all three of them where they stand, and call 'em names while he did it. But then the director yells "Cut!" and everybody stands back up. This is the real deal and I'm not the first thing like Bruce. I'm scared shitless.

The guys at Le Cue downtown, where most of the Houston late night action took place, told me I should stay away from north Houston, especially Laura Koppe Road, but as usual, I didn't listen–occupational hazard? Maybe I need a new occupation. If these guys only knew how little money means to me or how quickly I would open a window and drop it out, they'd quit tearing up my door. But what if robbery isn't their full intent? I don't know who these hoods are or what they want, but I don't think they have my best interest at heart. Plus, if my friends found out I surrendered my bankroll while I had a gun, they'd probably shoot me themselves. Some of the guys I hang out with are so tough they'd have these guys fixing my tires.

My stomach is twisted into knots and my hands feel sticky, even though it's cold in here. I'm sweating and shivering at the same time, with the occasional jerky inhale nervousness brings–all the symptoms of the Chicken Flu. One thing's for certain, if guns start doing their thing in these close quarters, there's not much room to miss; it's like fist fighting in a phone booth. Here's my quandary: I'm really not up for dying tonight, but when they come through the door, terrified or not, do I even have the grit to pull the trigger? Come on, Alfie, man up. You don't have a choice.

Cap those suckers as soon as they stick their heads through the door. Yeah, right! I'd like to establish, off the bat, that I'm not nor have I ever been or will I ever be, any form of tough.

This whole thing stinks big time. A low, almost unidentifiable, noise came from deep inside my throat that let me know I was approaching point break. "Come on, come on. Please," I prayed, "something tell me what to do." All of a sudden there's a loud punching sound and the scraping's turned into crunching. I can hear the aluminum framed, plastic composition door starting to dissolve and the voices are getting louder.

"Oh God! They're coming in."

It's 1959 and I'm watching the Pasadena (Texas) High School track team practice.

Let's see, I've watched those shot putting guys. I hold this eight-pound steel ball in the palm of my right hand, press it against my cheek, spread my feet apart until I feel solid, lean back as far as I can without losing my balance, like this. I prepare my body and arm to launch, twist around a little and . . . ahhhhhh! The son-of-a-bitch rolled off the back of my hand and popped my little finger right out of the socket. It hurt like a bitch and it looked like I was hitchhiking to hell.

Luckily my mind quickly forgot the pain from the break as it was preoccupied by a newer, fiercer one when Coach Brown grabbed my wrist and jerked the little digit back straight. That was my second and last day as track manager (fancy title for water boy). And I had so been looking forward to ripping the tape off those super jocks' legs, just to watch them jump. At 4' 9½" and rail skinny in my senior year, sports, like girls, had never been part of my life. Then my friend Mike Brown, whose father was the track coach, helped me get on as track manager. He said I could tell people my letter, "MGR," stood for "Much Great Runner."

The first thing the coach told me was not to play around with the equipment. The second thing I remember him saying (after my finger stunt) was, "You're outta here, Taylor." A two-day sports gig. At least I can tell people I did track for a while until an injury shut me down. In almost twenty years of hustling pool, hearing gunshots and seeing my fair share of blood, I never got hurt as badly as I did in my brief high school sports career.

The second effort Mike made to help me find my niche was telling me not to sweat it and, "Let's go to the pool hall." My older brother Jack was already a full-fledged golf, card, and pool hustler, but my family hung the "black sheep" label on him and my father used threats, volume, and pain to discourage any followers. It was to no avail. Little did Mike know that his invitation was my ticket away from Pasadena and a certain fate at the oil refinery, prepped by my three years of high school metal shop. Most likely, had I stayed, I would have wound up working at Sinclair or Shell and living in one of Pasadena's post WWII housing projects. I'd park my rusty car or pickup in the yard, like so many do, and marry someone who didn't mind my drinking a lot of beer and giving her an occasional slap.

Pasadena, Texas, was a rough little blue collar, redneck, white man's town. Growing up, a favorite pastime of mine was sneaking through the bushes at the corner of my street, East Thomas and Red Bluff Road, where the Ku Klux Klan had their meeting hall. Pasadena was one of the last towns in America to integrate their schools. There was something about them owning their own land grant that kept them fighting the inevitable. During this time, there were less than a dozen black families living in the town, all of whom lived on church property and whose children were furnished with transportation to Houston schools. A couple of times a month the Klansmen would drink beer and feed on their own hatred for entertainment.

There were two posters in the windows of the hall where they gathered. The first one showed a tall, blonde Swedish looking woman standing next to an African pigmy with a bone through his nose. The caption read, "Would you mix these two races?" The second poster showed an African American man with three tennis balls in his mouth. The caption read, "Tennis anyone?" It's hard to believe, today, that something like that could exist in a civilized society . . . or that minds that small were permitted to.

One time the Klan claimed they received a message from a black militant group from the East that they were coming to Pasadena on a designated date to "shut them down permanently." For the Klan members this was like yelling, "It's show time, everyone take your places!"

And take their places they did. Every shotgun, pop gun, squirrel gun and dumb son-of-a-gun crowded the hall and parking lot in eager anticipation. I had no idea there were so many pickup trucks in Texas. Those of us who hung around the perimeter to watch were hoping the visitors would show up on time. If I had it to do over, I'd open a concession stand selling beer and sandwiches, maybe rent out some lawn chairs. The police brought in a huge telescoping portable sniper tower, dropped it right in the intersection, and cranked it up. We waited 'till the late hours but it was for nothing. Nobody showed up, a disappointment for all.

Pasadena's only pool hall at this time had six pool tables which we hardly used, and three snooker tables that we never stopped using. We referred to pool as "slop" because, as snooker players, pool table pockets seemed huge. This dig at pool was my feeble and only attempt at snobbery. Later, I became a pool player which is where the money is and forgot about snooker altogether.

Most of our gambling was limited to playing for the 25¢ fee for the game. Almost overnight I surpassed Mike and our other friends on the snooker table. I don't know why, maybe being built closer to the floor gave me a line of sight advantage. I could usually stick a dollar or two in my pocket and play most of the day, and into the night, losing very few games. I lived on cokes, hamburgers, Hershey bars, and potato chips, most of which I won side betting or got from the proprietor for brushing the tables.

Dick Cook owned the pool hall and his uncle owned Cook's Hoedown in Galena Park, the next town over. His uncle's claim to fame was that he once hired Elvis and his band for twenty-four dollars a night. Dick once told me, "Alfie, you shoot so straight you won't be happy until you're the best player in town, then you won't be content until you're the best in Houston, and you still won't be satisfied. That's why you have a chance to become a regular hustler." Right then, any thoughts I ever had of pursuing a formal education or a job at one of the local oil refineries went three rails around the table, into the corner pocket, and down the drain.

Central Texas was one of the better states for pool action, other than west Texas, where the towns are so far apart. One of the advantages of playing a Texan, if you do go out west, is in case you forget his name, you can just read the back of his belt. The big talk around our little burg was the big money action in Houston and the surrounding little towns. Being an underprivileged kid from a family of twelve, I had never even seen a hundred dollar bill but I knew they were out there and I wanted a close up look at them.

For my first hustling excursion out of Pasadena, I hitchhiked thirty miles or so to La Porte, to Satterwhite's Pool Hall. I had about forty bucks that I had saved up for the occasion. I got into a five dollar nine-ball game with their best player and won about sixty dollars. I hitched back home eager to tell my brother and mentor, Jack, how I had beaten "the best player in La Porte out of sixty dollars." Jack kind of shook his head in disappointment and said, "That's too bad. I would rather you told me you beat the worst player out of two hundred. Now, you're finished in La Porte for sixty dollars. It's much more important in this racket to be a good manager than a good player." Then brother Jack followed this "heart to heart" by "borrowing" most of my winnings to play golf. But hey! That too was part of my education.

It's called "being bit by the pool bug" and when it happens, a pool player will think, talk, and breathe pool, morning, noon and night. No bridge game, Tupperware party or bridal shower can hold a candle to a bunch of pool players blabbing. One of my pool buddies said he thought about it so much that he was watching TV while his sister sat on the floor in front of him– he was trying to figure out the angle he would have to hit her to bank her into the TV. I've lost track of that guy but I bet he turned out to be a heck of a player. Most of our Pasadena palaver was about "playing the big time" in Houston. Finally, I worked up the courage to venture into the big city, and for the next few years, when I wasn't traveling elsewhere, Houston became my stomping ground.

In miles, Houston is not far from Pasadena, but for lifestyle and pool action, it was as if you were on another planet. Many pool rooms were open all night, almost all of them produced action and, in most cases, easy money. I rented one of the many garage apartments the city is famous for and altered my sleeping patterns to fit the wicked little subculture I had joined. Other than some quick in and outs for family funerals, Pasadena or "Stinkadena," as people called it because of our smelly refineries, paper mills, and toxic bayous, never saw me again. Oddly enough, many years later Pasadena became one of the biggest action spots in the state but I still stayed away.

Houston had T. J. Parker's Pool Room where a lot of the hustlers gathered after hours. T. J., a good player himself, had transplanted from Galveston where it was said he had been heavily into racketeering. T. J. had a diamond studded, solid gold car key and he liked to bet people his car key cost more than their car, a bet he always collected on because nobody could prove the amount he claimed he paid for it was false. He was also extremely big and a terrible bully. Typically, if T. J. got beat playing pool, he would pay up without squawking, but that was not always the case. Once he was spotting me a couple of balls playing One Pocket for fifty dollars a game. I was about seven or eight games ahead when T. J. started doing his knuckle dragger, mega volume, swear word routine on me. The straighter I shot, the louder he got, until I thought, if I didn't let up, I might quit hearing him and start feeling him. I apologized for upsetting him and offered to give him his money back, in front of the crowd, knowing that no self-respecting gambler would accept my offer. All T. J. said was, "Then give it up." I complied and settled for knowing that at least I had beaten him without him beating me . . . as in up.

This was the 1960s and diet pills were the rage for gambling and skipping sleep. They filled you with confidence and reckless abandon at the same time. Diet pills were known for three things and dieting wasn't one of them. They gave you the confidence to play your best game, they would not let you quit if you had a bad game, and when they were wearing off, nobody better say a cross word to you. Coming down from a "Dexie trip" could make a nun sucker punch a priest.

Once we had this young kid in a trap, losing to our player. He didn't have a chance to beat our man, although in his mind, we were on his side, pulling for him and telling him he had "the nuts." He slipped over to me and said, "Alfie, I'm down a lot of money and I should quit, but if I had a couple of pills, I think I can beat this guy. Can you help me out?" We didn't want our sucker to quit, so I went into the bathroom, took a couple of Bufferin and licked the "B" off them. Then I took them to the kid and told him they were "real good uppers." He swallowed both of them at once, then spent the next two or three hours never missing a ball and kicking our ass. The best laid plans of mice, men, and placebos.

T. J. had a free coffee table set up every night for a few months until he quit because the bums kept drinking the cream. Sometimes we would drop a handful of "uppers" into the pot, just to make the action go crazy. People got those drugs in their system and would hock their mother for money to play another game. In case they happened to win, they wouldn't even pawn her out. "Next time, Mom. I got a real good game coming up." The worst part about taking uppers, besides being goofy when you're up and mean when you're coming down...not to mention the chance of addiction... was, if you got beat before you came down, you couldn't even go to sleep and forget about it.

There were always a lot of local Houston area hustlers around T. J.'s and if you could stand the heat, you could even win some money from T. J. himself. All the traveling road players took a shot at him. The trick was to take him off without pissing him off. Eddie Taylor and one of America's top cue makers, who was also a tremendous player and whom I shall leave nameless, went into T. J.'s, hoping that one of them could play him. T. J. refused and Eddie, being the gentleman he was, didn't say a word. Eddie's partner, who was known to be a little smart-mouthed, kept popping off to T. J., trying to get him to play. Eddie warned him to stop poking the lion's cage, and then went to wait in the car. Eddie said minutes later his partner came out, bleeding profusely from his mouth and nose. It seems T. J. had heard enough and used one of his hamhock hands to give the lippy lad a good lip slap. Not on the cheek, but a full on, palm of the hand, frontal smack in the mug. It ended the cage poking but the lesson didn't take. The guy still has an attitude–but he does make tremendous pool cues.

For the extremely courageous or financially desperate, there was Red's Pool Hall on Nineteenth Street; a tough, tough joint. Even the toughest guys thought twice about going in alone. Once in Red's on a Saturday night, a man was shot dead by his opponent while playing. An hour or so later, when the cops finally arrived, they found every table still going strong and the players who took over the victim's table were just stepping over and around his body to shoot.

The trick to hustling in Red's after hours was to give one guy the bankroll and drop him off at the door, then park the car and not dally on the way in. I only went there a couple of times. Once, some plain clothes vice squad officers were infiltrating Red's on a Saturday night and I happened to be there. Oh, lucky me. On any given night, there were more drugs in Red's than at Libby Laboratories. The lawmen didn't serve a warrant so their plan must have been to nab people on their way to their cars. The place was packed and it was obvious that they didn't belong. Still, one of the house men stood up on a pool table and yelled at the top of his lungs, "VIIIIIIICE SQUAD!" There was so much contraband dropping on the tile floor, it sounded like a castanet solo but only the house man was arrested.

Another incident at Red's everyone talked about was the night a border patrol agent came in to play and hang out in the semi-underworld. He was still wearing his uniform, including his side arm, and was sitting on a pool table watching a game, when one of the locals came up and sat beside him. "Nice gun," the stranger said. "Are you a pretty good shot?"

They said the agent's answer sounded right out of his manual. "I practice at the range twice a month and am required to qualify, blah, blah."

His new companion asked, "Would you bet fifty dollars you could shoot better than me?" (He's a pool bum. Did you expect him to say "I"?) The agent answered with an affirmative.

"See that clock on the wall," the hustler asked, at the same time that he pulled his own pistol out of his belt and blasted a hole through it. People say only a few players even looked up from their games. "Beat that," the shooter said.

Totally rattled, the agent answered, "I can't fire my weapon in a public place. That constitutes a 4883 type of number, a felony, punishable for up to blah, blah, blah."

"Then, give me my fifty dollars," the gunman told him, now beginning to get pissed off.

"I haven't got fifty dollars," the agent said.

With his gun still comfortably resting in his lap, the shooter's last words on the subject (they say they were almost in a whisper) ended the incident quickly. "Well then, I guess you better give me that gun."

Someone told me that the last couple of weeks that Red's was open, even Red and his house men wouldn't go in there. Everyone just played it wide open without paying a dime until the equipment gave out. True or BS? Who knows, but it made for a good story. Still does.

Then there was the Heights Pool Room that was managed by a man named Dutch. Dutch liked order and in his place you would never find trash on the floor, dirty tables, or cues lying around. The tables stayed brushed and the floors swept. Even the one bathroom was tolerable. Dutch kept a neat dive. A nicer sort of riff-raff hung out in the Heights, with the exception of a ruffian named Country Smith. Country was a typical Texas redneck who liked to fight and talk about fighting, but he was always nice to me. To him, I was a kid. Rednecks are a breed of their own. They tend to act without reason. Once I saw another tough guy, Frankie Long, take a swing at someone who ducked the punch, causing him to hit a pay telephone and take it off the wall. Frankie was so busy throwing more punches he didn't even notice. One afternoon I walked into the Heights pool room right in the middle of a serious standoff. Dutch was standing behind the counter area, which was raised about three feet above the room floor. In his outstretched hand was a revolver pointed at Country, who was less than twenty feet away. "Back off, or else," Dutch told Country.

Country must have had another definition for "Back off." In his left hand, which was clutched in front his chest, he held three pool balls. In his right, stretched back and ready to throw, he had another one. I noticed it was the ever famous eight ball. It was a strange scenario, but easily readable that even though Dutch was armed with America's number one instrument of death, he was the one who was intimidated in the standoff. On top of that, Country was taunting him with, "Go ahead and shoot, you M. F. You might miss, but I'm gonna take your head off with these balls."

Dutch, who was older and infinitely more frightened, backed off, put down the gun, and apologized to Country for pulling it on him. Country told me later that he definitely had the upper hand in the situation. If that's the case, I wonder why cops don't blow off the gun thing and just carry pool balls instead. "Drop that money bag and get your hands up or I'll six ball you."

Joel Schatzman hung around the Heights. Joel was a world class card player and a friend of my brother, but nobody could figure out his pool speed. He had a terrible stroke and playing style. He looked like he couldn't play at all and backed up his apparent ineptness with a line of "po, po pitiful me"; BS a mile long. But Joel, a smart Jewish boy, knew about winning and most of the time played just well enough to do it. He couldn't beat me playing even nine-ball, so one time I spotted him the eight and the break. The eight spot means one player can win the game by pocketing either the eight or nine, while the other player must make the both balls to win. In nine-ball, the one through nine are racked in a diamond shape. The balls are pocketed sequentially, with the nine being the pay ball. The pay ball can also be pocketed out of sequence, making a win if the player combinations it off the lowest numbered ball. A lot of luck comes into play in nine-ball. The worst part about giving the eight spot is it gives the weaker player two balls that can win for him if either goes in on the break. Joel was beating my brains out with the spot, mostly because when he broke the balls, he smashed them harder than you'd think would be possible for anybody, and he was small like myself. His two pay balls went in on the break so often it made me dizzy. When I couldn't take any more and quit, I sat down where Joel had left his coat, his cue case, tip scuffer, can of powder, and such. I reached over and picked up the cue that he had been using for breaking the balls (players don't generally like to punish their playing cue by breaking with it, so they use a break cue). I could hardly lift it with one hand. Joel had hollowed out the handle and filled it with lead, taking the cue from twenty ounces up to four or five pounds. That's how Joel Schatzman broke the balls like a Mack truck. And it's also how he broke me in the Heights.

There was a top hustler named Ronnie Allen who did the same type of thing by hollowing out and weighting down a cue shaft, the front half of a cue. Ronnie's move was to match up with someone playing with only his shaft. People don't realize that for shooting, the weight of your stick means more than the length. Ronnie, who was a top player to begin with, was burning hell with his shaft. I saw the same thing years earlier when another great player named Marshall "Tuscaloosa Squirrel" Carpenter matched up using just his shaft. Instead of a lead load, he simply held a roll of quarters in his hand under the shaft which gave him the added weight and gave his opponent another kind of shaft.

There were other, even less civilized rooms, that hustlers avoided like the plague but I didn't bar any of them. There was Charlie Weaver's joint in the Fourth Ward, the darkest, scariest part of Houston. Nobody in their right mind ventured into the Fourth Ward, much less got out of their car to hustle pool. Charlie was too strong of a player for me to mess with, but he was a regular "customer" for my brother Jack. Charlie had a special jump, masse (curve), draw shot that nobody else could shoot or even figure out. The opportunity to use it didn't come up very often, but when it did the whole room would stop to watch him shoot it. I could beat anyone else in Charlie's except him, and there was good action there, so Jack and I became weekly regulars. I behaved like a quiet church mouse in Charlie's, but Jack wouldn't hesitate to get up in their faces and squabble back at them. Charlie Weaver's had the loudest jukebox you ever heard and there were speakers by each table. Ray Charles would blast out, "Hit the road, Jack, and don't ya come back no more, no more." As events unfolded one night, Jack should have taken that song as an omen.

There was this huge, very frightening man in Charlie's they called Champ who liked to play with his shirt off, as did so many in there. It was a little distracting playing Champ because of the four noticeable bullethole scars in his chest area. I asked what happened and was told it had happened there in Charlie's. Some guy had gotten mad over a game and started shooting at Champ point blank with a .38. I asked what Champ had been doing, meaning what had caused the shooting. Misinterpreting my meaning, the guy said, "Champ was steady cuttin' his ass."

Champ had indeed sent his shooter to the big pool hall in the sky. Once I walked up to Champ (who had always been friendly to me) and said, "Come on Champ. I'll spot you the break and play you some heads up nine-ball." He ducked down so close to me that I could close my eyes and one sniff would tell me it was Champ, quite possibly to give me a closer look at his scars. He smiled so big his top lip slid up over both of his front teeth, a half-inch up over his bi-colored gums, and boomed, "I'll spot you the break and play you some heads-up murder," with a heavy emphasis on the last word. I told him another time perhaps, that my murder game wasn't up to par. I didn't talk much to Champ after that . . . or even look in his direction.

Our playground at Charlie's was over the night Jack and his friend Rodney went in and Jack beat Charlie out of more money than usual. Charlie snapped, pushed Jack up against the coke machine and proceeded to crawl on him like they were going steady. Jack, not up for a close relationship at that particular time, grabbed an empty bottle from the top of the machine and gave Charlie enough of a head conk to have him back away into a knee buckling, ass-sitting position. It wasn't a good spot for the only two white men in the place, so Jack, in the words of Mr. Charles, did indeed "hit the road." He and Rodney ran out the door with several of Charlie's friends in hot pursuit. Fortunately, Champ wasn't part of the soiree. Rodney headed up the street for the car with nobody after him, while three pursuers chased Jack across the street to a closed service station. Jack pulled out the air hose, and using five or six feet of it, he swung the handle around enough to keep his pursuers back until Rodney arrived with the shotgun side front door open. They escaped. After that, we gave the Fourth Ward a pass for good. I'd hate to think about straying back in there without packing an air hose.

To put Jack's prowess with his dukes into context, I'd like to drift back to a very tense night in a bowling alley in a tough part of Houston. For those of you who read on and consider it a bit graphic, think how I feel. It happened more than a half century ago, when I was young and impressionable enough to remember each passionate moment. We were with Jack's friend, Johnny Roberts. It was the first time for any of us to be in the place to play pool. For me, it was the first time in that part of Houston. Other than another hustler friend, Wilson "Houston Whitey" King, we didn't know one of the many unfriendly faces looking at us. I got into action immediately. Youngster or not, I was winning against my opponent and, winning a sizable enough sum when a large young boy/man leaned against the table next to mine and began harassing me. I probably could have outwaited him, knowing his asshole behavior had to come from alcohol but Jack didn't like the disruption for two reasons: it was his brother and his money. So he eased up to the guy's right side and asked him to not bother his brother. I sensed the danger and shot my shots from the far side of the table.

This guy gave Jack a sharp jab to the ribs with his elbow, nothing to take him out, just a sharp taunt, to which Jack asked him not to do that. Anyone who has been around in the least would know that was interpreted to mean do that again and the man followed through a bit harder. I never saw someone punished so fast for their mistake. Jack came around with a right uppercut to his jaw that splattered him back on the pool table. By the time his head hit the slate Jack had his knees on the table pummeling the guy's face. Each time he hit the guy his head would pound against the slate. Sensing overkill that could kill, Johnny pulled Jack back and the guy's friends carried him out. Drama over? Not even close. Ten or so minutes later the guy, ready for round two, charges in toward Jack and is met with a mad ass fist right in the nose. With too much blood in his eyes, and knocked half senseless, he once more retreated to the parking lot.

We thought the fighting between the two would be over but the natives were more than restless. Fifteen or so minutes later a wide awake, shirtless bull charged through the door, his face still crusted with blood and snot, and wrapped his arms around the tops of jack's arms in a face to face, bear hug assault. This didn't look good for Jack, being so much smaller, until I heard the "smack, smack, smack" six or eight times as Jack was using just the strength of his forearms to beat the guys ribs until he couldn't breathe and made him drop his arms. The next sound heard, make that sounds, was the guy's jaw breaking in three places and his head hitting the floor first.

There was no early awaking this time. I quickly ducked out to Johnny's car and retrieved his long barreled .38 and slipped it to Jack, who told the guy's friends to keep their distance, while we backed out . . . never to come back in.

There's a difference between over and semi-over. A few nights later Jack and I were at a pool room called Pee Wee's, when the guy walks through the front door and up to Jack. I couldn't tell what they were saying but the guy's jaw was wired shut so my hunch was Jack was doing most of the talking. They went out the front door to I didn't know what or how many so I grabbed the same gun and ran out the back door. I bought it from Johnny after I saw it could prevent an ass whipping. There, leaning up against a car drinking a couple of beers like college buddies, were Jack and his victim. The guy apologized for causing the trouble and said Houston Whitey told him before it started that if he messed with Jack Taylor he was "going to get the top of his head tore off." He went on to say his mother asked him to find Jack and see if he would pay half of the two hundred dollar hospital bill. Jack gladly gave him a hundred and the kid said one more thing. "You're such a little guy. How do you hit so hard?" Sadly enough, the young man's penchant for trouble led to his demise in a bar fight.

You never knew where you would find action around Houston but you could find it daily. The whole Texas Gulf Coast area is a gambling Mecca, so there were hundreds of pool hustlers and thousands of wannabes to support us. But the room where action was most consistent round the clock was Le Cue Billiards, right in downtown Houston. It was on a second floor so all you had to do was tough out the panhandlers and junkies who hung around the slow elevator in the dark hallway when you went in or out at night. They were harmless, for the most part, but always annoying with their bumming. Why didn't they get a job? But look who's talking. I couldn't remember punching in anywhere in a long time. Minnesota Fats once said, "Working's for suckers. Playing, that's the secret to life." I was playing.

Some of the Le Cue regular characters were truly unforgettable. There was "Big Randy the Knife," who told us he "liked to get in and work close." Randy's idea of fun was to slip up behind people in the pool hall and put the backside of his knife blade up to their throats, just to make them hold still and guess whether it really was the backside this time. Once I was sitting on a pool table watching a game and "one trick Randy" did his blade thing on me. I didn't speak, or even swallow, lest my Adam's apple turn into Adam's applesauce, but by seeing the expression on my friend Neil's face when he looked my way, I could tell Randy was giving me the front edge, full thrill version. The worst part was when Randy laughed at the position he had you in, his body would move as would his knife. He was such a kidder.

Then there was "Coca Cola Bill," who got the name because they said he could get into a Coke machine faster with a church key (can and bottle opener) than the vendor could with a regular key. Bill had the type of speech impediment that sounded like collected spittle in the right back corner of his mouth, while the left side stayed closed. His "Js" came out like soft "Gs." The more excited Bill got, the farther you had to stand back to avoid a sprinkle. One day he told me his wife had died and they were burying her that same day, right around that time. I said, "You mean you're not at the funeral?" Expelling an inordinate amount of moisture with his first excited words, he answered, "Chesus Chrisht Alfie. I did everything in the world for her while che was alive. What do you echspect?" Once Bill explained it to me like that, I understood.

The last time I went into the Le Cue, a young black player they called "Youngblood" was sitting on a pool table. Youngblood had learned to play pool around Dallas where I hung out, and always looked up to my game, but since that time he had turned into a real good player and had taken to the road. When he saw me come through the door after not having seen me for years, he jumped a foot straight up off the table he was sitting on and said, "Alfie Taylor. I can't believe it's you. Get your skinny white ass up on this table. I'll beat you like your money was stole." I declined his offer but appreciated his delicate presentation and his accurate description of my ass.

A lot of top players came to Houston and always hit Le Cue. Some roosted there for long periods of time. Jack "Jersey Red" Breit played world class pool, any game on any size table, including the dreaded five by ten footers. He came from the East Coast in the 70s to hustle Texans; he fell in love with a woman named Dottie and never left Houston. Red was a gentleman with a great sense of humor. He was tall and just plain big. Stretching to any part of a pool table was no problem for him and since he could play with either hand, he never had to use the bridge (long cue holder). Red played tremendous One Pocket and the downtown businessmen, who came to Le Cue for long lunches, loved him. He gave them spots (handicaps) like ten to three, meaning Red had to make ten balls in his corner pocket before they made three in theirs. Red played such good safeties he hardly ever gave them a shot at their pocket. They never played for serious money, so nobody got hurt. The businessmen loved Red's proficiency at the game and even seemed to enjoy donating to his cause. On weekdays, from eleven to three, they lined up for the opportunity to play him even though he seldom, if ever, lost to them. For Red, pool was a grind out job, and when he had a cue in his hand, he too was pure businessman.

Greg "Big Train" Stevens, from Wichita, Kansas, hung out at Le Cue for years. Greg was probably the greatest pool shooter in history. I didn't say pool player, I said shooter. There were better players than Greg, but nobody could make the incredibly difficult shots that he could consistently make. And nobody ever shot so fast so accurately. As soon as his bridge hand hit the table, he would pull the trigger. To watch Greg play pool when his game was in top form was like watching a magic show. Everything he could see, he could make. He cut balls backwards and he banked balls in like rockets. Greg could shoot with the cue ball frozen on the end rail like it was nothing. He didn't care whether he was playing for a hundred dollars a game or ten, just so long as he was playing. And to Greg, it mattered little whether he won or lost. People liked backing him, just to be in his circle of greatness, so he played the toughest action he could find, no matter how many balls he had to spot weaker players, which all of us were. If he lost, he would just grab another stake horse (backer) and find another game.

Greg Stevens could play for days without stopping and he was the epitome of confidence. Once when he and I were on the road together, we went to Paris, Tennessee, so Greg could play the local champion, "Buttermilk" Brown. Greg could murder him on a nine foot table. I know because even I had no trouble beating Brown on that size table in Nashville. But on his hometown eight foot, slop bucket tables, where he could shoot one wild shot after another, Brown gave Greg and anybody else who came to Paris a run for their money. For three days they battled back and forth. Here's where it get's interesting. Although the Paris pool room shut down at 10:00 p.m., Greg's 'pharmaceutical intake powered him round the clock. Each night, after an all day session with Brown, Greg had me drive him the hundred and fifty miles to a twenty-four hour pool room in Memphis so he could practice all night and be ready for Brown, back in Paris, at nine in the morning. The next night he did the same thing. For Greg, sleep was out of the question. For me, it was out in the car. By the end of the third day, Brown and all his followers were broke and Greg offered to drive us back the couple of hours to Nashville so I could sleep on the way. He was still wide awake savoring his (our) victory, and I was whipped, so that was perfect. He was also still pilled to the gills.

Considering the late hours, quick, unplanned meals, booze, and all the rest that goes with hustling pool, ours was not a hydrating lifestyle and Greg had a particularly bad dry skin problem. He had a habit of picking at the skin on his hands when he wasn't playing. I was dead asleep on the drive back but I still woke up when I heard the heavy crunching of gravel from my car sliding sideways off the road, around a curve. Unscrambling my brain enough to become slightly coherent, I saw Greg steering into the slide with both elbows, while never missing a beat picking at his hands. Too tired to fight fate, I just closed my eyes and let the "Big Train" take us home.

I did learn one thing from Greg about his playing and mine. He explained that my style of stalling my game just enough to empty my opponent's pockets, coupled with the fact that I did it so easily and naturally, led to me missing a lot of balls. His words were, "If you want to play run out pool, get it into your mind that you want to make the other guy quit. You want to terrorize him, not baby him." I put his theory into practice once in Bessemer City, North Carolina.

"Bessemer City Slim" was an elderly gentleman by my standards at the time. Today, he would be my contemporary. Slim owned the local pool room and was a good house man and strong local player. He played just well enough to take on road players but he was a perfect score for any crossroader talented enough to make it to Bessemer City. My brother Jack set me up to play Slim some twenty dollar nine-ball. We had been out on the road for a couple of weeks so I was hitting the balls pretty solid. Instead of paying off after each game, Slim preferred to mark them up using the sliding beads over the table. After an hour or so I was ten or twelve games ahead and I didn't feel comfortable giving Slim endless credit, which was pretty foolish on my part since he owned the place. Also, I couldn't very well ask him to pay up when we had agreed to mark them up and he wasn't interested in raising the bet.

So I made up my mind to put Greg's theory into practice. I started shooting at every tough shot Slim left me, and making them. I cut balls in backwards. Every bank I shot at split the pocket. I was playing close position with almost perfect angles and running out rack after rack when I looked up and saw the entire pool room had stopped playing and everyone was watching our game, which made me run out that much more. I made up my mind to terrify the old man into quitting. When Slim's knees finally buckled, he owed me one thousand dollars for the fifty games that I was ahead. He quit like a gentleman and asked me to meet him at the City Cafe the next morning where he would pay me. When we got in the car, Jack said, "What in the world was that? That was the best pool I've ever seen you play. It's almost the best pool I've ever seen anybody play." I thought of Greg and the answer was easy.

The next morning at the cafe, Slim put ten one hundred dollar bills in front of me. Next to my hundreds, he put another stack of bills about an inch high. He said, "I've owned that pool room for more years than you've been playing pool and I've played most every road player that's come through the Carolinas–even beat a few of them. Buddy Hall took eight hours to get twenty games ahead of me. You beat me fifty games in four hours. I've never been beat by anyone, like you beat me last night. Fact is I've never seen pool like that. If there's anybody, anywhere, that you would like to play, that's what this money is for." I said, "No thank you," to Slim; but thought, "Yes, thank you," to Greg.

Greg was a nice guy and fun to go hustling with. He was also a great golfer and a capable card player . . . and a competent cheater. He had large hands so occasionally a card or two would get stuck in his palm. He said, "If you're playing gin, the only thing that will beat eleven cards (you're supposed to have ten) is twelve." With Greg, every day was a new beginning and his plans rarely extended past the following day and always included some fun. Everyone liked him but, sadly enough, Greg's was a lonely ending. He died fairly young with no family and, apparently, no close friends in his home town. His ashes sat unclaimed in the Wichita funeral home for weeks. When Jack, who was Greg's close friend and golfing companion, found out, he drove to Wichita and picked them up. Jack put the super confident, great player, Greg "Big Train" Stevens, in his golf bag pocket, played a couple more rounds with his buddy, took him into a couple of pool halls they both had liked, then buried him at the foot of his father's grave.

Confidence is a monstrous part of playing pool and when my own pool career was taking off I tried everything I could think of to improve mine. Reading books couldn't have been farther from my mind. That's why I escaped school. Still, realizing the importance of confidence, I bought three books: *The Power of Positive Thinking* by Norman Vincent Peale, *The Magic Power of Your Mind* by Walter M. Germain, and *Psycho-Cybernetics* by Maxwell Maltz. So much of playing pool is in the mind and these books became my reference source. In *The Power of Positive Thinking*, there is a list of ten rules to follow for success. Dr. Peale basically says you are like a camera and your body and entire being will seek to develop the picture that you put in your mind. "Formulate and stamp indelibly on your mind a mental picture of yourself as succeeding. Hold this picture tenaciously. Never permit it to fade. Your mind will seek to develop the picture. Do not build up obstacles in your imagination." (Peale) Moment by moment this effect rears its head while playing pool. If you are a capable player and your last thought as you pull the trigger is positive, you are most likely going to split the pocket and be ready to shoot the next ball. You know the ball is going in before you shoot. By the same token, if you draw back to shoot and picture in your mind missing the ball, Dr. Peale's same rule will punish you.

A lot of garbage goes through the mind while hustling pool, beginning with, "Now, where am I? Is this joint cool? Am I doing this place the right way? Can I make this long shot for my last money? Will this guy quit me while he's ahead? Now, where am I again?" I'm telling you, the mind gets going and it's a jungle in there. My success came from finding the one best thing and concentrating on it so intensely that the other rubbish couldn't get in. I would picture the ball I was shooting hitting the back of the pocket. Not just the pocket, but the back center of the leather rim, without touching a cushion going in, and it worked. I never thought I would reveal that secret, and if I were still out there hustling, I probably wouldn't have.

My younger brother Bobby liked to bet so heavily on me, that sometimes he wouldn't let me know how much he had down until after the game. Bobby said he could walk into a pool room and know by the sound what table I was playing on. My shooting style tended to be a little firm from playing on so many funky tables on the road and Bobby said he could close his eyes and hear the balls smacking the backs of the pockets on my table.

Back to Laura Koppe Road and my immediate terror. "Why in the world would I be in a hurry to get back here?" The pool room had been a solid action joint, just as I was told it would be, by the same people who warned me not to go. There had been lots of side bets and not much talent in the place. I won pretty good and everything seemed cool but when closing time came, the first person out the door ran back in and said, "There are some guys I've never seen before standing outside and one of them has a rifle."

Everyone gravitated toward the center of the room, down low, away from the front window and the house man called the cops. There must have been a police car nearby because they showed up pretty quickly, just as the suspects drove away. The cops took off after them, and then came back before we left and said they had chased them to the city limits and given up. The police left and the place emptied out.

When I walked into our motor home, my wife said she had felt something bump against the side. I looked around and found the two left rear tires were flattened. My horse was down! I flagged down one of the last guys leaving the pool hall and gave him fifty dollars to take my wife and five-year-old son downtown to Le Cue. Everything we owned was in the motor home and I wasn't about to leave it. I said to tell Eddie Stinson that I was in trouble that involved gun play and that I needed help right away. Eddie was my friend and a stand-up guy who worked the night shift, so I knew he would be around and would take my situation seriously . . . or so I hoped.

The car returned and now we were four. My hands are wringing wet and I'm burping the way you do before you puke. "I can't do this. I can't have a shootout in the middle of the night with who knows who or how many–or freakin' why?" With that trembling thought or sound, I can't remember which, I jumped up and rushed toward the door, which was the complete opposite of my preferred direction. Beside the door, which now had a tire tool sticking through it, set into the side of the sink cabinet was an emergency button for the alarm siren. Jumping in front of the door to push the button, while the door was shaking, was the tensest moment of my tense moment filled life.

I hit the alarm and got just the response I wanted–one more moment alone in the machine. The intruders stepped back in surprise, just long enough for me to jump into the driver's seat, start the motor, and screw the slashed tires, put the pedal to the metal. It worked. I was off, and they were running and grabbing at the door, which, like some scene out of a black comedy, was now open and flapping in the breeze. I watched them in my mirror as they ran across the street and swung their car around.

Within a quarter mile there wasn't a shred of rubber left on my tires and the rims were spitting out a line of sparks behind me. This nice, new rolling home of mine drove and sounded like a junker, but as long as it kept moving, it was my security. I was saved. I knew they could overcome my head start easily, but at least now I had given them a moving target, and one big enough to run their ass into a ditch. I'd wreck this thing in a nanosecond to get them. Who's the big guy, now? I felt better than James Brown.

A mile or so down the road, I spotted an all-night garage on the left. I swung the beast in, sliding on my rims, and jumped out. To begin with, running into a strange place in the middle of the night, with a pistol in my hand wasn't very bright. I could have been greeted with a bang. As soon as the mechanic looked up, I said, "Can you help me? These guys are trying to rob me." By now, their car was idling on the far end of the parking lot.

The mechanic grabbed the pistol out of my hand and said, "Give me that gun. I've wanted to shoot some of these punks around here anyway." This music to my ears hit a sour note when he followed up with, "You go out and chase them over this way and I'll shoot them."

Helloooo? I was running away while carrying a gun and now you want me to do what? Lucky for them they pulled out before I got into my running shoes. Actually, leaving then was good timing on their part because minutes later the cavalry arrived. Two cars came sliding into the parking lot and Eddie, with five or six friends, came piling out with guns, either in their hands or conspicuously sticking from their belts. The original guests had split before the party got going. There was a collective feeling of disappointment among my saviors that the drama was over and, with them by my side, I felt the same way. The mechanic took one of my rear wheels from the other side and put it where two smushed rims now sat. I limped my way downtown to pick up my family and a couple of new wheels, then headed back to Dallas, if not to a better class of hoodlums, at least to ones I knew by name, all the time concentrating on seven words. "Never hustle pool on Laura Koppe Road."

Jack "Jersey Red" Breit. Tremendous in all games.

THE FBI AND I

Dallas, Texas, November, 1963

. . . had our first meeting. I'm absolutely certain that nowhere on the planet is hustling pool a federal offense, so imagine my surprise when two well-dressed men, by business suit standards, were so anxious to talk with me that they offered to help me out of bed. I was visiting my mom in Dallas at the time (pool player lingo for back living at home) and the Kennedy tragedy was still in the air, so you can imagine her concern when the feds flashed their credentials, especially when they asked her to stay downstairs while they went up.

Hey, what's up? It's before noon. Who can function at this hour anyway? And how did they expect an all night pool scuffler to think straight with all this light coming in? OK, thoughts, sort your selves out. I did buy a hot TV awhile back, but unless it was stolen from a Post Office, that's not a federal offense. I'm twenty. I don't know anything criminal that's not petty or anybody worthy of ratting on. Even with these sleep deprivation tactics, I won't rat.

"Governor Alf Taylor?" one of them asked. I knew then it was serious. Few people knew my first name.

"Uh huh," I managed to get out. I thought I needed a cup of coffee to wake up, until I heard his next couple of lines.

"We're agents so and so with the FBI. We've been looking for you for more than two years. You're under arrest for draft evasion." Twang!!!
 I'm awake!

Ybor City, Florida, September, 1960

Two of the things I remember most about hanging around the little pool room in Ybor City, Tampa's "Cuba town", were the delicious smells from the heavy meat sandwiches made on French bread, sold out of the cafe windows that opened to the streets and, the street game the Cuban pool room hangouts and I played between pool matches. At night the boys and I would stand in front of the pool hall and lean up against the window sill. I was actually small enough to sit on the sill. When the street strolling girls walked past, just as each foot hit the ground (mostly high heels), we would all snap our fingers. It was fun to observe the rhythm of the snapping quicken with each step. Sometimes their feet sped up faster than we could snap. Occasionally, one of the more courageous ladies would stop and talk, nice or not nice. Either way, we loved it.

This area of Tampa was pure nightlife, full of impure fun. A constant stream of fancy dressed, heavily made up, perfumed to the max Cuban beauties strolled the streets, some for fun, some for profit, 'til the wee hours. Styled out 50s and 60s lowriders cruised by more slowly than a pedestrian's walk, most of them sporting Cuban studs hanging out the windows, catcalling at the girls in two languages. Many of the cars had "For Sale" signs in the windows, even though the owners had no desire to part with them; in the event someone did ask the owner "how much?" an amount similar to an overseas telephone number was on the tip of his tongue. A lot of the Cuban boys dolled themselves up as much as the girls, high styling in their fancy slacks, silk shirts, gold chains, and tangerine colored shoes with pointed up toes. These were the same shoes I had seen in high school, worn by the Mexican "cool daddies."

I hung out in this pool room as much in the daytime as at night, so I saw these same guys come in for lunch or after work covered in brown dust from their jobs at one of Ybor City's many cigar factories. And what does make a cigar Cuban? These were made in the states at "Cuban" cigar factories, by supposedly American citizens of Cuban origin. Is the difference where the tobacco was grown and was this tobacco grown in Cuba?

It was a couple of months before my eighteenth birthday and eighteen was the legal age to get into Florida pool rooms. I wasn't old enough to be in the neighborhood, much less the pool rooms but I beat the age rule by giving a fake birthday and signing up for the draft early, just to get an ID saying I was eighteen. Nobody expected anyone of signing up early for something everyone was trying to avoid. This little maneuver got me into the pool halls at the time and into my dilemma with the Feds a couple of years later.

Pasadena, Texas, 1961

My actual military stint began at a party by asking my friend, "Now let's see if I have this straight. You say they give you a chow card and you can go to the chow hall and eat as many times a day as you want? If that's true, where do I sign up?"

With an affirmative and his promise to join me, my buddy and I stayed up all night and caught a bus from Pasadena early enough to be first in line at the Houston Air Force recruiting station. My friend zoomed right through, but at four foot ten inches tall and eighty-nine pounds, I had to cheat to have any chance to pass the physical. (Requirements were a minimum height of five feet and a weight of one hundred pounds.) I stood outside of the induction center and shoved bananas down my throat and drank as much water as I could, trying to gain a few pounds. The bananas and water probably made little difference in my weight, but some pleading and standing on my tiptoes got me in and off to basic training in San Antonio. I remember telling the man in charge how I had come from a family of twelve kids so I knew a lot about fighting and about how my brother Lee had used me regularly for knife throwing practice so that I was really good at holding still too, if that would help. They must have been desperate for recruits. I was in.

Lackland Air Force Base, San Antonio, Texas, 1961

One of the many things I hadn't counted on was that the military wasn't prepared for guys my size. All of my uniforms had to be tailored. My brother Jack would tell people, "Alfie marches three paces before his uniform moves." Jack also tried to find the address for the Russian embassy because he said that if the military accepted me, he wanted to send in his surrender papers.

Lackland Air Force Base was no fun at all for most people and it was "hell's waiting room" for me. I was cut loose from home rule at a young age and I wasn't very good at taking orders. Oh, I could take them all right; I just couldn't follow them. I barely even learned to march with my right foot. For some unknown reason, those in command organized the flights of airmen with the tallest in the front right, graduating downward toward the back left. Then they placed the flights in a similar fashion. That left me on the inside corner in the back row of the last flight. At field parades, where we marched in a square, my right foot stayed in place while my left foot would pivot and a couple of hundred airmen would make a turn. I felt the power.

Another thing I wasn't prepared for in the Air Force was the Yankee contingent who picked on me like it was their hobby of choice. It got to the point that just hearing a New York accent or someone saying, "Youse guys," too often followed by, "grab Taylor," would make me shudder. No funny stuff or anything like that, they would just knock me around and, coming from a family of big brothers, I was used to that.

It was interesting how the Easterners would berate each other with the foulest of slurs and think nothing of it. I came from the South where cussin' someone out was usually a precursor to fisticuffs. Thinking back, the Eastern method, though louder, was considerably more civilized. Plus, the Yankees put their swear words in the middle of sentences where Southern boys used them at the end. For instance, the Yankees would say,

"I don't friggin' care where youse guys are from, get friggin' out of my face or I'll friggin' smack you." (I'm being polite with the "friggin.") A Southerner would say, "Y'awl from all the way over there? No shit?"

I remember my first Sunday at Lackland. Our training officer, Airman Hicks, said, "OK, let's move 'em out; mandatory church." Those last two words seemed to buck the Constitution so I bucked them. While marching to church, I heard pool balls clicking in one of the local day rooms. I side-stepped out of my flight, easy from my lowly position, and played twelve handed quarter nine-ball for a few hours until I heard Hicks calling cadence to my flight, on their return. While they were filling their souls, I was filling my fatigue pockets. I remember stepping back in line as they marched by and flashing my pool chalk green left hand to my buddies. Back at the barracks, I piled a small mountain of change, along with wads of one, five, and ten dollar bills on my bunk. That Sunday I gained a little respect for my bravado, but the Yankees still picked on me.

When I shipped out for the battle lines of Wichita Falls, Texas, and was plopped down in Strategic Air Command (SAC) to guard B52 bombers, I took it as a sign that I had no skills the Air Force needed. They used no talent guys like me for either cooking or the SAC Air Police.

Wichita Falls is a place in North Texas the God of wind chill calls home for eight or nine months out of the year. The only thing between the bomber flight line and Oklahoma, to block the wind, is a barbed wire fence situated about twenty-six miles north. We pulled eight hour shifts, walking alone around those mammoths of carnage, with only a coffee truck break every couple of hours. That's where I learned how to sing; my singing was not good, but good and loud. I could belt out "Mona Lisa" so loudly that nearby rabbits would wake up and tear up.

Even the guards were not supposed to get within twenty feet of the open bomb bays. Inside of each plane were four bombs that, together, yielded more destructive power than all the bombs dropped in WWII combined. But rules be damned–on extra cold or rainy nights, after the coffee truck's tail lights disappeared, I would climb up in the bomb bay, sit my ass on one of the bombs, whip out my magic marker and get to scribbling. Since we haven't nuked a country since that time, my graffiti is probably still there. And I wasn't alone with this idea. Witticisms like "F--k you, Russia," and, "Here it comes, you commie M.F.," were written all over those bombs. I never understood why our prose never became an issue at roll call. Maybe those in command felt that if you're going to nuke someone, it's alright to insult them.

Every bomber guard hated his job equally and there was an ongoing conspiracy on how to get out of it. One guy, a couple of pads away, saw the coffee truck coming and started swinging his rifle at the plane and screaming, "Don't you talk to me, you son of a bitch!" They made him a cook.

The only exciting thing that ever happened to me during this period was the night a rabid skunk staggered onto my pad. The base police came out and shot it because my gun wasn't loaded. Not even a single bullet for my shirt pocket. War was hell in Wichita Falls.

On my first weekend break, I went to Dallas and my brother took me to an all night bowling alley called The Cotton Bowling Palace where there was constant pool action. This night changed my life forever. From then on, every Friday would see me hit the front gate of the base and head 125 miles south to Dallas, either by sharing a ride with someone or using my thumb. I would play pool straight for the forty-eight hours I had off, then catch a bus or hitch back to the base and attempt to stay awake through my shift by singing. I was in a love-hate relationship at that time in my life. I loved pool and hated the service. Within a half hour after getting off work on Friday, I was out the front gate, holding a sign that read "Dallas, please" and sticking out my thumb. Coming back, each weekend found me cutting my departure time to the base closer and closer. Allowing the same amount of time for my return as it took for the trip to Dallas became my eventual downfall, in a manner of speaking.

I was winning money right and left in Dallas, so I used my bankroll to set up a small time loan operation on the base. Loan out five and get back six, or loan ten for twelve, with a fifty dollar limit. The guys all liked to play cards and would borrow money right up until the day before payday, then pay it back as soon as they cashed their checks. I was comfortable with my operation and the guys were paying off like slot machines. Even our squadron commander, Captain Mulligan, used my services, but with the Captain there was no limit and no vig,"vig" or "vigorish" being the interest charged on a street loan. The Cotton Bowling Palace was 'round the clock fun and full-time action, and each weekend found me less ready to return to Uncle Sam's house. I would check for the last bus that would get me there on time, and then sleep on the bus ride for the three or four hour trip. One weekend I slept right through the Wichita Falls stop and woke up eighty miles north in Quanah, Texas. I was going to be AWOL, but I was rested enough to hitchhike back and report to Sergeant Green, who told me not to leave the base again without his consent. Screw that. Friday I headed south, cue in hand, for forty-eight hours of nine-ball action. And Monday I woke up on a bus, this time thirty miles north of Quanah, in

Childress, Texas, rested again, hitchhiking back to the base again, AWOL again, and in trouble again. I got a sterner warning from Green this time with him saying that I was not to leave the base, period. He even hinted about the stockade, or brig, whatever their jail is called.

The next weekend I decided to listen to Sergeant Green until I saw the front gate and thought about green felt and greenbacks. Dallas was a blast again, but this time, instead of taking the bus, which made so many stops, I planned to leave at the same time the bus left and hitch a ride back. Hitchhiking in those days was easy if you were going toward Wichita Falls because so many military personnel did it. I caught a ride right away from a young guy who said he was going right through Wichita Falls. I told him of the hot water I was in for my AWOLs and then asked if I could catch some sleep as he drove. "No problem," he said. "I'll wake you when we get there."

He woke me up at an intersection where there were a couple of service stations and said to get out that we were here. I got out but didn't recognize the area. I needed to wash my face, so I headed to one of the service stations. When I asked the man at the station which way to Sheppard Air Force Base and what part of town was I in, he laughed and said, "Sheppard? Hell, boy, you're in Ardmore, Oklahoma." That son-of-a-bitch kid probably still laughs at what he did. And I was dead meat.

Hitchhiking with tears in your eyes can either work for or against you, depending largely on where you keep your hands. If you keep them down and stand up straight, you appear to be in a little trouble and people are happy to help, but if you have them covering your face, you're SOL. This time it helped, but I still arrived back so late that I didn't try to go to work, or even report in. I dropped on my bunk like a stone, thinking whatever happens, happens.

"Airman Taylor, you are to come with us."

I opened my eyes to see two base Air Policemen wearing their pretty blue uniforms. SAC Air Police, like me, only wore fatigues, eliminating any misconception I might have had about why they were there. It was the slammer for sure. Wrong again! To my surprise, I was taken to the commander's office waiting room and given some coffee. When I was called in, there was Captain Mulligan, Sergeant Green, and a woman with a small stack of papers in her hand. Could it be my file?

"Supp, Capin'? You short of money again?" is what I would liked to have said, but discretion being the better part of avoiding a court martial, I just stood there and effortlessly looked pathetic.

They were cordial but dead serious when they explained that they had never seen a soldier who was as uncooperative and bad for morale as I and then one of them asked me, "Just what is your problem?"

Pleading my defense, I told them how I had cheated on my physical to get in, partly because my friend and I went in on their "buddy system" where you are guaranteed to complete the service together. I explained that after the physical inspection in Houston they ordered my friend and me to get on different buses from Houston to San Antonio. I asked the recruiting sergeant why I wasn't going with my buddy and he boomed, "On the bus!" I only saw my buddy once, for a moment, at the BX. I had been scammed from the get go. I went on to whine to the captain about being picked on and humiliated, beginning in basic training, and said that I felt like I never fit in. He agreed, totally, and said they had prepared a special discharge for me, if I wanted it. It was a general discharge under honorable conditions, called a "3916—Unable to adapt to military life." I think there was a mention of, "To be used for civilian clerical work in event of an all out attack." Maybe I just imagined that last part, but I jumped at their offer to part company.

My "you're outta here" papers came with the stipulation that I was not to set foot on another American military installation, which couldn't have been easier to agree to. The captain went on to say that if I waited through the week, they would arrange for some mustering out compensation, to which I asked when I could leave if I didn't want the money. (The captain and I were square on our loan stuff and I could tell, even though he liked me, he had a personal interest in expediting my departure.)

He said I could leave as soon as I signed the papers and got my stuff from the barracks, to which I replied, just to push his buttons, "How 'bout if I don't want my barracks stuff, Captain?" My cue was in Dallas and I was wearing my civvies. The last words, and oh! what sweet words! I heard Captain Mulligan say were, "Sergeant Green, take Mr. (not 'Airman') Taylor to the front gate." I stuck one thumb up and the other toward Big D. At least the Air Force taught me "Mona Lisa."

Back to Dallas and the Feds at my bed. Fortunately, I had my Air Force discharge papers handy. They scanned them over with a puzzled look, then apologized for the inconvenience, but refused to tuck me back in.

If the Feds want me, they'll have to get up a little earlier . . . or is it later? A smile was on my face as I drifted back off. I'm not gloating over being such a rotten soldier. I just wasn't soldier material.

This story was just meant for fun and, in no way, disrespects the heroes of our armed forces who have put themselves in harm's way in defense of this country. God bless them.

THE COTTON PALACE YEARS

Dallas, Texas, early to mid-1960s

The question never was "Do you have a gun?" but "Where do you keep yours?" When I discovered the The Cotton Palace, while on a leave from Sheppard Air Force Base, I had no idea it would become my second home for the next few years. Actually, since I spent more hours in the place than away from it, I probably should refer to it as my first home. The Cotton Palace was open around the clock and, at any hour, you could hear bowling balls thumping, pins splattering, and the incessant clack, clack, clack of pin setter machines. And like any other bowling alley, your nose told you where you were (it was the mixture of lane coating, old shoes, and cigarette smoke).

Vic Domino ran the restaurant with café tables covering the center of the place where we all hung out, ate everything on the menu multiple times over, and watched the door like a bouquet of Venus Fly Traps. At any moment a sucker might walk in and the race was on. We'd trip over each other to be first to snap him up. Every scheme imaginable was concocted in Domino's, and had the tables been bugged, the information gained would have prevented or solved a lot of serious Dallas crimes. Not so with the pool hustlers; our misbehavior was boring by comparison to the activities of some of the people you are about to read about. The waitresses, who were privy to just about everything short of the details of the murders, passed on the table talk to the boss so Vic was definitely in the know. He was a pretty good guy and loaned me money more than once.

For the The Cotton Palace pool hustlers, our work was in a section of the place fifty feet and a world away from Vic's restaurant and the bowling lanes. Our shift began in the late evening and continued until dawn and I tried to be there for every minute, without failing to make it home before sunrise. If daylight happened to sneak up on me, I would either squint my way home or stick around and practice 'till nightfall, with the added possibility of catching some unwary businessman on his lunch break.

I was nineteen when I first went into the place but I looked about sixteen so getting action was no problem. Hustling pool was my only interest. I had the desire, the energy, and the chutzpah to hustle any living human. I said "hustle," not beat. There were a number of players around there who played better than I, but if I asked a stranger to play and he said no I nagged him, offering him odds or whatever. If someone said they didn't even play pool, I'd offer to help get them started.

A few months after I discovered the place I found myself out of the Air Force and hanging there full time. I had limited responsibilities and all I wanted to do was shoot pool. The Cotton Palace was a place where I could do as much of that as I wanted. My daily, or nightly, routine was to wake up at sunset to a couple of cups of java, and run through my version of "dress for success." A silk or faux silk shirt, perfectly tucked into tailored slacks, on top of freshly shined Johnston & Murphy alligator shoes, with matching belt, meant it was a good day and that I had some bucks in my pocket. With us, alligator, like our jewelry and bankroll, was a status symbol; how many pair, what brands, and so on. One of the guys wore size nine but bought elevens because he said he "wanted to get more alligator." Because onlookers were sure to notice when I stretched out for long shots, my socks matched or at least coordinated with my shirt. Buff the nails a bit, slip on my diamond pinky ring and gold watch (when they were out of pawn), a little dab of Dep hair gel to keep my hair in place, a splash of sweet smelling stuff, and I was one step from ready. Lastly, almost as a ritual, I would take my two cue shafts out of my case, clean the blue chalk off with a damp towel, and pour a little baby powder on a dollar bill. Having created the finest of fine sandpaper, I would buff the shafts until the bill itself was too hot to handle. My shafts were glass smooth and I considered myself to be the same. Throw down a little late breakfast (twelve hours late) and I was ready for the bewitching hours at the hottest spot in Texas, for hustling pool or just about anything else.

There are countless stories about the The Cotton Palace, some silly or funny, some exciting, and some, without coverage by any statute of limitations, or which contain the whereabouts of some of the players, that I cannot reveal. Pool hustlers, coin tossers, bowling hustlers, card and dice men, prostitutes for the aforementioned, and scufflers of everything you could bet on came from all over the country to take a shot at the The Cotton Palace "gang." Even traveling heist men put the place high on their list of favorites. Most of the people who got robbed at gunpoint, indoors or out, wouldn't even take it downtown. Besides ourselves, the twenty-four hour availability of the place lured in the characters of the night. Jack Ruby used to come in almost nightly with some of his girls after his strip joint, The Carousel Club, closed. Two of the ladies from his club who came with him, Chris Colt, "the girl with the 44s," and Toi Rebel, were particularly memorable; much more so than Ruby. In the restaurant, Jack was known as an extremely heavy tipper so the waitresses scrambled for him.

It was the 60s in Texas and money was flowing. Almost everyone who came through the door did so with deep pockets and almost all of them wanted some kind of action. Some of them had no skills of their own so they became side betters or stake horses. If you got emptied out in a bad game it was pretty easy to find a horse to put you back into the thick of things.

The Cotton Palace had a most illustrious beginning. It opened in 1959, with Jayne Mansfield rolling the opening ball. She was said to have used a gold (painted) bowling ball in a mink carrying case. Her first roll produced a rather questionable strike, seeing as all ten pins were wired together and even her gutter ball got her a strike. The chicanery perpetrated for this gorgeous starlet became our credo.

The place had forty-four bowling lanes that stayed busy most of the time, but other than a few trick bowling bets I knew about, or unless I was side betting on a bowling match, I stayed away from them altogether. My interest was in the walled-off area that housed twelve off-sized pool tables. "Off-sized" because standard sized tables have four feet by eight feet or four and a half by nine feet of playing surface. These tables, made by A.E. Schmidt, measured four feet two inches by eight feet four inches, a feature that, while upholding proper rectangular proportions, played differently enough to give newcomers some problems until they got used to them. The Cotton Palace tables also had yellow dot cue (white) balls that were slightly lighter than the standard blue or red dot cue balls, as well as the other balls in the rack. This made it difficult to put much English (spin on the ball) on the ball because the cue ball had a tendency to bounce off, but it made it easy to put a lot of backspin on it. Since we learned to make use of the way the ball played, it presented another home court advantage. Things like that only give you a head start. In pool, given enough time and ample funds, the best player will always prevail. No amount of luck can overcome talent on a pool table. Heart plays a large part of winning.

The dictionary defines heart as a hollow organ, and then explains how it functions. It goes on to add related words: personality, disposition, love and compassion, to name a few. Another is "courage," our preferred word for "heart," defined as mental or moral strength to venture, persevere and withstand danger, fear or difficulty. A certain amount of that was necessary each time you screwed your cue together. A couple of examples of how I perceived "heart" in various forms: In the later years of her life my mother became a bit heavy. One day as she was crossing a field in Dallas, heading to the store, a guy ran from behind and grabbed her purse which, unfortunately for the robber, the strap of the bag was over her arm and as he grabbed the purse, it swung him around causing him to fall on his back. My mother quickly sat on his chest and stomach. He wasn't very big so he couldn't budge. Then she gave him a long talk about how she had raised her six sons to be good boys and "It's up to you how you want to live your life" and so on. As mom got up she opened her purse to reveal the twenty-four dollars she had in it and split the money evenly with the man. That's "heart." Another example of heart I'll not forget is when a top notch player named "San Jose" Dick McMorran played me some one-pocket nine to six for fifty dollars a game. I was three hundred dollars ahead on Dick when I quit and walked out with only a quick goodbye. Dick was livid that I would quit him ahead for no obvious reason. When I came into The Cotton Palace the next day, he pounced on me with a heated "Why did you quit me ahead, you chicken shit?" I explained to him that my wife had just had a baby and that was all the money I needed to get her out of the hospital. Dick said "Hell, buddy. Why didn't you say so? I'd have given you the money for that." And he would have. I'm delighted to say, forty some years later, Dick is still my good friend.

On the outside of The Cotton Palace building there hung large, round, colored lights that represented bowling balls. The lights lit up sequentially, beginning at the back on one side of the building and continuing around to halfway across the front, attempting the image of a rolling bowling ball. The lights moved at just about the speed of a competent runner and many nights found us betting on or against a good sprinter who wanted to race against them. To beat the lights took a quick footed person to begin with. Then, the runner had to maintain enough energy rounding the corner to restart down the stretch. It was no race for the alligator shoes crowd. It didn't take long for somebody to sneak into the control room and install a rheostat onto the switch so he could adjust the speed, ever so slightly, just after his cohorts placed their bets. Typically, the faster the runner, the bigger the wager. The most fun was when the drunks, who, by nature of their substance think they can do anything, tried it. Before long the locals got hip to the rheostat scam but pity any quick-footed stranger who came by and put his money down. People were drawn to the lights like the proverbial moth and there was always somebody new taking a shot. Someone suggested pouring oil on the sidewalk at the corner of the building to win a particularly large bet. We dismissed that idea as too crude.

Along with myself, there was a consortium of a dozen or so hustlers and a couple of tush hogs (bullies) who relied totally on The Cotton Palace for their livelihood. Whenever a traveling player came through, if he stuck around long enough, he had to beat us individually and outsmart our collective scheming to leave town with the money. And, that's if they could avoid the heist. Double crossing, double dealing, and double trouble doubled our pleasure at The Cotton Palace. Backers fell, bookies thrived, automobiles and businesses were lost, and occasionally somebody would get sucker punched over a bet or robbed in the parking lot. In a couple of darker moments, blood was spilled. Wives and girlfriends moved in and out of the scene on a regular basis and with little fanfare. We were too self-absorbed to take in the big picture and our vision rarely exceeded our appetite. But, The Cotton Palace kept life interesting. We were captains of our own small ships only able to stay afloat by either sinking or at least damaging other ships. Someone close to me, who later married me, said we reminded her of a bunch of chickens surviving by scraping things off the ground. Ouch!

Pool cost sixty cents per hour, per player, and when your name came up on the waiting list, the rules stated the table was yours until you checked off. There were times when I would play an all-night session until I could no longer stand up or until it was too bright outside to leave. Not wanting to miss any action, I would keep the table time going and crawl under it to pass out for five or six hours. The guys behind the counter were my friends so they would poke me with a cue if a prospect came in. I would, in return, reward them should their poke pay off. What pride? Thinking about it now makes me shake my head but at the time, I thought nothing of it, and I was far from alone in this practice. A lot of the players who wanted to avoid a long drive or a short-tempered wife stayed over, or should I say under?

One morning...morning falling around noon to 3:00 p.m.... I woke up first to find every table covered with cues and cases, designating they were still rented, and each one housing a sleeping pool troll. Strict house rules allowed only one sleeping guest per table but, until this morning I had never seen every table occupied at the same time. If only I had traded my cue for a camera this day. After a good laugh and some coffee, proving once again the idle mind really is the devil's workshop, I took a piece of chalk and chalked everyone's nose a dark blue. A cube of pool chalk, worn more than half way down fits every sized nose perfectly so I made eleven masterpiece beaks with peaks. Bear in mind, some of these sleeping beauties were broke, foul moody, and armed, but I was confident messing with them for two reasons. These guys, I should say "us guys", refused to rest until they were totally dead on their feet, so when they went down, nothing short of a police siren or an unexpected wife's voice would wake them up. Secondly, we were a close group and everyone had a pretty good sense of humor. I did, however, begin my artistry at the back of the room so I would be working my way toward the front door, should I lose my soft touch. I painted eleven out of eleven noses, in perfect blue points, without a stir. Then I gathered everyone working in the place, from the front counter men to the pin mechanics and waitresses from the restaurant, and gave them an art tour of my "blue period." Everybody loved it but knew enough to stifle their laughter.

The first of my victims to wake up was Red Fisher, an easy going, very good player everyone called "Soft Strokin' Red." I'll never forget Red coming up to me in the bowling alley cafe, laughing, saying, "Alfie, come quick. You gotta see something so funny under the pool tables." All the time Red was talking, people in the cafe were having a gas watching his blue nose jumping up and down. He had no idea what had happened or who happened to make what happened happen, but figuring it out didn't take him long.

"Honest, Red. I don't know anything about it. I always walk around with blue fingers. It's eye shadow," was all I could think of to say. He wiped the chalk off of his nose and laughed his ass off and we both went back into the pool area for another look. Sleeping in a chair toward the back was "One Eyed" Richie from Irving. I guess he passed out sitting up when there were no table vacancies. Richie wasn't much of a player but he loved hanging around the element. I remember he was easily intimidated and when he got married, he took his wife's last name. He said she thought it was best that way. Anyway, Richie was out cold, with his chair leaning firmly against the wall and his left foot propped up on a chair. We switched his eye patch from his bad eye to his good one, and then placed six or eight matches strategically under his right foot. I remember how lighting the matches all at the same time wasn't easy because we were already cracking up at what might happen. And we did get our money's worth! Richie, as you might guess, woke up yelling and stomping his foot in the classic hot foot rapid beat tradition. As you also might guess, he was screaming, "I'm blind, I'm blind!" Today, I couldn't imagine doing that or even knowing anyone who would, much less laughing like we did, but hey, I'm not trying to portray us as nice guys. We were who we were. Richie was a gentleman and sportsman enough to forgive a couple of pricks for a couple of tricks.

One Saturday night Red, Billy Stroud and I drove over to Fort Worth looking for action and almost got more than we bargained for. Fort Worth is only about 30 miles from Dallas but the two towns couldn't be more different if they were on opposite sides of the country. Dallas, being the more cosmopolitan of the two, is home to the high tech and fashion industries, while Fort Worth, though modern in its own way, clings to its well deserved and honorable "Cow Town" image.

We walked into Glen Godfrey's Pool Room, right downtown. The place was Stetson thick and there was more "throw the money" on the table nine ball action than we could ask for. We each got into a game right away...and easy games at that. Red, whom I already described as "soft strokin" was also soft spoken and never gave anyone a hard time. As for yours truly, I played my timid mouse role to perfection. But Billy, who almost never missed a ball, also never missed a beat in the pop-off department. Fearless or tactless, you make the call.

This night would find Billy on both of his games He was playing either the owner's son or someone who worked there, and was running both the table and his mouth with equal proficiency, needling him with "crack wise" remarks like "You house men are all suckers" or "You play every day and this is the best you got?" While it's true a person gets more action getting people to not like them and wanting to beat them than they get playing the nice guy role... if ever there was a time and place for "time and place" this was it. Neither Billy's patter or playing was sitting well with the locals, as evidenced by the murmuring. This behavior made no sense to Red or me, but Billy was almost impossible to influence in any direction, on any matter.

Before long, a cowboy walked up to Red and me and said "You boys keep playing, but when closing time comes around you're all getting your asses kicked and that's a fact." It mattered not to him that Red and I had been perfect gentlemen, he was dead (I hate using that word at this time) serious. What we were dealing with were men who jump off running horses onto running cows for fun and since I weighed about 20% as much as a small cow and can't run near as fast, I knew this was a tough spot to be in. Thoughts like "the last roundup" and "the gunfight at the OK Corral" danced through my head. Time for the old thinking cap, for sure. I let my opponent win his money back, a chore made easier by my sweaty hands, and paid the table time for both of us. I offered to buy him a drink and would even have simonized his car if I thought it would make us tight.

About thirty minutes before closing time I slipped over to a pay phone and called the cops. All I said was "There's been a murder at Glen Godfrey's Pool Room" and hung up. About ten minutes later a small swarm of cops rushed into the place (a welcome sight, the only time in my career) and ten minutes later left, accompanied by three Dallas bound pool hustlers. It may be a jungle out there, but nobody makes a monkey out of Alfie Taylor...at least not this time. I learned two things that night: Don't go hustling with Billy and always have a quarter stashed for the pay phone.

For a period of about two years, between 1963 and '64, The Cotton

Palace was going so strong there was a waiting list for tables almost twenty-four hours a day. And the plain fact was the one who controlled the table controlled the action. By this time the crash pad aspect of the place had been suspended and we all received our permanent check out notices. It was stipulated that someone had to be playing on the tables or the house would give them to the next person waiting. Naturally, the house would rather have two couples on them, each paying sixty cents per hour than have one player practicing on them or some bum sleeping under them. We would rather do anything than give up the table when we finally got one, but no desire for keeping a table will ever surpass the passion surrounding the saga of Tommy Lambert and Johnny Littlepage. I wasn't there that morning (damn it) so I got the info second hand that evening. Johnny had a game where he was either winning or losing a considerable amount of money. Either way, he wasn't about to quit. Another regular, Tommy Lambert, had a problem with Johnny. I'm not certain if they were playing each other or if their spat had anything to do with Johnny's game, but Tommy shot him in each leg with a .22 pistol. Tommy was familiar enough with guns to know a .22 shot in the legs wasn't going to kill someone, unless they were alone and bled to death. But here, mid-morning in The Cotton Palace, there were a lot of people around, so it was obvious that Tommy was just trying to get Johnny's attention. It seemed a little excessive but Tommy was no powder puff.

Here's where this regular old mid-morning shooting turns into something memorable. Johnny was a man's man so he didn't lose his cool. He liked his game or his table so much that he paid someone to keep playing on it until he returned. He drove himself over to our friend (and gentleman pool sucker) Doc Simms, who was a veterinarian, and convinced (I dare not define "convinced") him to remove the slugs. With his gunshot wounds bandaged up, he then headed back to his table and his game. I know the two of them worked it out because they both continued to be regulars, or maybe what Tommy had done was working it out.

Pool players are natural negotiators and, other than the fact that they keep such odd hours, they would be natural politicians. In the pool room vernacular, pool players "shoot all angles and take no prisoners." There's a colorful example of pool player negotiating that took place in a town in Texas that's famous for its roses. I'll be a little vague and alter some names because I'm not particulary close to the players the tale's about and I don't want to ruffle any feathers.

In this town there lived a shortstop pool scuffler named "Lefty" Barns, which, in itself, was a strange moniker for a guy who played right handed.

Like a guy I met in the service they called "Tex" who was actually from Louisiana but said he didn't want to be called "Louise." Then there was this bald guy I knew named "Red."

Lefty pretty much controlled the action in this little room and was by far the best player the town had to offer, so grinding out a living from the other locals was no problem. One of Lefty's regular "customers" was an attorney named Robert Aaron White, who was reputed to not have the need for a regular practice, but kept his office just to escape the house. White was wealthy so the fifty or sixty, sometimes a hundred or so dollars he lost to Lefty meant little to him. His daily visits to the pool room were his way of escaping his mainstream element to hang for a couple of hours with the underbelly of the town.

Lefty was enough better player that Robert never won...except once: The "no gambling" rule in the place was enforced only to the point of money could not be flashed so it was standard practice to mark the games up with the overhead beads on the strings. Something almost magical happened that day for Robert. Instead of his usual meek style of play, he came out like a tiger, freakishly sinking everything he shot at and getting unbelievably lucky rolls.

Every time he blasted the nine ball it lucked in and when he missed a shot, Lefty was almost always snookered behind a ball. Before Lefty knew what was happening he was down far more money than he was able to pay. So, in a panic, he kept doubling the bet. And, in the same panic, he got wristlock so bad he couldn't pocket three balls in a row.

When the bead score said Lefty owed Robert twelve hundred dollars, Robert insisted on settling up. The whole pool room froze to catch Lefty's answer, everyone knowing he never had that kind of money and, if he did, he still wouldn't pay up. Lefty told Robert he had to get the money from home and would pay him the next day. The following day and the thirty or so that followed it found Robert coming into the pool room only long enough to ask Lefty for his twelve hundred dollars. It became a running gag to the locals around the pool room that at just past noon Robert would show up with the same question: "Lefty, where's my twelve hundred dollars?" to which Lefty always had the same empty pocket answer, "Can't do it today, Robert. Things are a little tight."

One Saturday morning, when the place was full, Robert came in a little more agitated than usual and said, "God dammit Lefty. Where is my twelve hundred dollars? I'm sick of asking you for it." to which Lefty jumped up from his domino game and barked, "God dammit back at you Robert. I'm sick of the question. Would you settle for six hundred?" In the blink of an eye, Robert said "Yes."

Lefty said, "OK, I owe you six hundred."

Some of us were sitting around in Dallas, after an all-nighter, talking about the worst equipment we had ever played on and with us, most discussions were fodder for a wager. We were constantly competitive and always looking for a little edge. How did the man put it? "I'm not here to rob and steal, I just want to wheel and deal." Don't believe him. We had entries into the bad equipment story pool about playing without chalk or even without a tip on the cue. Someone said the electricity went off in the middle of a big money freeze out (when money is put up and nobody can quit until there is a winner) and they finished the session by lantern light.

The hands down poor equipment story winner this morning was a little guy from Fort Worth who said he played in a small New Mexico mountain town, in a two-table pool room, on tables that had no felt covering at all. He told us they re-covered the tables each day with the local newspapers. He went on to say, "The tables were not that good for playing on, but the town had an inordinate amount of pool bums who were educated on current events." I don't remember if we paid that little guy before or after we beat him up, but we never welched on a bet.

I asked if I could use a story I had heard Minnesota Fats tell about bad equipment. I was denied using his entry for the cash under the "no coattail hanging rule," but was told to spill the story anyway, however sketchy the details. So here's the tale.

It seems Fats was hustling in this very old, upstairs pool room that had partly wooden, totally creaky floors. He said "partly wooden" because the other part of the floor was air. Fats said people had to actually step across some good sized holes in the floor, all around the table, in order to shoot. This would lead one to believe that the overall floor structure might not be too sturdy. Even walking to the bar or the bathroom could lend pause for concern, and we're not talking about Minnesota Skinny here. Fats said the only advantage was that wherever he was in the room he could look through the holes and see who was coming up the stairs. The other thing this particular room had were the very old style tables where the balls rolled into the pockets and down a metal track to a gathering shelf beneath the racking end of the table. These were called gutter tables and you rarely see them today, except on some of the bar-sized coin tables. Fats started playing the house man One Pocket, with the house man insisting on kicking it off for a hundred a game. Having only a hundred dollars in his pocket didn't bother Fats, even knowing if he loses the first game, it's over. Fats had a lot of gamble in him. What a treat it would have been to know

Fats when he was in his prime. No matter that he wasn't the "greatest player ever" as he self-proclaimed, he was a world class character and a high roller. At his Billiards Congress of America (BCA) Hall of Fame speech he said, "I was driving Dusenbergs when them other guys was puttin' air in their tennis shoes." Fats knew the game of One Pocket inside and out.

One-Pocket: It takes eight balls, pocketed in any sequence, in one of the two top corner pockets to win playing One Pocket. Each player has their own pocket. The balls are broken softly, in a safe manner, from one side of the table, which determines what player has which pocket. The object of the break is to push as many balls toward your pocket as possible while leaving the cue ball in a safe place on your opponent's side of the table. One Pocket is a game of playing your opponent safe where he or she cannot shoot toward their pocket, until you get a shot at your own. The game involves a lot of strategy and is one of the better games for stalling against a weaker player because you can beat him more slowly, a few balls at a time, as opposed to nine-ball where you have to open up more.

In this particular game with Fats, the score came down to seven and seven, with the one deciding ball left on the table. Because of the safety play involved, the last ball can be on the table for a long time. The rule on a "safety" is the cue (or white) ball has to touch a rail after ball contact. Failure to do so penalizes the player one ball. This game was one of those times when each player shot close to a dozen safeties. Even for Fats, who was known to have a lot of patience playing One Pocket, the slow answer to whether he would be broke or not was becoming maddening. Suddenly Fats saw an opportunity, a long shot, in both the figurative and literal sense. His opponent left the game ball close to the middle of the end rail, on the end of the table where their pockets were. The cue ball was halfway down to the other end of the table, a little off to one side. The shot was too thin to cut in so Fats elected to shoot at a four rail bank, knowing he was going to have to turn the cue ball loose. It was a win or, more likely, lose shot. The table's cloth was damp from the humidity and rolled sluggishly, which meant Fats needed to put his weight into it and fire the cue ball hard to get the object ball four rails around the table, which is just what the fat man did. The object ball came shooting off the first rail like a Roman candle and the cue ball went wild in the opposite direction. The audience, who had come out of their seats and were standing as close to the table as they were permitted to be on this now or never attempt, made a collective noise that sounded somewhere between a gasp and a deep breath, then went silent for just a moment. Some of them quickly moved even closer to the table as if being closer to this final shot made them part of the event.

Speculative comments came in at a murmur.

Rounding the first two rails perfectly and then coming off the third rail, the ball looked right on track and Fats' prospects were looking good. But the instant the ball came bouncing off the fourth rail, heading directly but slowly toward Fats' pocket, there was first heard a low creaking noise, like someone dragging their fingernails across a blackboard. The room went silent and everyone stood dead still. Then a loud crunching, splintery, sound filled the room as the floor under Fats' feet disintegrated into almost wood chip sized pieces, and the round man, cue still in hand, disappeared through the floor faster than David Copperfield's assistant.

The way Fats tells the tale, just as his head was following his body through the hole in the floor, heading to who knows what fate down below, he saw his successfully pocketed ball rolling down the chute to join the other seven. It was rolling alone so he knew the cue ball hadn't scratched and he had, indeed, won the game. Before Fats hit the bottom floor, the whole pool room heard him yell, at the top of his voice, "Play for two hundred!" There was nobody like Minnesota Fats.

Some of The Cotton Palace stories had a more serious tone and involved some very scary characters who based their operations out of there. One of these characters was Stanley Cook, a known hired gun. Stanley was a mellow, soft-spoken guy who was always nice to me and all of us who knew him. He didn't play well himself, but he loved to practice with me or bet on my games. When I met Stanley, he was washing windows on highrise office buildings. His resistance to wearing safety belts earned him the name "Creeper." One time his co-worker friend was slipping from their scaffold and Stanley held onto him as long as he could until they both fell eighty feet, seemingly to certain death. They hit a concrete ledge on their way to the pavement below that flipped them over. His friend hit on his head and was killed, while Stanley landed on his back and survived, with multiple broken bones throughout his body and a serious concussion. He was slow walking mush for the longest time and no sooner recovered when he suffered more major injuries in a horrendous car accident. He was crushed and once again spent months in the hospital. I don't know if it came from a feeling of invincibility or, at least, super resiliency, but that was about the time Stanley ditched his window washing career and started in a new direction that would earn him the label of "Texas' most feared hit man."

Al Reinert wrote in Texas Monthly Magazine, in December, 1993, "Regardless of statistical records, there is little doubt, the king of Texas hit men, until this time last year, was a Dallasite named Stanley Cook, cheerfully known to his friends and fans as 'The Creeper.' Variously credited with between ten and fifty murders, Cook was easily best known as the most feared hit man in the state, labeled by both The Texas Rangers and The Dallas Morning News as an enforcer for The Dixie Mafia." Reinert went on to quote a friend of Cook's as saying, "The thing that made him so bad is he didn't care about killing. He'd shoot you right in the God damn middle of Times Square."

The media made certain the public knew a lot about Stanley but his friends had an even closer look. In a moment of secrecy Stanley told me a story about one of his escapades. He had fulfilled a contract and put someone to death for a man whom he said owned an insurance company. Later, Stanley said the insurance man asked him to take a ride with him. In an attempt to cover his tracks, the man stopped in a dark neighborhood and told Stanley to look out the window at the house where the man said he lived. When Stanley turned back around the man was pointing a .357 Magnum pistol at him. Stanley said the first slug hit him around the center of his ribs on his left side and came out his right side, just under his shoulder. He said the worst pain came from the back of his head and shoulder being slammed into the ceiling of the car as the bullet went through him. He opened the door and rolled out just as the second slug hit him in the right side of his neck and traveled down and out the left side of his body.

With the biggest crisscrossed holes through his body that almost any pistol could make, Stanley still managed to run into the fenced in back yard of a house. When he looked back, the man was standing by the gate at the only exit from the yard. The moon was full and Stanley said he could see the man holding the gun up by his chest and watching him. With no alternative escape route, Stanley charged right toward and by the man, avoiding two more shots, got into the car and drove to the hospital. Weeks later, when Stanley was released, the insurance man had sold his company and his home and moved out of town, sans forwarding address, lest he meet Stanley again.

Stanley came out to Tucson and stayed with my wife and me for a couple of weeks, later in my life. Regardless of his occupation, he was our friend and had always been a gentleman to both of us, but he was the first visitor we ever had who came with twenty flasks of mercury in his car. Don't ask. Don't tell. When the FBI came to our home, after he left, they asked my wife, Beverly, in what capacity did Mr. Cook serve while in our home? (Those little peekers had been watching us.) Bev told them he was our babysitter. The Feds smiled, handed her their cards and their "call us" line, and left. Stanley did, in fact, watch our six-month old boy for us more than once while we went out. We knew there was a chance the baby's

Pablum might not be mixed just right, but we were absolutely certain nobody was going to push him around.

Stanley "The Creeper" Cook's luck ran out in 1972 when he walked out of the Lemon Twist Bar, on Lemon Avenue in Dallas. First he opened the passenger door of his car and let his friend in. Then, as he opened his own door and the interior light came on, he was shot in the chest from across the street with a .30 caliber rifle. Stanley died instantly. An attendant at the service station across the street said he saw "two clean cut, well dressed men drive hurriedly off in a late model car." It is suspected he was taken out by the mob for maintaining such a high profile. Mr. Reinert's article also stated that, the last Texas attorney general's 'Report on Organized Crime' virtually gloated over Cook's demise, "when he found himself on the other end of one of those contracts." Nobody was ever charged with the murder.

Many pool sessions in The Cotton Palace continued for two or three days without stopping. This was accomplished thanks to the miracle of pharmaceuticals. When someone mentioned needing an "L.A. turn-around," they weren't talking about a bus ticket. Diet pills or "Uppers" were the rage. Dexedrine, Benzedrene, Dexamyl spansules (time-release capsules), and for those who wanted to stay up for days and bore their friend to tears with endless jabbering, there were the super powerful Black Mollies. All of these drugs would keep you awake and, when you hit your stride, make you play to the absolute best of your ability. We didn't smoke pot. Texas was the most draconian of all states on that matter and first offense for possession, at that time, was an automatic prison sentence. The criminal aspect aside, my thoughts were who would want to smoke a joint and hang out and listen to music and be cool with friends when you can be out robbing some sucker on a pool table?

Our definition of a pure sucker (though small as he was) was "Crackalou Jim." Jim was some sort of businessman who came in every Saturday night, always dressed in a business suit and always half lit. I had two things going for me with Jim. He wouldn't play anyone but me and secondly, he couldn't make a ball in the ocean playing pool. But Jim had a stipulation; we had to play one game of six-ball, which took about three minutes and one game, of his own design, called Crackalou, each for five dollars, back and forth, and we would usually play for hours. The rules to Crackalou are as simple as anyone who would play the game. The floor outside of the pool area was some sort of tile or parquet in squares. We each would throw a coin into the air, behind our heads and whoever's coin landed closest to any crack between the tiles wins. Absolutely skill-less, but Jim loved it because it was his own concoction. I would figure to win half of the Crackalou games and all of the pool games so I could count on "Crackalou Jim" to donate fifty or sixty bucks a week to my cause. Jim was probably this very successful guy who told his cohorts at work about making some pool hustling kid throw coins in the air to make a living.

Here is a quick story that properly defines our "suckers." Two straight shooting pool hustlers were shivering in the cold outside of a closed pool room, with no place to go, when a big Cadillac drove by. One of them said, "Hey! There goes Doc Barnes. Remember when I beat that sucker out of two hundred dollars? It was like stealing. Man, what a sucker." Next came a new Mercedes and the other hustler said, "There goes that lawyer that we used to team up on and beat playing dominoes every Thursday until he wised up. I got that sucker for eighty dollars in less than an hour." And so on. The "suckers" drove nice cars and lived in nice homes, while we "smarts" slept under pool tables. I never understood the importance of that story until I went straight and I haven't slept under a pool table in years.

The diet pills did, indeed, make you play better, gave you the confidence to bet high, and helped you stay in action longer. When the formula kicked in just right, a kitty cat would turn into a mountain lion. The downside of uppers, other than risking addiction, overdosing, jail time, and not being able to quit playing when you were getting your brains beat out, was that coming down from them spelled a hard crash, no matter who you were. People could turn mean as snakes for no reason. A lot of early morning confrontations in The Cotton Palace were attributed to someone crashing from a "Dexie trip." A side benefit of the diet pills was we stayed slim.

My own contact with pills was limited, thanks to good advice from my older brother and fellow hustler, Jack. So much of my career and knowledge of the game was influenced by him. He taught me a lot of good hustling tips and, over the years, he also ironed out a couple of "toughs" who were messing with me. Jack had grown up hustling pool around Houston in the 50s when fisticuffs went hand-in-hand with pool playing and he was equally proficient at both. My approach to getting by was more "rabbitesque." I could ride my bike away from a pool room at full speed, unscrew my cue, and count my money all at the same time. America's Funniest Videos would have had a field day with me.

In the school of hard knocks, my brother Jack was my professor. Late one night, in The Cotton Palace, a guy named Jimmy something, who was as crazy about Jack as he was about pool came up to my table and said, "Alfie, make this ball and I'll give you twenty dollars." I was straight in on the easy shot and couldn't figure his angle but I shot the ball in and he threw a twenty dollar bill on the table. I had never seen money that was a pea green color but before I could (or wanted to) question it he said, "Another ball, Alfie, another twenty." I collected again and he played one more round. I looked at the funny money, laughing. The three bills were dated around the 1920 or 30s. I asked the guy what was up. He took me to his car and pulled the back seat up to show layers of the stuff. "I got it out of my grandmothers safe. She has stacks of it and never goes in there." A light went on and I asked him, "Well, has Jack been able to reach you?"

"What?" he said. "Jack wants to see me?" I told him, "Yeah, he's been asking around about you. We should go wake him up." He was so anxious to see him that he jumped into the front seat without even dropping the back seat down, an errand I quickly took care of lest we get stopped by a constable. We did indeed wake Jack up but Jack Taylor was never fully asleep. He knew if I was there with a stranger it wasn't for high tea. "Jack," I said. "We have a problem. I'll explain after I use your bathroom," at which time I told his wife, who was in the bedroom, that the kid was "packin' heavy loot."

Then I went back into the front room while Jack excused himself to talk with Betty. When he returned I said, "Jack, Tommy Lambert beat me out of eighty dollars and we're both broke. Can you help us out?" Jack said "Well. I only have thirty dollars. Here Alfie, I'll give you ten, but Jimmy, I'll give you twenty." Jimmy's eyes almost teared with joy as he pulled up the front of his shirt to three stacks of money under his belt, which he threw up in the air and said, "Don't worry Jack. I have plenty of money." The rest, as you might guess, is history, but to continue the history lesson, Jack asked Jimmy if he wanted to take a road trip to Oklahoma City. When they arrived Jack held the bankroll while he sent Jimmy to the hotel room upstairs with a hooker. What the lady of the evening was doing to the guy upstairs, Jack was doing to him down below. The pool game was over and the money was gone. The kid didn't care; he got to go on the road with Jack Taylor. Besides, he still had Grandma's combination. Later, when Jack showed up at a bank with the goofy bills the banker was hesitant about cashing them in. Jack told her "Read this bill: it says 'pay to the bearer on demand.' I'm the bearer and I'm demanding." He got his money. But, that's what they say about Jack: "Win or lose, he always gets his end." Some events in The Cotton Palace were of a more serious nature.

The following incident happened around five or six in the morning when the action was cold and tempers were warm, a time when everyone who had gone up the night before was coming down. The place was still crowded with leftovers, everyone guzzling coffee, comparing notes on the night, and cutting up jackpots (an industry term for telling pool stories).

There was one man in the place who had a group of the regulars following him around. Whenever a bookie or other high roller came around, everyone liked to stay close to him in case he got into action. We called it, "playing to the strength." I was practicing nine-ball with a guy who was about my age and physical stature named Danny Mayfield. Danny was a preppy, nice guy bowler, the type of guy who not only had a social security card, but actually carried it. For kicks, he liked to play pool with me. I didn't know that the big man who everyone was trying to stay close to was Russell Douglas Matthews, a name that meant nothing to me. I would surely have been more diplomatic had I known that Mr. Matthews had been labeled by one well known columnist as "the most dangerous man in America."

The sound of R.D. Matthews' name made the local tough guys tremble. He made Charlie Boyd (a very dangerous man himself, as you will see further along in the story) fetch drinks for him. In the book, *Contract on America: The Mafia Murder of John F. Kennedy* (1989), based largely on the findings of the Warren Commission, Matthews was described (in an FBI report) as a "burglar, armed robber, narcotics pusher, and murderer." They also linked him as a key figure in the Kennedy assassination conspiracy, all the way to him being a possible trigger man.

In an article from The Las Vegas Review Journal, September 3, 2000, John Smith wrote the following about R.D. Matthews: "Organized crime and gambling sources just whistle and whisper about Matthews, a 60-year friend of Benny Binion and operator of downtown Old Paddock Race Book. They think the world of him but would never want to cross him. The man's reputation stretches from Texas, where he ran with the Hollis De Lois Gang, worked in the gambling rackets with Binion, and was arrested fifty-nine times, but served only a single prison sentence; to Havana, where he helped operate casinos linked to Meyer Lansky and Santo Trafficante; back to Dallas and the heart of the Kennedy assassination, where his proximity to Jack Ruby and other key players raised the suspicions of the 1964 Warren Commission Report and 1979 House Select Committee on assassinations; back to Las Vegas where he found refuge and a job with his dear friend, Benny Binion." Mr. Smith described Mr. Matthews as "one tough piece of rope." To a punk like me, who knew nothing, the man was just one more of the many strangers who ventured nightly into the Cotton Palace.

R.D. walked up to my table, in what appeared to be an angry mood, and barked at me, "Are you Jack Taylor's brother?" I answered in the affirmative.

He said, "Tell your brother I'm going to kill him."

It seemed Jack had scammed Titanic Thompson, one of the most famous gamblers in history, out of some money, and R.D. had decided to champion Ti's cause. I don't know why he was so upset when Jack had simply conned a guy who had conned a million. Titanic ("Ti"), who was seventy-six at this time, was hustling cards in New York, in 1928, when Arnold Rothstein (the gangster widely believed to have fixed the 1919 World Series) was killed, and was called to testify at the alledged shooter's trial, so he was definitely a player. I was lucky enough to be Ti's friend and even took a road trip with him. At seventy-six, he was one of the few men in the country who could shoot his age on the golf course. And Ti could do it with either hand. He was a world class horseshoe player, a competent bowler with a well-disguised, slow rolling game, a fair pool player, and a top card man.

Once, when I was about twenty, I was driving with him from Shreveport to Dallas. We had been in Shreveport trying to trap a guy named Sarge. Ti had me lose money to several of the lightweight players in our three day attempt to get Sarge on the table. When Sarge wouldn't bite, I asked Ti if I could go ahead and bust those guys who I had lost money to, but he said no. I should save them for another day and another play. On the way out of town, we stopped at a golf course where Ti introduced himself to a group of doctors as an oil man (he had actually done some wildcatting in his younger days). In eighteen holes, making various bets on every hole, he recouped all our expenses and the money I sluffed off playing pool back, and then some.

I was feeling particularly close to Ti as he told me stories on the drive home, and so I opened up and told him how much I envied him.

"What?" he said. I told him how everyone respected him so much and how he was so capable in so many games and he was the only person I ever knew who carried thousand dollar bills. He blurted out at me like I was nuts: "Don't you dare envy me. I'm seventy-six years old. I'd like to be your age, standing out there on the highway, hitchhiking, dead broke, and buck naked."

I learned a lot from Ti, but now, at age sixty six, some things ring truer than others.

I wasn't brave, just a smart aleck and badly uninformed, when I said to R.D. Matthews in reply to his threat to kill my brother, "Tell him yourself. I'm not your message boy." It wasn't the best answer because the big man jumped in about two feet from my face and snarled, "Then, I'll just kill you."

He then turned to a girl we all knew and said, "Linda Lou, take me to get my gun," then stormed out the door with her close behind.

I didn't think much of it and continued playing when another tough guy named Billy T. Dyer, who was Linda Lou's boyfriend, came over and told me who I was messing with and said he really would kill me. I remember he said, "Alfie, you're a boy in a man's world and you might die tonight. Leave now." Billy was always nice to me, even this time when he was issuing a command; especially this time.

How tough was Billy T., you ask. Charlie Boyd once shot Billy T. point blank in his upper torso six times with a .38 while they were sitting in the front seat of Charlie's car, then kicked him out into a ditch. One would think that would be that. But no; Billy, whom we had labeled "Davy Crockett" because he was big and hearty, crawled across a field to a farmhouse and got help. Miraculously, every bullet missed a vital organ. Days later, when Billy awoke in the hospital, he found Charlie sitting beside him with flowers in his hand and an apology on his lips. Charlie claimed the pills had gotten him "upset" and wondered if they were still buddies. They were.

Another time Charlie came into the bowling alley with another "tuff" named Jimmy Anderson. Jimmy had fresh stitches showing down one side of his throat. When I asked what had happened, Jimmy told me that Charlie, who was standing right there with us, had gotten pilled up the night before and cut his throat. I looked at Charlie and asked, with fake awe, "Really, Charlie?" whereupon Charlie pulled out his knife, put his thumb about an inch down from the point, and said, "Yeah, but I held my thumb here so I wouldn't kill him." Now, that's a considerate fellow.

Charlie terrified me so much that one time he robbed me over the telephone. He called me when I was playing in a bar and asked how much money I had. I told him sixty dollars. He said, "Alfie, you little son-of-a-bitch, don't you lie to me." I apologized and said I had two hundred and forty. He told me to leave half of it with the bartender for him and to be gone when he got there. No problem. The cash was there and I was far away. I didn't tell him about the two twenties I had tucked into the old alligators.

Charlie liked any kind of crime. We walked out of a restaurant once, and a workman was repairing the front door. He was on his ladder with his tool chest on the sidewalk behind him. As we walked by, Charlie reached into the tool box and grabbed a can of Liquid Wrench and stuck it in his pocket. He surely didn't need that can. I don't even know if he realized what he was taking. He was just putting in his time at work.

On another occasion, Charlie and his very dangerous accomplice, Chester McElvane, robbed a sweater salesman for his samples, right in the bowling alley parking lot. Charlie had been barred from the bowling alley (via the mail, because nobody would do it in person), so he operated an extortion game from a phone booth across the street. The sweater salesman was a young kid who came in regularly. I remember him walking into the bowling alley and flashing a newly purchased pistol to all of us. Knowing that Charlie had been barred from the place, he announced, with a swagger, "I'd like to see that Charlie Boyd mess with me now."

Later in the evening Charlie called and asked to talk with the "sweater man." After their conversation, the sweater salesman put down the phone, walked over to me, visibly terrified, and said, "Alfie, Charlie wants me to come across the street and talk to him. Hold my money and gun until I get back."

Without a doubt we had a mole who had tipped off Charlie. Pool games came to a halt. Everyone was waiting for the outcome. While we didn't think our friend would get hurt, we were certain he wasn't going to get helped. Ten or so minutes later, with his bravado properly drained, our courageous sweater man called me on the phone. Everyone crowded in to hear.

"Alfie," he said, his voice cracking and stammering at the same time, "I'm with Charlie. Would you please bring my money across the street? He wants to borrow it." I told him I would.

Before I got out the door, he called again and said, "Alfie," his voice now in the second phase of tears, "Would you bring my gun? He said he wants to borrow that too."

Right then we knew this was no more than a late night Cotton Palace, Charlie Boyd hogging, so it was getting really comical. I'm sure Charlie was having a good time, as well. I took the goods across the street as instructed and set them down near the phone booth, then left without making any eye contact whatsoever. I wanted this to stay funny and I wanted myself to stay out of it. We all watched what transpired next, from inside the front door, and the house came unglued with laughter. Charlie and Chester escorted their guest back to the parking lot and the trunk of his car, where his sweater samples were kept. As sweater man opened his trunk, his car alarm went off accidentally. What a show we got watching him as he frantically ripped the wires out of his own car alarm because turning it off with the key might take too long and piss Charlie off. He carried his garment bags to Charlie's car. When Charlie left, sweater man looked up at us watching him and left without coming in.

The next day Charlie called me and said he wanted to give me a few sweaters and would I come to his apartment. I didn't want any sweaters any more than I wanted stolen merchandise, and I didn't want either as much as I didn't want to go to his apartment. But, most of all, I didn't want to say no to Charlie.

When I arrived at Charlie's apartment, Chester McElvane was sitting on the bed reading. Charlie said, "Alfie, watch this." Then, in front of both of us, he emptied his .38 revolver out on the table holding the gun about three feet over the table illustrating his flair for the dramatic with the unmistakable firecracker like noise of the shells smacking the Formica. Charlie said, "Hey Chet, look here," as he stuck one shell back in the gun, spun the chamber, then instantly snapped off a "click" point blank at Chester.

I remember Chester throwing both arms and legs in front of himself, out of reflex, long after the shot would have done it's thing, and screaming, "God damn it, Charlie, I wish you'd quit doing that!" I wondered how many times Charlie had done it before, but there was no way I was going to ask because I knew Charlie and I knew, sure as shootin', another spin and click, or bang, would soon follow. I just wasn't sure in which direction. Claiming an allergy to wool, I left without a sweater...better known as evidence.

Two very nice pool hustlers, Don Watson and Joe Cosgrove, from Atlanta, spent some time in The Cotton Palace. These southern gentlemen were classic hustlers of the old school who would never cause any problems. Not ever. I was delighted to be their friend. Both of them had been winning regularly so they had a pretty good bankroll. Charlie, who was still a Cotton Palace member at this time, marched the two of them into a small bathroom in the back of the pool area (that was closed for good, immediately afterwards), where he robbed them and ordered them to not come out for thirty minutes. Then Charlie went into the bowling alley cafe to relax and count his earnings, actually thumbing through the bills with an air of impunity as he walked through the pool table area. I watched Don Watson, who couldn't be more mild mannered, come out of the bathroom and pool area, into the cafe, a little prematurely. When he saw Charlie sitting in the cafe, he turned and actually ran between the pool tables, back into the bathroom. We couldn't laugh at Don because any of us would have done the same. Charlie was scary.

One night Charlie called me at the bowling alley and said the Sheriff told him not to ever come back home to McKinney, a small town just outside of Dallas. He went on to tell me how, earlier that day he had shot his wife in each leg for "giving him a hard time," but she refused to press charges and it had "pissed the sheriff off." That's what I call a wife. We knew the two of them worked it out because months later his wife shot him in the chest with a .22 rifle. Again, that's what I call a wife. As is typical with .22s, the bullet hit a bone or bones and did a folk dance through Charlie's torso. It punctured a lot of stuff. Charlie hung on, in critical condition, for weeks, but all of the prayer sessions we had were for nothing. Charlie pulled through.

Mr. Boyd wasn't so lucky later when he went to prison for trying to rob the Princeton, Texas, post office. Not very long after his imprisonment, he died during gall bladder surgery in a Galveston, Texas, hospital. The rumor that went around for years, that he had been killed by a fellow inmate while in prison, made for a better story and, until recently, that's what we all thought. One way or the other, Charlie's dead. You think I'd be writing this stuff about him if he were not?

Back to Mr. R.D. Matthews and me: With my newly gained information about my young life possibly ending this morning at the hands of "America's most dangerous" (I hate it when that happens), I suddenly remembered a prior commitment elsewhere. Stopping only long enough to pick up my cigarette from the table rail and put the wrong end in my mouth ...a mistake, quickly detected... I made this one of the times I braved the sunlight home. As my friends relate the story, about fifteen or twenty minutes elapsed when R.D. came barging through the door and up to Danny Mayfield, who was still playing, stuck a long barreled hand gun in Danny's face and cocked the hammer back. Billy T. jumped in and told R.D. that Danny was the wrong guy. If I could have been a very small fly on the wall, I would have loved to have seen Danny's face. R.D. then put out the word that I had twenty-four hours to pack my things and "get out of Dallas," but sticking to my principles that I was not to be pushed around or told what I had to do, I made it in twelve.

Actually, the last line was for humor. The next day Titanic called R.D. and told him that I was his friend, a "good boy," and had even traveled the road with him. It's funny how R.D., who had come down from whatever he was on the night before, could barely remember the next day, an incident that I haven't been able to forget in more than forty years. But listen, if any of you reading this know R.D.'s whereabouts, don't mention my name to him, O.K.?

Another very lethal individual who hung out at the Cotton Palace a lot was George McGann. George was a poker player with a reputation for being a poor player who sometimes left poker games with all of the money, even when he lost. He once played in a game with Richard Nixon, and lost. The Secret Service agents kept George from pulling his act this time. George liked to bet on me and was always a nice to me. One time I asked him if he had recently seen a certain person we both knew (the name eludes me). This guy hadn't been around for weeks, after becoming a semi-regular. I knew he and George had been having some problems over money and I think I was just bored and stirring up embers by bringing his name up to George.

George said, "You know, Alfie. It's the damnedest thing I ever heard.

Talk about a crazy suicide. That guy walked almost twenty miles south on I-45, crawled up in a drainpipe, and shot himself six times." I felt no need for elaboration on George's blackest of comedy.

There's a story about George that was written up in Bluff Magazine (July 2007). It seems he robbed the players in a poker game and the next night came back, bought chips, and joined the same game. Everyone in the game was afraid to quit or even mention the previous night. Once he arrived at a game early and just robbed and tied up the players as they walked in. When some of his captives began objecting, George pulled out a knife and held it to one person's ear and said "the next M.F to say a word loses one." There are a lot of threats that won't quiet a person. This wasn't one of them. Another time when he was in a poker game, he had taken off his watch and put it on the table. It disappeared. He stood up, pulled out a very large gun and said, "Everyone in here is getting searched. You can get it standing up or laying down." The watch reappeared and the game continued. But George McGann was alright with me. We even took a hustling trip through Oklahoma together. What did I know about the people I was hanging around with? I was just a young pool player.

In 2007 Johnny Hughes, writing for Bluff Magazine, said George McGann was responsible for thirty murders, and was a suspect in the murder of the wife of Buford Pusser, of the movie Walking Tall fame. He too was listed in the Warren Commission Report as a key figure and possible trigger man in the Kennedy assassination conspiracy.

In the classic tradition of living and dying by the sword, George Albert McGann, at thirty-three years old, while in Lubbock, Texas, was shot to death by the man he was allegedly holding hostage. It is said that "everyone has skeletons in their closet." The Cotton Palace crowd lived in the closet with theirs.

In what amounted to an obituary for pool action at the The Cotton Palace, an article in The Dallas Morning News on May 3, 1966, reported that the Dallas City Council had "voted to revoke the billiard hall license of the Cotton Bowling Palace." This followed a raid by the police the week before to "stop billiards' gambling," and marked the end of the The Cotton Palace era.

The four or five years that I hung around the The Cotton Palace could be described as my "R-rated formative years." It took the touch of an angel and one amazing looking California girl to help me escape intact. And I did it just before the big raid.

Alvin Clarence Thomas, AKA "Titanic Thompson"

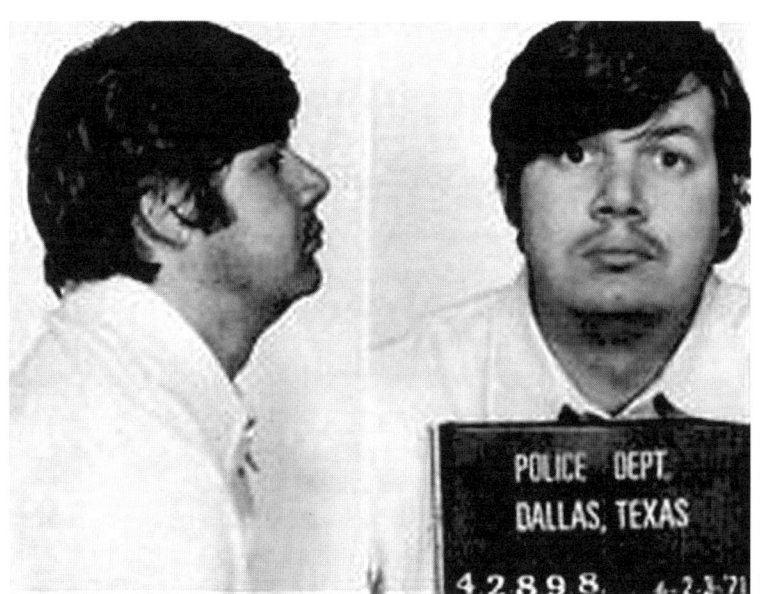

Stanley "The Creeper" Cook – Texas hit man and Chris' babysitter.

THE POOL WIDOWS:
THEY'RE SWEPT AWAY BY THE INTRIGUE

Pool Widows; (pül widōz)–noun, plural. *Wives or girlfriends of pocket billiards hustlers and pocket billiards suckers, whose patience and fortitude are taxed regularly by long hours of sitting and assisting their counterpart while he is trying to win money to pay bills that you can bet even money are past due. (20th C. Am.)*

Pool widows are a breed of their own. They're sharper in general than the typical wife or girlfriend. They have to be; they're exposed to secrets about the semi-underworld that are hidden from the working class. They develop a sharper intuition so they can tell when someone is trying to get over on them – it's called being "with the show." The pool players creed is "Be sincere, whether you mean it or not" and the widows see right through it.

Pool widows can sit quietly for hours on end, while their man tries to bring home the bacon on the green felt. Talking or moving in a distracting manner while he's shooting is out of the question. On the other hand, when his opponent is up to the table, gab is permitted, or even encouraged. They sometimes handle side action, hold the stakes, or fetch coffee, sandwiches, booze, or cigarettes. In more intense situations, when some form of equalizer is necessary, a widow's purse will leave the building and return five or six pounds heavier. Some of the ladies will work crossword puzzles or bring a book or some needlework type of falderal to keep their hands busy. The more experienced ones will bring a toothbrush and a pillow to sit on, never knowing how long the sit might be.

Widows make the best messengers, whether it is to the backers for more scratch or to deliver something of a more cryptic nature to a co-conspirator behind the scenes. This was before cell phones, so widows made all of the necessary phone calls, lest their man miss a game. Their mission included encouraging their man to win or coaxing him to quit if he has a bad game. If he gets broke there are only two options for the widow. Stay far away from him 'till he cools or get extra close and cool him out herself. Widows wait at home, sometimes for days on end, for their husbands to arrive, never knowing when, with whom, or with how much or little money, but knowing for certain, whether he was a smoker or not, he would smell that way. His clothes would require a written estimate at the cleaners. Even the money he pulls from his pockets reeks of stale tobacco. His hair, forget about it.

Widows prepare odd meals at the oddest hours because even the few pool hustlers who wear watches don't live by them and the standard fare doesn't dictate what he eats. Greg Stevens, a hustler from Wichita would, on occasion, eat two or three deserts before his entree arrived. There was a trick bet going around that a person couldn't eat a quail a day for thirty days straight. The few who tried it vomited after a week or so. They're too rich. I heard someone offer the bet to Minnesota Fats and Fats replied, "I'll bet you I can eat thirty of them little birds in one sitting and throw in a tom turkey. If you don't pay up, I'll eat you too."

Pool hustlers punch out and go home when someone gets broke. Keeping the TV turned down for twenty hours or more while he catches up on his sleep is not unusual. My older brother Jack told me that when I crashed after a long session, I was like a cadaver and no amount of yelling, shaking, or water splashing would roust me. The house could be on fire and I wouldn't budge. But try to take my diamond watch off my arm, in my deepest dreamland, and I was on you like a hobo on a ham sandwich. It's a matter of priorities.

Widows have to live with the constant mood swings that come with their chicken and feathers lifestyle, sometimes quietly, sometimes with futile resistance. They're exposed to the underbelly of society, no matter what good soul is shooting for their team. They are a society of their own, keeping hours that would make their mothers lose sleep along with them. Their conversations rarely stray from the latest action or who should be able to beat whom, playing what game. Once in a pool room in Tucson, I heard some of them talking outside of their bathroom. The men's room was out of order so sharing the ladies room was in order. One of the girls who had just come out said, "I just don't understand it. Those guys can hit a six-inch pocket dead center from nine feet away and they can't hit a two foot toilet from two feet away; must be something wrong with their stick." . . . followed by feminine guffaws.

Some widows are more animated. Once, in The Cotton Palace, I saw Savanna Red Peterson run in covering a deep, bleeding cut on his forehead. Running a few steps behind Red was his wife who was carrying one of her high heels by the sole and screaming through her gums, "You son-of-a-bitch. You better give me back my false teeth." To which Red grabbed the lump in his front pocket, shook it and replied, "Got 'em right here but I ain't gonna do it, baby. You'll leave me for sure." Like a good widow, she stuck around and Red returned her choppers. Ain't love grand?

The best pool widows were the ones who had day jobs that paid the nut ("nut" being the minimum expenses to keep a roof overhead and food on the table). To their credit, most pool widows, in the words of the late Patsy

Cline, do stand by their man.

Typically, as a young pool hustler (22 at the time), I didn't like girls hanging around the tables or even playing on them. They killed the action. In The Cotton Palace the rules stated a person could not hang around in the pool room area if they were not checked onto a table. When girls gathered around in the pool area (chicks dig pool players), I would usually summon one of the rent-a-cop guards to shoo them out. I made a lot of enemies, guys and girls, but this wasn't a popularity contest to me. I was on the job.

This night was different. It was a little after midnight and I was waiting for the late night suckers from the closing bars to show up, where they could play 'till dawn and on. Freshly showered and shaved, I was at my best. I was leaning over a table smoking a cigarette and watching a young woman, whom I had definitely never seen before, playing pool. On this night I was more than content with the gender encroachment. She was on the back corner table, playing alone, with all signs pointing to her wanting to be left that way. It didn't matter that she couldn't play well, putting it mildly. She was a knockout. She was shapely for sure, about five' five", with short brown hair in a pixie cut, emerald green eyes, soft, full, unpainted lips over sparkling teeth, and perfect dimples, the kind that jump at you with the slightest smile. She was wearing a knee length, sleeveless lime green dress, a color that was popular in the mid-60s. Until tonight it wasn't my favorite color. The dress had a small white collar giving her ensemble the same look of innocence as the woman herself, as if her mom had picked it out. She was wearing small, gold ball earrings and a hair thin gold chain that circled her neck so tightly it hardly moved as she bent over to shoot. Her skin was light olive and her arms and hands were silky smooth, like someone who had used lotion all her life.

She made a solid bridge with her left hand and had a pretty fair stroke, like she had received some personal coaching in her college student union building. I can see how college boys would love the task, not to mention this high schooler. No polish was used or needed on her short, well trimmed, buffed nails, and here I was with a double coat of clear enamel on mine. The best part was there wasn't a sign of a ring on her silky left hand. Her white pumps were kicked aside and her stockinged feet sank softly into the carpeting. She moved around the table slowly and methodically, like a pool cue wielding Ninja. Five or six minutes went by without her pocketing a ball and I still thought this was the best pool I had ever watched. Something about a girl playing pool in stockinged feet is extremely sexy, like when they dance with their arms over their head. Whoever this dreamboat was, whatever she was doing here, wherever she came from, she was, as the country song says, "Close enough to perfect for me." The most exciting thing about her performance was, I could tell she knew I was watching but she didn't look up once. I've always had a high regard for girls who had no time for me.

I boogied behind the front counter and took a look at the name on her driver's license, which was required for a table deposit: "Beverly Goodenough." Beverly, a hostess on American Airlines, had just returned from a New York turnaround flight and had stopped in to play a little pool. She was freshly based in Dallas and, to my utter delight, had not yet made any friends.

My opening line probably could have been better thought out. I buffed off my alligator shoes on the back of my Sansabelt slacks, tucked in my dress shirt real tight, did the "hah" thing on my diamond pinky ring to moisten it for shining against my pants pocket, used my hands to make sure my hair was flattened properly, and sniffed the back of my wrist, happy that my last splash of Canoe was still working. Then I sauntered up to her with what I considered my coolest demeanor and asked, "You're either a stewardess or a hooker. That's all that comes in here this time of night. Which is it?"

Silence and a cool glare came from what was clearly a nice girl. Too bad, really. Had she been a hooker, at least I would have had a chance. So here's the skinny. I'm a two-bit pool hustler, using a line like that on this heartthrob who the previous year was voted Sophomore Princess at UCLA and had been a tennis companion of the great Arthur Ashe. I was in over my head more than Jacques Cousteau on a bad day.

But this night, I had an ace in the hole close by and his name was Minnesota Fats. Fats had come to Dallas and we were running around together. His interest was in crowd pleasing, not hustling, and for me, hanging out with him in front of my homies couldn't have been more fun. Minnesota Fats could draw a crowd on a street corner in Osaka, Japan, before you could say konichiwa. Everybody knew him, everybody was aware of his exaggerated braggadocio, and everybody loved him. And I was sure this little babe would be no exception.

I remember my words to him clearly: "Drop everything Fatty," I said. "This is serious. I need help with an unbelievable girl."

Now nobody ever loved women more than Fats. I heard him say, "I used to play cards for a week, play pool for a week, chase the tomatoes for a week, and sleep for a week." It wouldn't surprise me if it were true. My point being, Mr. Minnesota Fats Wanderone understood my need and was on top of his game. He shot some trick shots for Beverly, he told some pool stories to her, he made her laugh and he said he would be willing to "play one game for a million dollars against her." Fats put stars in her green eyes. If she didn't run away now, I knew I had a chance. She didn't run, she smiled at me, and I did get the chance. Beverly Jean Goodenough was swept off her sheer stockinged, size five and a half feet.

Then this sweet fat man uttered fourteen words that changed two peoples lives forever: "Beverly, I'd like for you to meet my agent here in Dallas, Alfie Taylor." Tah Daa!

A little down the road, a few tricks of my own and I made Beverly into a Taylor wife, never mentioning those two very scary words, Pool Widow. If you make it through this book you will see how my occupation made Beverly temporarily abandon her sheltered upbringing and stick a gun in her purse more than once to help her man, who was in trouble, in a manner that would R-rate a TV show. Seven years later she hung up her "moll" label and escaped from this jungle as much a lady as she was upon entering, and much, much more street smart.

As a note, almost forty years after Beverly left the racket and this racketeer, I'm delighted to say I am writing this particular story on her computer, as her house guest, in Santa Barbara. I told you she was a lady.

I will follow this with a letter from Evelyn Wanderone, written in her own hand, about her travels with her husband. She sent it to me as I was producing a video tribute to Fats, after his passing, for the Billiard Congress of America's Hall of Fame. Evelyn's is a gentler perspective.

DuQuoin, Ill
July 10, 96

Dear Alf & Wife Judy?
Yes I am happy to say that having been married to Minnesota for 44 years, was unlike most girls enjoy.
He taught me what it means to be Street smart. ~~I doubt that knolage~~
We were married in 1941 In those days it was great for a young wife to travel by Car and see the ~~sights~~ across country especially the inside of some of those old pool rooms. ~~But~~ you would be surprised to know that I was well respected, I acted like a lady and they treated me as such.
Minnesota was most happy at our home in Dowell, Ill. With dogs and cats most Cast offs. He hustled food for them every morning, he went to McDonalds and other places that gave good hand outs.
Cats was away on a trip the wheather was bad and ~~I~~ decided we didnt have ~~ads~~ enough shelter for the animals, ~~&~~ I called our lumber co. ask how ~~soon~~ I could get a big animal ~~house~~ built, Soon they erected a block building for the Cats & Dogs — It was known as Evelyn's Cat house. Cats approved and liked it very much.
Please excuse this try.
The Best Of Luck to you Both
Evelyn Wanderone

A GLIMPSE OF BEV'S LIFE TO COME

Dallas, Texas, 1966, The Cotton Bowling Palace

"OK, baby," I told my girlfriend, "as soon as I stuff my 'hoodlum clothes', as you call them, and my alligator shoes and belts into the trunk and back seat, we can be out of here. I'll take the jewelry. I can always hock it. It's a 1959 Cadillac (the same model the first bat mobile was made from) so if I leave the keys in it and the window down, someone will see the stuff and take it, car and all, by morning. I signed the title and left it in the glove box. Then we'll hop in your little Karman Ghia and head for the West Coast. I never want to see this place again."

Bev perked up and just grinned out the words, "First a stop in Las Vegas to get married, right?"

"Right," I said. "That's a for sure." Good girls always seem to come with strings attached.

Then she added, "You're going to love California. People out there don't even carry guns."

"They don't? How do they solve their problems?"

Williams, Arizona, 1966, Grand Canyon, pre-marriage honeymoon

"I didn't run away with you to sit on a smelly donkey, Alfie. And my toes are freezing. I can't wiggle them. I think they're going to break off and look how close to the edge this thing is walking. You talked me into this."

"First of all, it's a mule, Beverly" I answered and added, "Do you think my toes are any warmer? Look at it this way, if your mule slips and falls into the canyon you won't have to worry about cold toes, am I right or Amarillo?" I thought I might add a little levity to the situation.

From there to the trail's end, I got more conversation out of my mule. Our guide kept repeating the same line. "Keep up the pace, people. I have to spend a certain amount of time in this canyon and a certain amount out." He repeated the line so much everyone in the party wanted to spend a certain amount of time thumping him. Did we really shell out money for this torture?

It was sunny all the way to the bottom when we left the South Rim of the canyon and most of the people in the party, like ourselves, didn't plan on the hours we would spend in the shade coming back up. Had we been informed of this when we bought our tickets I'm sure we would be lounging comfortably at the lodge and Bev wouldn't hate me. One woman in the party couldn't bear the discomfort and opted for a very expensive helicopter ride to the top. The only redeeming feature of the mule ride is that in almost a hundred years, no mule has ever slipped off the trail. Bev was pulling for mine to be the first.

Las Vegas, Nevada, 1966

Judge Potter, the Las Vegas Justice of the Peace, was filling out papers after the ceremony when he looked at my new bride and asked "How do you spell your last name?" Out of habit Bev spelled out "Goodenough." He smiled. "Well, I guess the ceremony didn't take. Should I perform it over?"

We laughed like crazy over the silly line, but consider who and where we were. We had the sweet birds of youth thing going for us. We hadn't the foggiest idea of what awaited us but we were carefree and fearless, and that was enough. We just knew they played pool in California and I felt like a walking secret weapon. We laughed at everything. The question was probably the judge's standard joke or should Bev have taken it as an omen?

Dunes Hotel, top floor suite, 1966

So! I thought to myself. How much of this fancy room hanging, wine drinking, snack snacking, and honeymooning can a guy stand all at once? This fool needs to shoot some pool. I tiptoed out of the room into a jam packed casino. No windows, no clocks or watches on any employees, and pure oxygen pumped in so nobody gets drowsy. Money and chips piled high in every direction (except mine) to create the illusion that it has little to no meaning, except as more coupons to join the fun. Do these Vegas people know how to milk a sucker, or what? Unfortunately, my racket required a little more effort and sometimes with a more unruly crowd. I caught a taxi and told him to just cruise the strip. He said the only pool hall was downtown but there were some tables at the bowling alley right down Las Vegas Boulevard. Sure enough, the place had six Brunswick Gold Crown, nine-foot tables. They were good tables but they were covered with a yucky orangey-gold colored felt, with chalk to match. To me, any color of felt other than green was for home tables. I like to get on the green to bet my green. But color be damned, everyone was gambling and throwing the money right out on the table to pay off. I had never seen that before. In Dallas, it was "keep it down or go downtown." I instantly got into action, with all of the side action I could want, and more. "God, I love this city."

My God, I thought. How did I get so broke so fast? Leaving almost two thousand dollars in that place made me sick to my stomach. The guy wasn't even a very good player. I don't know if it was from over betting my bankroll or just plain dogging it from playing so high. I'm a twenty dollar hustler trying to play for two hundred. Noisy ass bowling alley. Stinkin' orange cloth.

I was so immersed in self pity, I didn't notice the guy walking up to me until his fist caught me square in the chest. I remember my back hitting the construction fence behind me was more painful than the punch, but neither bothered me as much as trying to catch my breath, coupled with the taste of blood in my mouth. I was hoping I'd bit my tongue. I kind of slid down the fence 'till I was half standing. Reaching into my pocket and taking my last twenty dollar bill was no chore for my assailant. I didn't get much of a look at his face but his stink was overwhelming. "God, I hate this city."

My wife and I were staying in a cheesy little budget room back behind the casino at the Stardust Hotel. "Honey," my new wife said, sweetly, "Sorry about last night but you seem to be OK. Would you mind terribly if I drove on down to Inglewood and stayed with mom until you're finished here?"

"Sure, babe, no problem," I said. "But, I can't imagine why you'd want to leave here. This place has it all."

My sarcasm was answered with a slight laugh, which was a shade sarcastic in itself. I'm sure the thought of being back with the airlines was going through my new wife's head. As for me, punctured lung or whatever be damned, I'm sticking around until I get my money back, which I accomplished over the following week by playing more games, with more people, for smaller denominations. It was similar to the story about Mae West coming into the house with a new fur coat. When her housekeeper asked where she got it, Mae said, "I found me a man with a thousand dollars." A few months later the housekeeper showed up with a similar fur coat. When Mae asked where it came from, the housekeeper said, "I found me a thousand men with a dollar."

I love drawing a parallel between Mae and myself.

When you could smell the action, but not the air.
Southern California, 1966.

I flew into LAX with my bankroll back intact and got picked up by a stunningly beautiful and completely forgiving wife. That alone can lead to a man's sweetest dream. So here we find "Sophomore Sweetheart" Beverly Jean Goodenough Taylor, this new Pool Widow, spiraling into a lifestyle she didn't know existed, but comfortable that she's going to learn it on her own turf. A nice girl who had stepped from Kappa Kappa Gamma to Alfie's Gonna Scamma. Little did she realize how much excitement was coming into her life. And little did she figure that all excitement isn't so good.

On the other end of the family spectrum, Beverly had a brother who couldn't have been living a more different lifestyle. He was a young, brand new, super gung ho Los Angeles policeman. He was a good enough guy but I could never see beyond his uniform and I'm certain the uncomfortable feeling I had being around him was mutual. Plus, there's a saying, "A cop is a cop is a cop." Once Beverly and I were having dinner with him and his wife at their parents' house. Brother cop dominated the evening with stories about all of the people he had arrested that week, making certain to include all of the 3916s, 4223s, and other coded cop lingo. He even fired a couple of cryptic zingers at me, but in my mind he wasn't any more hip than the suckers I skinned on a regular basis. While he was in cop school or growing up playing volleyball on the beach, I was packing heat and living on my wits. However, since this was going to be the new me, and many of my stories were cause for his handcuffs, not a "baah" came from my black sheep mouth.

Bev and I settled into an apartment in West L.A. and I began my period of hustling pool in shorts, Hang Ten T-shirts, and flip flops. Los Angeles County is made up of eighty-eight cities, each with multiple pool rooms. Beverly took an academic approach and bought a hardcover book map that contained all of them. She then took phone directories and looked up the address for each pool hall in every city, circled their location on the map, and added a number that corresponded with a directory of the names of the rooms. Each day I would hop into her Karmann Ghia, with her book in the passenger seat, and head out in any direction. Daytime pool action was everywhere and so was I. Being a newlywed, my nights were deliciously occupied. I hit city after city and not only was I making money, but I was also having a blast. Nobody knew me and hardly anybody I ran across could beat me, not until I ventured into the Tropicana Bowling Center in Inglewood where the word "beating" took on new meaning.

Like the Cotton Palace in Dallas, the Tropicana Bowl was open 24 hours a day, seven days a week. The pool area housed a half dozen or so nine-foot pool tables and one five by ten foot one. It was a serious action spot with nonstop gambling on pool and bowling. I headed into the billiard area looking for a young pool player named Richie. Richie Florence was a name I was familiar with long before I left Texas. For years he was called "Little Richie" because of his youth. He later earned the nickname "Little Bulldog" because of his fierce play and refusal to give in. Still, all the things I had heard about Richie over the years didn't prepare me for the ass whipping he handed me that day in Inglewood.

I had gone to the Tropicana Bowl specifically to trap him. I knew he would give any stranger a big handicap and it wasn't difficult to find him. He was a celebrity and everything in the room clearly revolved around him. It also wasn't difficult to get him to give me a spot (handicap). The first mistake I made (other than even trying to get on the same table with that kind of talent) was playing him six-ball instead of nine-ball.

With nine balls on the table there was a small chance he might miss. I talked him into spotting me the three ball playing six-ball, which is a tremendous handicap unless you're playing someone who never misses a ball. To begin with, I was forced to hold back since I presented myself as a super weak player, but to hold back even a fraction of my speed playing someone like Richie was equivalent to my giving him a handicap. I had never seen this caliber of pool. He put me in a fog. He just would not miss and the worst part was the way he laughed while he tortured me, saying things like "this guy comes all the way from Texas to get the three and six and can't take it off. How 'bout that?" I couldn't make a ball on the break, no matter where I broke them from, and he had perfected a break where the two back corner balls would run four rails around the table and one or both would go in almost every time.

To rib me further, he asked me if I wanted to break them every time, and when I declined, he asked me if I wanted him to break every time, knowing I couldn't say yes. So there I was, playing one of the best players in the country, make that the world, on his home court, with all of his friends and admirers around. Plus, the small amount of money we were betting meant a lot to me but little to a high-roller like him. Both the six-ball game and my playing were a joke to the "Little Bulldog." Richie Florence was the first world champion player I had come up against and it wasn't fun in the least. It was almost as bad as having a job. Luckily, I played so terribly that immediately after I quit, "Lose Easy" Joe Veasey from Philadelphia offered to spot me the four ball. I accepted and got all my money back. Later, Richie and I became good friends and remained so until his passing in 2002.

In California, I made money consistently, our expenses were small, and Bev and I were a super tight twosome. Life was simple and good. However, to supplement my income while I was in L.A., I put another talent that I had to use. I never was a poker player, or dice shooter for that matter, but I knew a bit about building crude but effective "juice joints." Juice joints are made for cheating at dice. As I mentioned, I didn't play dice, fair or unfair. It wasn't a matter of principle; I just wasn't cut out for the rowdy side of the life that accompanies the participants. But as a straight business proposition, I could invest three or four hundred dollars in a relay, a couple of truck batteries, a magnetic coil, and a remote control switch and get twenty-five hundred for the end result. People (cheaters) were waiting in line for them since that much money could be recovered in a crooked dice game in a matter of hours or minutes. By themselves, the pieces I used were only various electrical components, but hook them together in the right way and they became an extremely illegal device.

A juice joint works like this: By installing the coil, batteries, and relay behind a wall and using dice that are magnetically charged, you can control the game by simply hitting a remote switch in someone's pocket or a floor button, while the dice are in the air. The joint can also be used with 110-volt AC current but occasionally, when you hit the button, the lights will dim. And das when de trouble gwan begin.

At this time there were two places that I knew of in the U. S. where you could purchase gaming equipment that, how shall I put it, would give you a better chance (spelled "C I N C H"). There was T.R. King's in Los Angeles and Jackie Kress in Oklahoma City. Juiced dice, marked cards, fixed roulette wheels, things that would boggle your imagination and have you cashing your Social Security checks to play more. All for fun, you understand–wink, wink. I did my shopping locally at King's because shipping these items across a state line involves the feds.

On a smaller gimmick scale, I could invest fifty dollars in a powerful two-inch flat magnet, a cloth pocket, and a leather strap, and make a knee joint that could easily sell for three or four hundred. A knee joint is used in playing various dice games out of a cup (Ace Away and Ship, and Captain & Crew are the names of two of them). As the name implies, you strap the magnet around your knee, making sure you're wearing baggy pants. Cup games were usually played with four or five dice. You couldn't roll the dice out of the cup when using a knee joint because some of them would miss their mark and others would come to a suspicious halt, or maybe do a double back flip. You would simply dump the cup upside down as you use your toe to push your knee up under the table. Then you would drop your knee, lift the cup and, voila! You win again. How 'bout that? I sold two knee joints to a couple of guys in Anaheim who, without knowing it, played them against each other.

Another gimmick we used T.R. King for was marked cards. Bicycle brand cards were always the choice for marked cards because the pattern on the back of the cards is complex. There are various places they can be marked, mostly in the top left corner. A favorite approach was to dot out a speck in one of the bicycle spokes. There are just about as many spokes as cards in a suit, so it made quick counters out of slick cheaters. The secret to looking for marks wasn't to look for what's there but to stare at the whole pattern and look for what's missing, since they always remove a piece of the design. You could even buy contact lenses that would show you obvious marks that were otherwise impossible to spot, but you either had to be a lens wearer to begin with or spend a lot of pre-game warmup with watery eyes. It doesn't look good if you're winning and crying. With contacts, you could even buy dab ink that lets you make thumb sized marks as you play that are invisible to others.

My ethically compromised pals and I had a favorite card scam that defied exposure. Before Texas Hold 'em took over, Lowball was the card hustlers' and card suckers' game of choice. As the name implies, the player with the "worst" hand or lowest cards wins. Bee brand cards came in two finishes. Written on the bottom of the packs was "smooth finish" or "cambric finish." To look at the two, you couldn't see any difference, but the finish on the backs had a slightly different feel. We would buy twenty or so decks of each, separate out the tens and face cards from one deck and swap them with the high cards from a deck with a different finish. We would take these "special" decks to T.R. King to be repackaged and cellophane wrapped, complete with a new seal, like they were straight from the factory. With practice (which we did by the hour), we could feel the difference as we slid the cards out from under our thumbs while dealing. We had a practice routine where we would each go through the deck by ourselves calling each card high or low by its finish. For each one we missed we would throw a dollar in the pot and the one who missed the least would take the pot. For these no pressure, play with your buddies, "Can I pay you later?" stakes, I ruled. One guy sanded his thumb raw thinking it would give him more sensitivity. A sensitive card cheater, isn't that sweet? When it was your deal in Lowball games, it became easy to tell when your opponent had a high card; sort of like cheating in Braille. This was called playing the "rough and smooth" and nobody, except a few other card hustlers, was hip to it. We were like a thief's Olympics. As competent as I became at feeling the difference, I still never had the cojones to put this skill into action. Could it have been that I was inadvertently feeling conscience pangs? Nah! Someone once told me I would steal the pennies off a dead man's eyes, but that's bullshit. What could you buy with a couple of pennies?

The only times I ever saw one of my contraptions can be broken down into two times, my first and my last. A man called "Highway" Paul Baker and I trapped a guy in Santa Paula playing pool. Dave Leal, who owned a trucking company, spotted me the eight ball for a hundred a game when he couldn't beat me even. Paul and I had put down a "spread" for him the night before, where Paul beat me out of some serious money like I was a pure sucker. Dave took the bait and I taxed him pretty good. Afterwards he said he would play anyone he didn't know some three-cushion billiards for big money. A three-cushion billiard table is usually five by ten feet and has no pockets. Instead, there are two white balls and one red ball, all larger than pool balls. Each player plays with a different white ball (one has a dot on it to avoid a mix up). The object is to hit one of the other balls and have your cue ball contact three cushions or more before hitting the other ball. It's essentially an old man's game and a suck action game. The bet is usually low and games take a long time. A road hustler couldn't stay in hamburger money hustling it. I once heard Minnesota Fats say, "Three-cushion players like to play twenty points for a cigar."

We flew in a champion three-cushion player from Albuquerque named Fez, but Fez beat Dave too quickly, causing him to quit after just two games. I told you it was a suck action game. Finally, Dave said, "If you guys want to win my money it's going to have to be shooting craps." Calling Mr. Taylor!

My good friend, Bob Feste, from El Paso, was going to join us for the game. We rented a motel room in Santa Paula and cut through the wall from the closet to install the coil and relay for a juice joint. We ran the wires to a floor button under the carpeting by first cutting out a little patch of carpeting and using a coat hanger to pull the wires under it. To avoid repercussions for the damages, we rented the room in a phony name. If nothing else, we were experts at covering our asses. The game was scheduled a couple of hours away, so the three of us went to eat and meet up with Dave, leaving Paul's wife in the room. Error! I can't remember her name but I do remember how much she despised all hustlers, her husband the least, but still keeping him in the mix.

We'll never know if it was by accident or intentional, but when we got back to the room, white smoke was pouring out from under the wall. It looked like the opening of a rock concert. Paul's "little rascal" wife had placed a chair leg directly on the button and left, causing the relay to stick open and the coil to go red hot. Flames couldn't have been far behind. Awkward was the least of our feelings. Four guys smelled smoke and one smelled a skunk and that was the last we saw of Dave Leal. It was also the last time I messed with crap games. I can't imagine what the housekeeper thought when she saw a two by two foot hole in the closet wall. Big rats? Pretty close.

Put and Take tops were also a big item sold at places such as T.R.

Kings. The top is about two inches tall with eight beveled sides and spins on an axis that goes through the center. Each side says something to the effect of "take two," or "take one," "put two," or "put one," "match the pot," or "take the pot." I've heard that Put and Take games derived from an old game called Dreidle that's played on Jewish holidays. If you get three guys playing Put and Take with a juiced top, for a quarter, you can win hundreds of dollars per hour. "Match the pot" turns into a sucker's worst nightmare, like the old thing where you take a penny and double it each day for a long month. You will be into millions of dollars.

Crooked Put and Take tops work one of two ways. Ninety percent of the people will spin with their right hand in which case the top is beveled to land on "put" a high percentage of the time. When you are ready to win, you simply spin it with your left hand causing it to come up "take." You can achieve the same result by spinning it in reverse with the right hand but doing that creates suspicion and copycatting.

For a full on assault, three matching tops are necessary; a fair one for starting the game, or in case you have to take a break during the play, the standard righty, which will take care of most of your customers, and one that's beveled the other direction in case you run into a left hander. One of my compatriots accidentally left a righty in with three suckers while he left for a phone call. When he returned fifteen minutes later, the players told him the pot had gotten so big, with nobody ever hitting "take," they had panicked and split it up among themselves. You cannot control a game that has both right and left handed players, so you leave the square (or fair) top in and gamble with them or bow out for a while. Each player will win so many spins he will be ripe when his closeout time comes. This move is called "babysitting." Another type of Put and Take top has a sliding axis that is secretly pushed through the top, with the middle fingers and palm, to achieve right or left hand advantage. Using this type of top left no room for fair play, so bathroom breaks and phone calls were out of the question. People tend to bet lower and lose less on games of skill like pool, whereas games of chance like cards, dice, or Put and Take, or the infamous slot machines, will cause a sucker to do almost anything for money to play more. When a sucker became willing to really bet it up and wouldn't quit, it was called "getting their nose open."

If the opportunity to make a score came up, we certainly didn't let anything as meaningless as "principle" get in our way. I was playing twenty dollar nine-ball in El Monte with a guy named "Fat Ronnie" when my friend who was handling the money called me over. He showed me the twenty dollar bills I was winning had identical serial numbers. The guy was paying me in "queer" but the game was so easy I didn't care. We won a bundle of twenties and spent the next day at Hollywood Park betting the horses with them. I think that was my only experience with "easy come, easy go."

Early one morning while Beverly was fixing breakfast, I was sitting on the floor surrounded by batteries, magnets, and other items necessary for my craft when my brother-in-"johnylaw" popped in for a surprise visit. Only a cop would consider knocking three times and walk right in as "knock before entering." He was dressed in his full cop regalia. His blue shirt was tucked in so tightly that sitting down, which he didn't, seemed impossible and his creased pants didn't show a sign of a wrinkle. His kill, maim, choke, and restrain paraphernalia were snapped snugly in place on his patent leather belt. His shoes, which were inches away from me, were shiny enough to make a drill instructor squeal with delight. He was head to toe cop. He looked around at my funny articles and said, "Alfie, what in the world is all of this stuff for?"

I've always prided myself at being able to think on my feet, but this time I would have to do it on my butt. I thought back to my childhood summers on the farm in Tennessee. My older cousins would take crank telephones, strip the wires, and put the bare wires into the small cattle watering ponds. When the crank was turned, it would shock the smaller fish enough to have them surface where they could scoop them up with a net. I explained to my brother-in-law how we were going to use these things to go for bigger fish in a local pond (a golf course at night). My weak story, and my down on the floor, crick in the neck point of view, combined with his scary uniform, made him look like the biggest cop I'd ever seen.

I'll never forget the half smile, half suspicious cop look that came on his face as he said, "Now I don't know if I believe that." I could tell he loved catching me with my toga up, but feeling under the protection of little Sis, I went at him head on. I picked up a shoe box from under the chair beside me. In the box there was a dozen or so pairs of juiced dice, in every different color and style, from Vegas reproductions, complete with various casino names, to small Monopoly and other board game dice. I flipped the top off the box with my thumb, rolled all of them out on the floor in front of me, and hit the switch five or six times. The dice jumped up and down like the last dance at a Saturday night country hoedown, as I asked, "Well, do you believe this?"

Officer Brother's hand went over his eyes, which seemed unnecessary since he had already made a point of showing us how tightly he shut them to begin with. His brogans did a 180 and he made a dash for the door substituting "I didn't see anything" for goodbye. This event didn't do a lot for family relations but it did end our early morning constable pop-in visits. Mission accomplished. Meanwhile, my new pool widow wife never turned away from her cooking. Ahhh! I knew Beverly was going to be a good one.

FROM GEORGIA SKIN TO MINNESOTA FATS

Early 1960s

When I took off from Pasadena, Texas, to meet up with my brother Jack and get some road experience, I should have left early and driven straight through. It was only about three hundred and fifty miles to where we were supposed to hook up. Instead, I left in the late evening, became road weary, and wound up spending a cold night listening to various things chirping and croaking at a southern Louisiana roadside park. I was too sleepy to drive, too broke (or cheap) to get a room, and too cold to sleep; a vicious predicament. The crack of dawn had me back on the road and looking for the closest McDonald's.

Jack was living in a little town called Houston, Mississippi, but I didn't have the foggiest reason why. Tupelo was close by and I had heard of action there around the college, but Houston? When I arrived he fixed me a sandwich and introduced me to the house men at the two local pool rooms in town, a mile or so from where he, and now, I were living. The following morning my big brother Jack delved into his bag of tricks and asked if he could borrow my car. He said his wife was waiting for him and he needed to "pick her up." I pitched him the keys and gave him the answer he was looking for: "Sure brother, help yourself." I figured the laundromat or such.

A couple of months passed without word from Jack before I started to wonder where he had to go to "pick her up." It didn't bother or surprise me because Jack was just being Jack. I was getting two, five, and sometimes ten dollar nine-ball action daily which kept food on the table (or, in my case, in paper containers) and paid the rent at our mobile home. I kept a hundred dollars socked away under a rubber mat in the silverware drawer, in case I had to catch a bus home. It was my first savings account. It was an easy walk to the pool room so I didn't need my car, although I held the thought of getting it back eventually. Nothing about the future and no part of my past entered my thoughts. I just wanted to shoot pool every day, and I was getting to do just that in Houston, Mississippi.

At this time, a type of pinball machine, setup for gambling, was either legal or tolerated in Mississippi, and the pool room where I hung out a lot had two of them that operated almost constantly. The machine screen displayed four squares of four numbers. Players could move the squares around various ways and move the numbers around the squares, to get winning numbers to line up. The more nickels you fed into the machine before you pulled the ball launcher, the more options you were given to move the squares and the bigger your odds and payoffs would be if you won. It was pretty scientific stuff for the times but with today's technology, a thirteen-year-old kid might walk in with a gadget in his pocket that he built himself and make the old machines go crazy.

Daily, I would watch people buy rolls of nickels by the hands full and feed them into the machines, slapping the sides, shaking them and kicking the legs, and talking to them as if they were alive. In most cases, the players left with just enough of their paychecks left to bargain their way into the house. When someone won, the machine credited them with the amount of nickels which they could cash in at the counter but the players would most often ring off their credits one at a time to beef up their odds for the next pull. Don't be thrown by the fact that they were just nickels. The amounts on the dials totaled in the hundreds, so it was serious gambling. Brown and blue coin wrappers littered the floor like peanut shells in a country bar. The house paid off just enough to keep the players coming back. Few people left money ahead, but enough that, in a bored moment, I decided to give the machine a try. I bought a roll of nickels and sat down to play my first pinball machine, ever. After plunking only a few coins in, an old man slid a stool up next to mine and sat down so close his knee was touching mine. He was one of the nice farmers who came in daily and only spent money on coffee and chewing tobacco. These gentlemen didn't play anything except for an occasional two dollar domino game, where they would scream some victory statement and slam the winning domino down on the flat wood table with a noise comparable to that of a medium-sized pistol. I knew that underneath the overalls and old boots lay the wealth of the county. This particular man loved to watch me play and even bet a few dollars on me when he could find someone willing. When I made a good shot he would say country things like "I'd like to have a pup out of that boy" or "This kid'll break you of sucking eggs." I didn't know the exact meaning of these witticisms but I could tell by the way he was saying them they had to be in my favor.

When he scooted his stool beside me, I thought he was there to pull for me to beat the unbeatable. Instead he put his right hand in front of the coin slot and his left arm around my shoulders in a fatherly way, and said, "Hold on youngster. Answer me this. You got this pool thing down right fair but how do you expect to beat anything that backs its ass up to the wall and challenges the world?" I pulled and released the launcher five times quickly, watching the shiny balls drop into the abyss and, at the same time, picked up the remainder of my nickels, thanked him and walked away. In the forty-seven years since that Mississippi farmer's advice, I've never played a pinball machine, slot machine, or video game of any kind. Very few, if any, one liners in my life have had such a profound effect, except maybe when I was born and my father said to my mother, "We have to keep him, regardless."

The most exciting thing that part of Mississippi had going for it was twelve miles down the road from Houston in the town of Mantee, home of Sonny Springer, "The Mantee Raider," a great Mississippi pool player and a well-mannered, fast and smooth talking country gentleman. Sonny wasn't exactly a sucker but he did have to stay in the action at all times. Jack, who was Sonny's good friend, said, "If there's no other action, Sonny will play parking meters."

Sonny's father owned a small barber shop in Mantee. In the back room of the barber shop were two very old pool tables where Sonny learned to play as a kid. He was so small when he began that he would drag a couple of Coca Cola cases around behind him to stand on. It paid off. Around that part of Mississippi, Sonny Springer was a pool God. Sonny's family had a fertilizer business and I used to ride around in the fields with him while he spread lime, just to talk pool stories. Once, after I had stayed up all night, I went out to work with him and fell asleep in the front seat of the truck as it bumped along over the fields. Sonny said I would bounce off the seat onto the floor, where I would continue to bounce around until he would grab me by my belt and drag me back up onto the seat. Then, he said, the sliding, dropping, bouncing, lifting process would begin again, without my ever waking up.

One afternoon I beat one of the better local players out of about a hundred and twenty dollars. Combining that with the eighty or so that I started with put my bankroll at a little over two hundred dollars. I was particularly proud of the victory because Sonny had been watching and I had played well. Following my match, Sonny started telling me about this card game called Georgia Skin that they played a few miles down the road. He said he was broke, but if I staked him with my two hundred, we might "win real big." I didn't know Georgia Skin from pig skin but Sonny was my hero *du jour*, so my bankroll and I were in.

We drove for an hour or so and pulled up to a shack in the woods, far from any sign of civilization, outside or in. There was a fight going on in the parking lot between three guys, each of whom seemed to be on different sides and all grabbing and swinging and kicking at the other two. None of them could punch very hard but every swing came with a good swear word. I couldn't believe the way people were walking around them like it was no big deal and how nobody tried to break it up. I wanted to see every kick, scratch, and screaming eye gouge but my older, wiser, and broker partner ushered me inside.

Sonny and I were the only white people in the place, probably ever. This was the other end of the pendulum from the KKK meeting hall two blocks from my home in Pasadena. I was about nineteen and had grown up in the 50s when one foul word around someone's wife or girlfriend could earn you a bloody nose. I hadn't been around many women who swore at all without a mouth washing, much less big, mean looking, hard cussin' black women who had a gun exposed. I mean exposed on the table in front of them. The guys at the table looked equally mean, only most were smaller.

Every other utterance contained a bet, a threat, or a mention of someone's mother and every other sentence, by man and woman alike, involved the "N" word. They were all black, so that in itself was totally confusing to me. On the other hand, when they laughed at something together, they howled. They knee slapped playfully, shook and grabbed at each other, and followed with remarks like, "Shit, that brother's tellin' you like it is." Or, "That sho is how it was where I come from." Chalk it up to "fools rush in" if you like but I wouldn't have traded this evening for Saturday night at Monte Carlo.

The rules to Georgia Skin, like the players themselves, are pretty simple. You open a new deck of cards and tear off the box top. Then you remove all of one suit, say diamonds. The players, up to thirteen, sit around a big table and select one of the thirteen cards that have been removed and, in games that lack thirteen players, the balance of that suit is set aside. The other three suits are shuffled and shuffled and, "Gimme dat deck, M.F. I wants to move 'em 'round too," shuffled. Everyone has the option to shuffle. The cards are then slipped back into the topless box face down. The size of the bet is predetermined and each player puts his money in the pot and his card, face up, in front of them; in most cases, alongside their gun. Tonight's bet was twenty dollars per player when Sonny sat down and was raised to thirty, then forty over the course of the night. The box of cards remains on the table and the dealer pulls one card at a time off the top and turns it up. The cards can only be touched and dealt using one hand. When the card matching yours appears, you turn your card face down and you're out of the hand. The player whose card doesn't turn up wins the pot. The card selected by each player can be used for multiple hands. The other three suits are shuffled again for the next hand. In other words, Georgia Skin is pure luck unless the last person shuffling manages to move any of the cards that match his or her card down toward the bottom of the deck. This form of cheating is called "killin' the cub." No telling where that expression came from, probably from some fool named Cub who got caught doing it. For a little punk like me this was, indeed, a scary, but very interesting crowd.

Whiskey, money, and "mothers" flowed throughout the night as I sat very close to my "honky" counterpart, a small prayer on my lips with each turn of the card that it wouldn't be Sonny's. Sonny's hell! Ours! Players went broke and left and came back, without ever leaving a seat empty. There was a constant waiting line to get in the game. Cases of complimentary beer and sweet drinks were dumped into two ice-filled washtubs and a couple of platters of sorry looking, Saran wrapped, whitebread potted meat sandwiches sat on a shelf over the washtubs. I couldn't imagine being hungry enough to go for one. Pints of whisky were sold by a little grey-haired man who looked a hundred years old. His job was to do nothing but handle the bottles of whiskey, which he pulled out of a long coat with multiple pockets sewn into the interior for that purpose. He carried a brown leather bag strapped around his neck and shoulder under his coat that he pulled out to collect the money and give change. In robot-like fashion he would open his coat and flick his left arm out and the bag would sail out of sight under his coat. There was a cigar box on a table beside him that he used for the sandwich money. When he sat on his bar stool, the coat surrounded and touched the floor evenly all around him. He looked like a white tipped black bottle rocket. He never moved from his seat to refill his pocket but he just kept pulling them out. He was fascinating.

The house raked the pot after each hand so I'm sure they overcame the expenses of the complimentary drinks. This Georgia Skin game was a full on, back woods, "tax exempt" independent cash business.

Soft drinks were all that I was holding in. I say "holding in" because there was no way I was going to leave the room for a minute, even if there had been an indoor bathroom. Sonny, who was ahead about $1500 dollars, got skunk drunk and staggered outside to pee. On his way back in, he laid his head down on an old kitchen table and passed out cold. I sat beside him or, in this case, beside his body, for three or four hours. I was holding his gun and our money in my lap the whole time and even though I was nervous, the other players couldn't have been less interested in me. And that's without them even knowing that if push came to shove, I would side with them over that white Sonny fellow. Hey! It's a jungle out there. Not one of them ever glanced at me or the bundle of money I was protecting so closely. For these ladies and gentlemen, this was just another day at the office.

Sonny woke up, took another trip to the outhouse, shot down "a hair of the dog," and sat back down to play. It was morning and I told him I had had enough and wanted to take my share of the winnings and hitchhike back to Houston. Like the cat said while making love to the skunk, "I've enjoyed this just about as long as I can stand it."

I had a little more than nine hundred dollars when I walked the mile or so through the woods to the highway. It was daylight and very few people were moving around outside so thoughts of trouble never entered my mind. I was too busy thinking about where I would spend my newly gained fortune. I remember the money was in my left pocket because I had to use my right hand for hitching and no way was my left hand leaving this bankroll. I was fat city. Hell, I thought, I'd probably never be broke again. Yeah, right!

I caught a ride right away with a guy who liked my story about the skin game. I offered to buy him a sandwich so we stopped at one of the many backyard barbeque stands that dot the highways throughout the South and pigged out. This particular stand had a sign out front, the kind that rolls out with movable letters that said "Eat here even if it kills you. We need the money." Apparently others liked their food or humor because the place was packed. After eating, my new friend went a little out of his way to take me to Houston and dropped me off at the pool room. I didn't know how Sonny got home so quickly, but he was already there and he was as broke as the Ten Commandments; and, he was waiting for his "little buddy." Thinking back, maybe Sonny being broke and waiting for me had a connection. I was curious how he passed me getting home, probably while I ate, but I never brought it up. He told me about this hustler's jamboree called the Johnston City Classic World One Pocket Tournament that was held in southern Illinois, and how we might go there and turn my bankroll into "something really big." He said the top players in the country would be there and I would get to meet them, so I bought a couple of tickets on a Trailways bus and "The Mantee Raider" and the "Pasadena Newcomer" headed for southern Illinois.

Sonny was a tall, good looking fellow with a lovable country charm who played the ladies man role well. I remember him meeting a woman on the bus and playing night games with her in the seats across the aisle from where I pretended to be sleeping. What I witnessed that night was well worth the crick I got in my neck from the armrest. I didn't know what was waiting for me in Illinois but this life beat the hell out of working at a Pasadena, Texas, oil refinery.

In Johnston City, Illinois, George and Paulie Jansco owned the J&J Guest Ranch where they hosted and sponsored the tournament. The Jansco brothers had been bookies in Evansville, Indiana, but returned to their native Johnston City after the late Senator Estes Kefauver began his famous racket investigations in the 50s. One day a couple of crossroaders came by the Jansco's bar and met George, and the idea for a pool tournament was born. At this time there were no major pool tournaments in the country, other than straight pool tournaments in the East, and there was no action in or around the game of straight pool. The first year they played only One Pocket and the prize money was $5,000 which "Connecticut" Johnny Vevis won. The next year they raised the prize to $10,000 and played nine-ball, straight pool and One Pocket. Before long, Sports Illustrated and ABC's wide World of Sports had latched on to the Johnston City event and it was no longer a small matter. Keith Jackson and Jim McKay attended the events, sporting their Brooks Brother's suits and impeccable manners. The prize money was pushed to $25,000 which was huge in those days. The Janscos even had their own golf course where crossroaders and celebrities tee'd it up together as if the tracks had no different sides. In this little southern Illinois town, George and Paulie Jansco had created something unique in the world: A Pool Hustler's Jamboree.

The Johnston City tournaments were legendary for their high stakes action. Everyone brought bankrolls or backers. Some brought both. With names like Marshall "Tuscaloosa Squirrel" Carpenter, Joey "The Cincinnati Kid" Spaeth, "Detroit Whitey," Joe "The Meatman" Balsis, "Tugboat" Whaley, and the legend in his own time, Eddie "The Knoxville Bear" Taylor, the scene was straight out of a Damon Runyon novel. There were two tables in the front room where the tournament was played and where everyone who bought a ticket was allowed entry. In a small building in the back there were two more tables that were set aside for all night action for anyone over twenty-one. Immediately after the tournament games were over, everyone raced for the action room, except yours truly, the under aged one. There has never been anything to match the action in Johnson City. Everyone wanted a piece of everyone else's bankroll. Those who couldn't play somebody would ask for and get odds. Proposition bets were created out of thin air, from betting on tournament matches to trick shots. George Jansco wasn't a very good player, in fact he was pretty awful, but he came up with a game of his own that he would play for big money with any of the pros. He called it Stars and Stripes. It was one-pocket where each player has to make eight balls in his own corner pocket. In Stars and Stripes, the pro had to shoot in a solid colored ball (1 through eight) then a striped ball (9 through 15) while George could shoot his in any order. It was almost impossible to overcome the proposition. A lot of pros tried but Eddie Taylor was the only player to beat George at his game. Clem, a strong player and brilliant proposition man turned the tables on George when he told him he would play him but George had to shoot the balls in the solid and striped order. Clem, who was a right-handed player, would only shoot with his left hand behind his back. Clem beat him every game. The Johnston City jamborees were the most celebrated pool events ever held, but in 1972 they came to an abrupt halt when thirty IRS agents raided the place, locked the doors, and confiscated all of the money.

Sonny's first money match in Johnston City was with Hubert "Daddy Warbucks" Cokes, a wealthy Omaha oil man who played well and found this little pool playing subculture interesting enough to dabble in. Sonny won, but to my dismay, he said he was playing on someone else's money so I wasn't in on the winnings. The next night Nicki Vatch beat Sonny and this time, again to my dismay, he said it was my money that he was playing on and, with it gone, I was pretty much out of the gambling scene. Was I a tad gullible or what? It didn't matter all that much to me. I was here, I had eating money and I was hobnobbing with the country's best pool players. And, little did I know that the following night dire circumstances and an overweight sweetheart character were going to change my life forever.

October nights in Illinois run the gamut, from pretty darn chilly to downright frigid. This one was closer to the latter and I had nowhere to go to get inside even if I had wanted to. Sitting in the car would have been an option, had we a car. Our motel was too far away to walk to and Sonny was nowhere to be found. I pulled a Coca Cola case up to a window outside the action room and stood it on end for a seat. I set my pack of Kools on the window ledge and scraped/wiped the frost off of the window so I could see inside. Thinking back, I can't imagine how anybody could smoke menthol cigarettes in the freezing cold, if one has to smoke at all. The place was packed. There was a five-handed ring game on the front table with four players I didn't recognize and one player everybody knew—one who could hang with John Wayne and have John grateful for the privilege. That was the western looking fella, "Cowboy" Jimmy Moore, from Albuquerque, New Mexico, with his long slip stroke, seemingly never missed a ball in the ring games. Moore was a big man who wore tall-heeled cowboy boots and smoked a cigar, both of which made him look even bigger than he was. He dominated the nine-ball so fiercely, running out every game, that they finally changed the ring games from nine-ball to ten-ball. Just having one more ball on the table, plus the balls not spreading on the break as much makes ten-ball much more difficult. They did this so that others would get a chance to shoot. What did the Cowboy do? He still ran out consistently.

He was also a tremendously straight pool player and was known to have bested Willie Mosconi's official high straight pool run of more than five hundred balls multiple times in practice sessions. Jimmy was a real gentleman and everyone thought the world of him. "Cowboy" Jimmy Moore was inducted into the Billiard Congress of America (BCA) Hall of Fame in 1994. He passed away November 17, 1999.

"Handsome" Danny Jones, who later went on the road with "Lipstick" Jack Terry (what great girl catching names!), was talking to soft spoken "Pocketbook" Don Watson who always carried a book in his back pocket to read between pool sessions. Jones and Watson were both from Georgia and each of them had won first place in different events when I saw them at the Macon tournament a few years earlier. Georgia produces a lot of good nine-ball players and most of the bar tables only have nine balls so that's all they play and action is plentiful. The small towns have a lot of good action in them, but stay out of Atlanta. The natives are not friendly.

Norman "The Jockey" Howard, who people had seen spurt real tears upon defeat more than once, was "woofin'" at someone to play a $500 freeze out. Like most jockeys, Norman was small but he could really play. And nobody dared mention playing nine-ball to the great Luther "Wimpy" Lassiter. There had to be better ways to commit financial suicide. Wimpy had this funny little jab stroke but he played uncanny nine-ball. Larry "Boston Shorty" Johnson was arguing about not wanting to play with at least one foot on the floor, as was required in tournaments. He wasn't much over five feet tall and he insisted on crawling up on the table to shoot shots he couldn't reach. And shoot he could. Eddie Taylor said there isn't any pool or billiard game invented that Shorty couldn't play great. No longer with us, Mr. Johnson is also a BCA Hall of Fame member. Larry "Boston Shorty" Johnson passed away in 1996.

One of the participants all of the players wanted to beat was Bill "Weenie Beanie" Staton. Bill was a great player and could give anybody fits playing almost any pool game. But more than that, Bill Staton was also the nicest and most honorable gentleman to ever pick up a cue stick. Bill didn't play for a living but he loved playing tough action, whether he was on a pool table or in a casino. Bill absolutely loved casinos and played blackjack as well as anyone. He got his nickname because he owned a chain of hot dog stands called "Weenie Beanie's." In the 60s and 70s Bill owned the Jack and Jill Cue Club in Arlington, Virginia, where he promoted a number of tournaments. The club was known for round-the-clock action and in fourteen years the Jack and Jill never closed its doors. Bill was a guest on the Steve Allen Show and Johnny Carson Show, where he shot the only trick shot known that involves pocketing all fifteen balls in one shot. In 2004, he was inducted into the One Pocket Hall of Fame.

But here in Johnston City, Bill was just "Beanie", the guy to beat. All of the hustlers knew that if you beat Bill, "You could really get your teeth fixed," which is pool room vernacular for "win a lot of money." To actually use perfectly good gambling money on dental work seemed frivolous to some of these characters.

I was just a kid in those guys' eyes so there was no reason for them to know me, but I'm delighted to say that later in life after our pool years, Bill Staton and I became best friends. Along with our wives, we took cruises and saw a good part of the world together. He taught me blackjack card counting techniques as we sat on the deck of the ship; then, man of honor that he was, warned me that using what I learned is frowned upon. We visited casinos in Turkey and the Greek islands. He even caught a dealer in one ship's casino trying to make a move on him with a blackjack two shoe and embarrassed the dealer so much he couldn't speak. Beanie was triple smart at any card game and could hang with any hustlers, no matter how tough the crowd. But with his family, Bill was a softie and a joy to be around. We took a vacation to the Yucatan with his whole family where we climbed pyramids and swam in underground rivers. We toured the temples of Japan and produced a documentary together on the All Japan Nine-Ball Tournament. Wherever we went, Bill and I never had an unpleasant moment. None of his three children ever heard him raise his voice. His grandkids said that when they visited him, he would show them each their favorite trick. They would give him a one dollar bill and he would fold it, and fold it again, and fold it again and, magically, it would unfold into a hundred. I loved Bill like a brother. Bill "Weenie Beanie" Staton died February 18, 2006. The void he left in the world of gentlemen gamblers will never be filled.

At the tournament that year, there was a lot of excitement about a young flashy kid from California who had come with "Tuscaloosa Squirrel." Ronnie Allen was his name and One Pocket was his game. He wanted to match up with anybody and play as high as they wanted. His aggressive style of play, his uncanny knowledge of the game of One Pocket, and his precision cue ball control in tight spots around the stack made him a threat to run out any time he got to the table. Ronnie had a charismatic way of controlling his game, his opponent's game, his backer, his opponent's backer, and the audience. He looked good, he talked fast and in peoples' faces, and he backed it all up with his awesome play. I wanted to be him.

Another great California player in attendance was Richie "Little

Bulldog" Florence, from Torrance, California. Richie played with his chin down over the right side of his cue (an unorthodox style), but his follow through on every shot was a sight to behold. No shot possible was too tough for him. Richie had a great attitude about pool and gambling and was always a pleasure to be around unless, as I found out when I played him in Inglewood, you were his opponent. When a top player would emerge somewhere around the country and beat everyone who messed with him, Richie would find him and beat him so severely, the player's reputation would fade away overnight. I heard about him for years before I ever felt his might.

My eyes were dancing around the standing room only, 2000 square foot room, where time stood still, cash became entertainment coupons, and everyone had a secret agenda. I remember many of the participants from the three or four Johnston City tournaments I had attended forty-odd years ago, but which of those players were there each year is a blur. Little did I know at the time that I was witnessing American pocket billiard's history. These gentlemen I'm speaking of, the old guard who made this history, are no longer around and pool tournaments, like tennis and golf have lost much of their color.

The October cold was reaching my bones and my nose was doing that little drippy thing. I was scrunched up on my box seat with my hands tucked under my armpits and my collar turned up on my neck when I heard a voice behind me say, "Whatcha' doin Shorty?"

I turned around and there on that cold October night, backlit by the moonlight, closing his car door, was this round figure of a man with a pool cue case in one hand and a glittering diamond ring, make that two rings, on the other. He pronounced "Shorty" without an "r" so he was definitely from the East Coast. Since I had just seen America's all-time top pool movie umpteen times, and he was the buzzword around there anyway, there was no doubt in my mind that I was having a personal audience with Rudolph Walter "Minnesota Fats" Wanderone. Pinch me, I thought. I must be dreaming. "New York Fats" had been his handle up until the movie *The Hustler* was released, but many of his contemporaries just called him "Fats" or "Fatty." Fats felt that if Hollywood could take a real person and make him fictional, he could certainly take that fictional person and make him real. From that time on Mr. Minnesota Fats "did more in his lifetime to help promote pool than anyone, ever." Those are the words of Fats' long time, close friend, Eddie Taylor.

When Walter Tevis wrote *The Hustler*, he was going to school in Lexington, Kentucky. On the side, he worked at his long time friend, Toby

Kavenaugh's pool room. Mr. Kavenaugh spent countless hours talking to Mr. Tevis about Eddie Taylor's and Minnesota Fats' (at this time New York Fats) exploits. Even though the events in his book and movie are fictional and the names were changed slightly, these two colorful Hall of Fame characters and what they added to the history of the game were certainly influences for Mr. Tevis' writing. The movie even begins with a seemingly impossible bank shot which "Fast Eddie" makes twice in a row to win the money. Eddie Taylor was heralded by his peers as the best bank pool player ever.

Eddie thought the world of Toby Kavenaugh and in 1994 called me and said he couldn't sleep night after night since he heard Mr. Kavenaugh was beaten to death in his home by robbers. Eddie asked me, "Son, how can people like money that much?"

As an example of fiction vs. fact in the movie, Paul Newman, playing Fast Eddie Felson, and Jackie Gleason, playing Minnesota Fats, meet for the first time and begin playing a game of straight pool for one hundred dollars a game. This would have been huge money in the early 50s, when this game was supposed to be taking place. While producing a documentary entitled "Eddie Taylor and the Legends of Pool", I asked Mr. Taylor to tell me about Minnesota Fats. Eddie said, "The first time I met Minnesota Fats, I was fourteen years old. (This would have been in 1932.) Fats came to my home in Knoxville, Tennessee. We played back and forth all night, a game of Bank Pool, a game of One Pocket, then bank, and so on. We played for two dollars a game and broke dead even." Thinking about

Hollywood's version with the $100 a game scene made me crack up laughing. I liked the real story more.

Fats was as famous for his storytelling as he was for his pool playing. One of his stories, a tale that has been around the pool world for many years and has been told in many ways, involves a one-eyed pool hustler and a newsboy. Everyone who heard Fats tell the tale has their own version. Here's my spin called "Willie and the Newsboy."

There was a newspaper boy who used to come into the pool room every day, but lived for Saturday after he collected money from his route when he could come in with money. Few people knew his real name, he was very quiet. Everyone just called him "News" and he liked it. Besides delivering the paper, News read it front to back and always had a section sticking out of his back pocket. If he wasn't playing or watching a game, he was reading. News had been a polio victim of the 50s which left one leg a little shorter than the other so he wore one shoe that had a raised sole. When he played pool, he walked slowly, sideways around the table in a crab fashion, to disguise or minimize his limp. News loved pool more than anything. Whether he was playing or watching, the pool room was his life. Sadly enough, he wasn't a good money manager so his hobby cost him a lot. He wasn't really a kid and nobody knew his age but he seemed younger than his years. He still lived at home with his mom and never spoke of girls. He didn't speak much at all except about pool. His expenses were small so all of his money played.

News would head to the pool room as soon as he got his pay where, waiting to take his money, as he did every week, was a local penny ante hustler named Willie Stumpf. Willie had lost an eye in a fight with his wife one morning when she poked him with his own toothbrush. He denies it happened that way, but it was rumored there was an eye witness. Willie had a bit of money he'd saved from milking suckers but he was a cheapskate, so in order to save money, he replaced his missing eye with a used glass eye that he found in a pawn shop. It matched his real one in color fairly well, but the pupil was a totally different size and shape. It wasn't lined up correctly with the other one and it didn't fit very well, causing the pupil to sometimes get stuck up in the outside corner of the socket. Sometimes Willie would be down on the table shooting and his glass eye would get stuck turned up as if Willie was watching the people who were watching him. It was creepy to begin with but sort of comical after you realized it was a fake. Everybody knew how sensitive Willie was about his eye and made a point not to mention it or even look at it closely when he was talking to you, which was a feat in itself because it was so terribly interesting. Another thing about Willie Stumpf was he wasn't a nice guy. He gnawed and chiseled his way through life, a bone at a time, like an alley dog. He had a bad temper and was pretty tough with his dukes, which was the motivating reason nobody mentioned his eye.

But, favor Willie or not, everyone respected his pool game. He could cut balls in backwards, so thin you'd swear he only touched the ball's paint. He ran hundreds playing straight pool regularly. The reason Willie could shoot so straight, having only one eye, brought out a number of opinions (that everyone kept to themselves) but the real reason remained a mystery. As a side note, England's all-time top snooker player, Joe Davis, had only one eye and he stunned the nation for decades with his precision shooting. Perhaps when an eye and depth perception are lost something is added to the vision to compensate that works for pool. No, I'm not advocating impairing your vision to improve your game, but it's up to you.

Straight pool is sometimes referred to as call shot, and is played by racking all fifteen balls in the beginning. The balls are broken softly for safety play. After the balls are broken, a player can pocket any ball in any order into any pocket he designates beforehand. After fourteen balls are pocketed, they are racked up on the spot. The shooter then pockets the fifteenth ball and uses the cue ball to break the stack apart so he or she can continue the run. The game is played mostly in the East, where there are countless players who regularly run hundreds of balls without a miss. The world record was set by the great Willie Mosconi when he ran five hundred and twenty six balls in an exhibition. Straight pool isn't a good hustler's game because one game can take an hour or more to finish. News was also a very good player who had run a hundred balls more than once, but just in practice games.

Each Saturday, News and Willie would meet to play one game of one hundred and twenty-five point straight pool on which Willie would make News bet the full amount of the paperboy's paycheck. And each week without fail, Willie would break the kid who would then limp out the front door hanging his head and hiding his tears. Though he never won, News wouldn't complain and everyone felt for him except Willie, who gloated incessantly about his "weekly pigeon." Also, nobody could talk News out of playing him. Sometimes the games between the two were pretty close so everyone made a point to watch the weekly shootout. To the man, they were pulling for a different outcome.

One Saturday afternoon the weekly match between the two became especially entertaining. News had only twenty balls when Willie made a tremendous run of more than a hundred balls, bringing his total score up to one hundred and twenty-four. He was leaning over to shoot in the game ball and break News one more time and, no doubt, needle him the rest of the afternoon, prick that Willie was. Unable to contain himself, News stopped Willie and said, "Willie, wait." By this time, tears were forming in the paperboy's eyes. "Each week you take my money and I can't ever seem to beat you. Not even once. Would you please give me a chance and bank that last ball instead of shooting it straight in. I'll do anything you tell me to do." By this time even the audience felt the kid's pain and Willie didn't have one person in the place that he could call his friend.

With News only having twenty balls, Willie snickered and said, "Tell you what Newsboy. I'm feeling generous. That's the kind of guy I am. If you stand up on the table and sing "Ave Maria" at the top of your lungs, I mean really belt it out, I'll bank the ball."

Humiliation took a back seat to desperation and News agreed to Willie's offer. He took off his shoes and climbed up on the pool table. This was the first time anyone had seen News without his raised shoe. He was standing straight, with the foot of his shorter leg standing on two sides of the racking triangle to give him balance. Feeling one of his life's worst moments, but not letting it get in the way, News screeched out every word of "Ave Maria" to the best of his very limited ability. He even threw his arms out at the crescendo, stumbling off the rack under his foot. That desperate little newspaper boy couldn't have put more effort into his production if he were in Carnegie Hall. As funny as this would have been under ordinary circumstances, nobody except Willie laughed at the poor kid. Willie, still smirking and singing, Ahhhhhhh vaa Mariiaaaaaa under his breath, but loudly enough that News could hear him, shot at the bank and missed by a fraction of an inch. "Oh no!" said Willie, with the utmost sarcasm. "Now the little singing newspaper boy is going to get me." News went to the bathroom and freshened up, a trick he learned from the movie *The Hustler*. He took his time composing himself. By this time the crowd, feeling News had no chance anyway, began dispersing.

    News always wore a baseball cap and everyone knew when he turned it around backwards it meant he was on his game. When News returned to the table his hat was turned backwards and pulled down low over the back of his neck. His bangs, which usually hung down below his eyebrows, were tucked under the strap of his hat. Nobody could remember seeing his eyes before. He was, indeed, feeling the reprieve and his confidence was building. And in the words of my dear friend, and the hands down greatest woman pocket billiards player in the world, Allison Fisher, "It's all about confidence, isn't it?" Whatever News said to himself in the bathroom, he came out ready for battle. Before long News had fifty balls, then up to sixty, seventy, and on he went. Rack after rack was disappearing, with News playing perfect position and every ball splitting the pocket dead center: eighty, ninety, a hundred. The paperboy was on fire. Even his limp seemed to have abated as he almost ran around the table firing balls in. The crowd regathered quickly, even larger than before, first murmuring, then whispering, then totally silent, collectively hoping the kid wouldn't fall apart at the last moment. Nobody on any other table in the room shot in another ball. People at the counter, trying to pay their bill were told to wait, lest the cash register disturb News. The three pinball machines that were constantly annoying with their bells and flipping and zinging sounds, were unplugged, something that never happens.

    Two old Tick Hounds who usually roamed around the tables were taken by their collars and led reluctantly, but quietly, outside. Nobody really knows where the dogs came from. They had been around since anyone could remember. They lived inside the pool room when it was open and under the front porch at night. They weren't the kind of dogs that fetch or get lovable or would ever be up for anything active. They didn't even care about being petted. They just wanted to roam the room, with their noses to the floor, looking for crumbs from the white bread bologna sandwiches the owner's wife made and sold at the counter. The strange thing about these curs was that they were exactly the same size and build, both were the same old dusty red color and both with no markings except one white left front paw. They were identical, yet one was named "Big" and they called the other one "Little." It never mattered that nobody, except the house man and his wife, could tell them apart because they wouldn't acknowledge any kind of call whatsoever. Not from anyone. To get them to move you had to take them by the collar and lead them, to which nobody received any resistance from either hound. God never created a more complacent creature but, between them, they didn't possess one "man's best friend" trait. There was one slight difference in the two dogs but you had to look closely to see it. One of them, I think it was Big, had a small knot over his right eye (that started out much larger) where Willie had jumped the table with his cue ball hitting the dog square on in the face. From that day on, every time Willie got close to Big the dog would let out a low growl that continued without pause, like no air intake was needed, until Willie, who was terrified of him, would move away. People loved to watch their paths cross because Big was the only one not intimidated by the bully. More than once someone slipped up to where Willie was playing and threw part of a sandwich under the table, in hopes of luring Big to Willie. Lastly, to quiet the place totally, someone pulled the string cord to stop the clack, clack, clack of the overhead fan. The pool room was like an operating room.

 People crowded as close to the table as they dared. A hallmark event was looming on the horizon and everyone wanted to be part of it. Sure enough, the paperboy continued his run until he, too, had one hundred and twenty-four balls, and was leaning over to shoot his game ball straight in, for his first ever victory over Willie. It was an easy shot, a "gimme". The taste could not have been sweeter for News or the audience. Everyone was holding their breath. One more ball and this place was going to come unglued. News took a couple of warm up strokes and drew his arm back slowly when, all of a sudden, Willie jumped out of his chair, laid both forearms and palms on the table, directly in front of the pocket and said, "News, wait." News stopped and looked up, aghast that even Willie would be so bold as to interrupt him that way. Willie said, without moving even one finger from the table, "We both know I've beaten you every time we've played and it looks like you've got me here, but if you'll give me a chance by banking that last ball, I'll do anything you say."

All eyes turned to the News, who didn't speak but casually limped over and sat on a bench, put his feet up on the arm of a chair in front of him, pulled his newspaper from his pocket and fanned himself with it, while he thought and thought, in no particular hurry. The little paperboy was clearly savoring his moment of Nero like power over Willie. Shall it be a thumb ups and give him a chance or thumbs down and lop off his head? Everyone in the audience was pulling for News to turn down Willie's offer and take the sure win. The prospects of banking the shot in front of him were not very good.

The crowd let out a collective "at last" type of noise when News sat up quickly and shook his head rapidly back and forth, not as a "no" answer, but more like the last move of a shiver that began down below and worked its way to the top of his head. He jumped straight up, stood taller than anyone remembered him being before and looked across the table at Willie, as he said "Tell you what, Willie boy; I'm feeling generous. Take your eye out and spin it as hard as you can on the table and I'll bank the ball. I mean spin it like you mean it." The audience froze . . . as did Willie. Not only had News broken a long standing taboo about mentioning the tough guy's affliction, he was actually ridiculing Willie. This incident was straying from being comical and Drake, the house man, who the locals referred to as "Drake the Snake" behind his back, moved in closer to the two of them in the event of trouble. The sawed off baseball bat that usually hung over the cash register under the cardboard sign that said "Touch this and die" was conspicuously missing. Drake had one hand behind his leg so its whereabouts were not a mystery to anyone paying attention. Time stood still. People were looking back and forth at the two players as if they were watching a tennis match, hoping the next move from Willie wouldn't come in the form of a lunge at News.

You could feel the steam rising from Willie as greed prevailed over both anger and embarrassment. He didn't speak, but glared at News hard. Nobody had ever seen Willie breathe so hard. It was close to a snort. Then, using his thumb and first two fingers, Willie plucked the damp, misshapen object from its socket, gave it a quick wipe on his jeans and, with his thumb and middle finger, sent the eye into a whirling dance across the green felt. No one knows if it was Willie's anger or what, but something gave him the strength to spin that eye like no eye has ever been spun before or since or probably ever would be spun again. If glass eye spinning was an Olympic sport, Willie stole the gold. They said the eye spun and spun on the old worn cloth, until it circled the pool table more than once, barely slowing a bit when it bounced off the triangle News had stood on to sing.

Then it finally slowed enough to check out everyone standing around the table a couple of times, while all watching were twirling their eyes or head in unison with it, until it wedged itself up under the end rail, staring right into the back of the corner pocket. The scene was just too bizarre for description. Later, most everyone agreed they enjoyed the spinning eye immensely but could have passed on the visual of Willie's empty socket.

News looked at his opponent with a smile on his face, wider than anyone had ever seen come from the kid and, as he shot his game ball straight in the pocket, he said, "Not that eye, Willie."

Now back to Fats and me at Johnston City. Here I was, somewhere in southern Illinois, alone and cold, with less than a hundred dollars to my name and I couldn't be happier. I was hanging with Minnesota Fats. He listened to my under age and "can't get in" story then laughed and said, "They can't keep my buddy out here. You ain't even wearing no coat. What's the matter with them mooches?" With that, the most famous man ever to pick up a cue took my hand and walked me into the action room and a great friendship began. These were the top gunfighters of the pool world; the best of the best and I was here with them. If my education really began when I escaped Pasadena High, I had just entered grad school.

Years later I was watching another Jansco tournament at the Stardust Hotel, in Vegas, while sitting in the bleachers next to Fat's wife, Evelyn. Fats was entertaining the audience between matches with his jokes, speeches, and fancy shooting. As usual, he didn't make many of the trick shots he attempted but, also as usual, he still had his audience in stitches. Minnesota Fats was as close to a Vaudeville act as somebody my age would ever see. He claimed he never worked at anything. He once said, "Change a tire? I'd rather change cars." He told one guy "You wouldn't bet two big dogs could whip a little dog." He told another "You wouldn't bet fat meat's greasy."

Evelyn and I had never officially met but I told her how much I thought of Fats and that he and I would see each other from time to time around the country, and about how he had introduced me to the woman I married. I told her about riding around in Dallas with him, in his big Lincoln, when he saw a pack of hungry looking dogs. Fats pulled over and opened his trunk to reveal a case each of dog and cat food and a can opener sitting on top of a stack of bowls. He delighted in feeding the strays and sweet talking them while they ate.

My brother, Jack, was living in Houston with Fats for a time. He said once he and Fats were walking down the street when they saw two mongrel dogs digging through the trash behind a Weingarten's supermarket. He and Fats only had eighteen dollars between them but Fats went in and bought twelve dollars worth of ground chuck and took it outside to the dogs. Fats loved all animals and claimed he wouldn't even swat a mosquito. He said he took a long road trip once with a car full of mosquitoes and not one of them bit him. He said that was a better deal than he could get from pool players. Evelyn told me they had more than a hundred stray cats at their home in Dowell, Illinois. She went on to tell me how Fats liked to tell his audiences the story about the young boy he took in out of the cold and looked after in Johnston City, years earlier. She had no idea she was talking about me. I said nothing.

How was I to know my investment of a couple of hundred dollars in a Georgia Skin game, in a shack in the Mississippi Delta, thirty some years earlier, would lead me to a lifelong friendship with Minnesota Fats? Even more, how was I to know the nature of my final contact with his life?

In January of 1996, I heard on CNN that Minnesota Fats had passed away at his home in Nashville. I couldn't stop thinking about him all day so I sat down and wrote a letter about what Fats meant to me, which I sent FedEx to his most recent wife, Theresa Bell. A few days later Theresa called to thank me for my "kind words." She went on to tell me they hadn't prepared anything to say at Fats' funeral so they elected to read my letter as his eulogy. I was honored.

Epitaph on Gravestone: "Beat every living creature on earth. St. Peter rack 'em up."

"SPOOK," "BREAK EVEN BILL," AND ALF BEAT THE GREATEST GAMBLER OF THE 20TH CENTURY

I'd like to step aside for a moment and turn the next part of this book over to my long time friend, preliminary editor, and pool associate, Bill Porter. This story pertains to our mutual association with The Cotton Palace and Titanic Thompson, but it's more about Bill than me. Bill retired after thirty years as a college professor, so his eloquence with a pen will give you a break from my simple storytelling. On the other hand, had I spent that much time in college, I wouldn't have my story to tell.

Dallas, Texas, early 1960s, The Cotton Bowling Palace
"In a bet there is a fool and a thief." ~Proverb

Bobby "Spook" Stephens, a regular at Cotton Palace in the early 1960s, slipped around the billiard area so quietly that he seemed to appear out of nowhere, like a ghost or spook. He was a solid nine-ball and One Pocket player and a very bright guy, with three years toward a college degree in mathematics. Our friendship began when we started discussing math puzzles and gambling odds in Vic Domino's restaurant at Cotton Bowling Palace.

My own pool game wasn't much, but it was strong enough to beat the "straights" and drunks that wandered unwarily into the billiard area. Like other Cotton Palace regulars, my "work day" began when I awoke in the late afternoon and my "lunch time" was about midnight. So I was rested, practiced, and sharp at 2:00 a.m. when the barflies were shooed out of the Dallas taverns and drifted over to The Cotton Palace and its 24/7 gambling action. Since many of my money sessions ended up with me having to struggle from behind to finally get back to even, I was saddled with the nickname "Break Even Bill." Hey, breaking even is a big step ahead of booking a loser! Actually, I was proud to have any nickname at all in that crowd.

The third member of our crew was Alfie Taylor, and you already know about him because this is his book. Even though only about 20 years old at the time, Alf had developed more hustles and scams than guys twice his age.

The gambler we teamed up to beat on a bet was none other than the famous, or infamous, Titanic Thompson. Of the several books about Titanic, I'd recommend *Titanic Thompson: The Man Who Bet on Everything* (2010) by the excellent writer, Kevin Cook. Another book about Titanic worth reading is the Carlton Stowers biography, *The Unsinkable Titanic Thompson* (1982).

To appreciate the story I'm about to tell you, you have to understand a bit about Alvin Clarence Thomas, or Titanic Thompson as he was known to high rollers in the world of gambling. (After a misprint in a New York paper, Thomas conveniently let people think his name was Thompson.) Born in 1892, he was about 71 years old and hanging around Cotton Bowling Palace when we first got to know him. He had lived the life of a gambler since leaving his Arkansas home at 16 years of age with nothing but a few bucks in his pocket. He became one of the best known and highest betting gamblers of the 20th century and is the subject of numerous magazine articles and several books. The character of Sky Masterson in Damon Runyon's *Guys & Dolls* (originally a 1950 Broadway musical and later a movie) was based on Thompson, a good friend of Runyon. His extraordinary eye sight and eye-hand coordination enabled him to become a world class golfer who, back in the 1930s, bested golf immortal Byron Nelson in a high stakes golf match. When asked why he didn't become a pro golfer and play on the tour, Titanic quipped, "I could not afford the cut in pay." He wasn't kidding about that because in those days the best pro golfers were lucky to make $25,000 in a year while Titanic might win that much in a week hustling rich country club golfers. He was also deadly accurate with a shotgun or pistol and was known to have cut short the lives of at least five would-be holdup men who tried to rob him. He once played in a poker game famous for being the scene of Arnold Rothstein's death; Rothstein was the gambler reputed to have fixed the 1919 World Series.

More important for this story than Titanic's skills at golf, guns, or poker was his uncanny knowledge of proposition bets. He is most remembered as the most creative proposition bettor who ever lived, many of his exploits having found their way into television shows and movies. There are hundreds of stories about Titanic making and winning bets on a wide variety of propositions such as which pigeon in a pair will fly away first, how far he could hit a golf ball, whether he could throw a peanut over a building, or how many cars with license plates ending in a zero would pass by in the next five minutes. Most of his proposition bets were set up so that there was no way he could lose. For example, while walking down the street with a fellow gambler, he bet he could find at least 100 hairpins on the sidewalk within the next two blocks. The night before, Titanic had dumped several thousand hair pins along that block and so had no trouble finding 100 of them the next day. The golf ball he bet he could hit an unheard of distance is probably still rolling on frozen Lake Michigan.

I remember when Ti (short for Titanic) busted Danny Matthews, a local bookie, with an unusual dice bet. He asked Danny how many rolls of a single die he would need to roll a six. Danny was a pretty shrewd gambler and probably told Ti he'd have to think about it. Maybe Danny had read the then recent John Scarne book on gambling (*Scarne's New Complete Guide to Gambling*, 1961) in which Scarne gave a method for calculating how many rolls would be needed in such a bet. Using Scarne's method, the number needed for a fair bet would be just less than 3.5 rolls.

What we know for sure is that Ti offered to bet against Danny rolling a six, giving him three rolls alternating with four rolls for an average of 3.5 rolls per bet. If Danny had read the Scarne book, he would have been sure he had somewhat the best of the wager. What Danny almost surely didn't know was that Scarne, a world-famous authority on betting odds and gambling, was just plain wrong on this one! And what Danny *should* have known was that Ti would never knowingly offer anyone a fair bet. The true breakeven point on that bet is 3.8 rolls, so Danny, getting an average of 3.5 rolls per bet, was "sucking hind titty" so to speak and taking over 5% the worst of the bet. Over the course of a long evening of rolling that single die for many, many bets, Danny left The Cotton Palace almost $2,000 lighter. I tell this story to emphasize how sharp Titanic was when it came to odds and probabilities.

As Ti sat around The Cotton Palace, regaling us with stories of his hustles and scams, he would occasionally toss out a proposition bet and ask which side of the bet we liked. None of us pool hustlers and scufflers were anxious to bet on a proposition with the world famous Titanic Thompson, but we enjoyed listening to his stories.

Bobby Stephens and I got into some of these discussions and Ti seemed to enjoy describing proposition bets and asking us which side of the bet we favored. Bobby and I might spend a day or so analyzing the bet and eventually we'd go back to tell Ti which side of the bet we liked. Ti, seeing that we had figured the bet out, would just smile and come up with another bet for us to analyze. This went on for a few weeks until Ti finally came up with a card bet and offered to take *either side* of the bet. And he then told us that we could bet as much as we wanted on the outcome. How could he make such an offer? Surely one side of the bet was a lock or cinch, right? Or so we thought.

The card game Ti described is known as the Game of 31. It's a simple game to describe. The game uses the lowest 24 cards in the deck, Aces through sixes; just create six stacks with the Aces in the first stack, then a stack of four deuces, and so on. All the cards are face up on the table. The two players alternate in drawing cards, keeping a running total of the cards drawn (so that if the first four cards drawn were a six, a four, an Ace, and a deuce, the running total would be 13). If you hit a total of 31 on your draw you win; if you are forced to exceed 31 on your draw, you lose. It's kind of like Blackjack where the object is to hit 21 or have your opponent bust by going over 21.

A little analysis reveals that hitting the key number totals of 3, 10, 17, and 24 will ordinarily allow you to win. For example, if you draw a card to make the total 24, and there is at least one card left in each stack, your opponent can't win by hitting 31 on his next draw and can't keep *you* from hitting 31 on your next turn. So is it really that simple to win this game? Can you simply go first and draw a three, then on your next turn draw a card to hit a total of 10, then 17, and then 24? If you think this will work, gather up some cash and let's meet up. I'll let you go first and draw a three. You can bet as high as you want.

This little game, so simple to describe, has some interesting twists to it. The reason that knowing the key totals of 3, 10, 17, and 24 doesn't guarantee a win is that it is possible for one of the six stacks to be exhausted before the end of the game. For example, you may draw to hit the total of 24 and feel like you are now certain to win, but if I draw a four to make the total 28 and the stack of threes has been used up, you're dead meat.

After Ti offered this proposition, Bobby and I left The Cotton Palace, got out our pencils and paper and began an analysis of the game. We started by determining whether there was a way to force a win by drawing first. By the next morning we found that drawing first could force a win 100% of the time. It was just a matter of memorizing a sequence of draws after our initial draw. (You can read a detailed description of this game in the 2003 book, *Billion Dollar Bunko*, by Simon Lovell. If you read the section on the Game of 31, you will find that you can force a win by drawing an Ace, deuce, or five on the first draw, with a five giving you the easiest route to a win.)

Having assured ourselves that we had this bet completely figured out, we went back to Ti and told him we were ready to make a serious wager. Remember, Ti said he would take either side of the bet, meaning he offered to draw first *or* second. Didn't he realize that we might figure out the game? Would he try to twist the bet in some way to gain an advantage? He just looked at us and told us he was willing to bet as high as we wanted and as he had told us, we could draw first or second.

Wow! We didn't show our excitement at the time, but Bobby and I could hardly believe that we had Titanic Thompson, the legendary gambler and acknowledged king of proposition bets, trapped in a bet he couldn't win.

And he was willing to bet big. Instead of playing pool with some sucker for hours to win a few bucks (or just get stiffed for the money), we were on to something that could net us more cash in an hour than any of us had won in a month.

There was a big problem standing in the way of our cashing in on a big bet. You have to bet big money to win big money and Bobby and I together had only a few bucks at that time. We asked around to find someone willing to put up some cash, explaining that we had a total lock on a proposition bet and that there was no way we could lose. But as soon as they heard we were betting against Titanic, it was no go. As one potential "investor" said to us, "You guys are betting on a card proposition with Titanic Thompson? And you have a mortal lock? Yeah, right." No one wanted to put up money for a bet against Ti. And as it turned out, he had an angle or a way to twist the bet that we had never anticipated.

I have to give Alf some credit here. Despite his knowing Titanic's fame as a gambler, he trusted Bobby and me and took our word when we told him that we were certain we would win the bet. Alf was willing to chip in his whole stack, but he was on the shorts too and had little to contribute. Vernon Litton, a Cotton Palace regular who usually carried several hundred dollars in his pocket, had told us he'd be there that night to throw in with us on the bet, but he never showed. We might have been a bit peeved at Vernon for letting us down, but considering his reputation for violence, we let it slide.

The time came for us to "put up or shut up," so Alfie, Bobby, and I went over to Ti's apartment, just a few blocks down Lemon Avenue from Cotton Palace. Ti wasn't much of a host and didn't offer us anything to eat or drink; he just got out a deck of cards and asked us to show our money. It's embarrassing now to admit that we had less than $100 among the three of us, but we put up all the money we had and Ti started pulling out the Aces, two, threes, fours, fives, and sixes from the deck and tossing them onto a coffee table.

While putting the cards on the table, Ti asked whether we had decided to go first or second in drawing a card. (It turned out that asking us this question *while* spreading out the cards on the coffee table was highly significant.) I told him that we'd go first, and Ti, spreading out the cards on the coffee table, told me to go ahead and take a card. Ti hadn't placed the 24 cards in neat stacks with the Aces, deuces, and so on in stacks of four cards each. The cards were just spread out, face up, in no apparent order or pattern.

Ti seemed so confident that it made me suspicious. With the cards all jumbled up on the table, not in neat stacks, I couldn't tell for sure that all 24 cards were there. I told him I wanted to make sure he had put out all 24 cards, and when I checked, there were only 23 cards. An Ace was missing. That missing Ace would have given the person drawing *second* a sure win if they understood how the game worked. Maybe I should have told you that Ti was a known card mechanic who could deal seconds or palm a card as slick and fast as anyone. He had palmed an Ace to change the bet around.

Now it was clear why Ti was willing to let us go either first or second. He knew that if we let him go first, he could force a win with honest play and if we chose to go first, he could palm an Ace and force a win by going second.

With all 24 cards now on the table, I promptly drew a five, the easiest path to force a win. I was secure in the knowledge that there was no way Ti could win; no matter what card he drew, I had a memorized response.

Ti also drew a five to hit the key total of 10 and I quickly drew a deuce, just playing out a memorized sequence. He drew the third five to hit 17 and I pulled a deuce again without a second of hesitation. Now he looked at me hard, the way a seasoned poker player might study the face of an opponent. I looked back at him, no need to even look at the cards now. If he drew a five to hit 24 it would exhaust the fives and I'd just draw the third deuce to make 26. With no fives left, he couldn't win. Ti didn't even draw a card; he knew he'd be drawing dead.

Ti pulled out some small bills and paid off his debt, but he was clearly on tilt and started suggesting variations on the bet and then proposed several other bets, none of which appealed to us, at least not without time for analysis. It was clear that he was seriously upset about being beaten on the bet, even though the dollar amount of his loss was too small to be of any consequence to him. You have to understand that in our little world of hustlers, grifters, and scammers, the most shameful thing was to be played for a sucker. It was no shame to be broke; it was only shameful to *stay* broke. It was no shame to have been convicted of a crime that might even boost your status in our crowd. But it was shameful being suckered into a bet that you had no chance to win. And Ti, despite having beaten more suckers out of more money than just about any living human, was for those few moments the sucker and we were the "smarts." If every bet has a fool and a thief as the quotation at the beginning of the chapter suggests, in this case, Alfie, Bobby, and I were the thieves.

A few weeks later I was hanging around the front desk of The Cotton Palace talking to the counterman Frank Murray over the constant racket of 44 bowling lanes. Dick McMorran (aka San Jose Dick) had just walked past on his way to the billiard area. Ti walked in wearing a cardigan sweater and looking like an elderly member of the country club set. Seeing me at the counter, Ti pulled out two dollar bills and his car keys and said, "Here

Billy, run out to my car and get my golf clubs out of the trunk."

I thought for a second and told him, "Sorry, I have something else I've got to do right now," and walked away. It's rare that you can know the exact moment when you become sure about the nature of your relationship with a person, but it was clear to me at that moment that Ti didn't consider me a friend and might never have thought of me as one. If he had just asked me to get his clubs, I'd have been glad to do it, but offering me the $2 showed me clearer than words that he saw me as a go-fer and not as a friend. I know Alf did become friends with Ti and Alf's brother Jack was really close to Ti for a while and has some great stories about him.

A point should be made here about the dollar amounts we gambled for back in the early 1960s. I once beat Billy T. Dyer out of $140 playing $20 nine-ball and that was enough in those days for Bobby Stephens and me to take a weeklong trip to Colorado, and that included gas, food, and lodging. Sometimes the amount of the bet just wasn't as significant as the context of the wager. I recall watching Billy Stroud play Jerry Trigg for $3 a game, finally beating Jerry out of more than $50 but more importantly taking the unofficial title of the best nine-ball player in Dallas away from Jerry.

So Alfie, Bobby, and I did indeed outsmart a man who was arguably the smartest gambler of our or any other time. We didn't "sink" the great Titanic, but we did cause him to spring a little leak and got to watch him steam about it.

Not long after this episode, I made my mom happy by leaving the somewhat seedy and definitely dangerous environs of Cotton Palace and going back to college. I'd been hanging around pool players and Dallas late night characters for a year and figured I'd better head back to the straight life while I still could. At the University of Denver in the fall of 1963, when a bit of homesickness set in, who was I missing as I sat alone in my room on the seventh floor of Centennial Hall? Yep, I was missing Alfie, his brother Jack, Bobby "Spook" Stephens, and the whole crew of hustlers and heroes back in Dallas. The characters I knew and hung out with during the year I spent at The Cotton Bowling Palace live vividly in my memory even now, almost 50 years later. By the way, Bobby Stephens eventually went on to work for Texas Instruments as a Senior Member of the Technical Staff in the Geophysical Services division where he helped develop advanced technology seismic processing software used to find oil deposits.

The Internet put me in touch with Alfie, whom I hadn't seen face-to-face in over 45 years. The email he sent me when we first reconnected began, "Gosh, Billy, you finally called. Do you have any idea how many disappointing trips to the mailbox a guy can make in 40 years?"

"PLAYING THE DUCK" WITH THE KNOXVILLE BEAR

September 9, 2005, Anderson County, Tennessee

I looked around at the handful of Tennessee country folk who had come to say goodbye to their old friend, Eddie Taylor. Most of them were older people, some of whom were his childhood friends. Many of the same people had gathered here with Eddie and me years before when we buried Eddie's wife, Violet. Other than an occasional flower pinned to a dress, no fine or special ceremony clothes were present. But everyone looked freshly showered and neatly clad. "Salt of the earth" could not have better defined than this group. No tears were shed by these people this day, that I could see, but their faces could not hide the sadness in their hearts. Tears were clearly on the inside. Country people seem to accept death in a different manner, perhaps, because they live around farm animals and the cycle of life on a more regular basis. People in rural areas also tend to live and act the same in most, if not all, countries around the world because their needs are so basic. Eddie was special to these people. He was their friend whom they watched transcend his country roots to achieve fame as one of the greatest pocket billiards players and most famous pool hustlers of all time. And he accomplished that without losing his country gentleman's heart.

Born October 1, 1918, Eddie's uncanny ability as a pool player arrived early in his life and, in spite of the rewards he reaped from his talent, it cheated him out of a childhood in the normal sense of the word. Sports, girls, and schooling couldn't grab his attention. Eddie's only interest was playing pool and for good reason. By the time he was fourteen he could beat almost anybody in Knoxville on the green felt. His specialty as a youngster was playing snooker, but the gambling money was on nine-ball and bank pool so he switched his game to them. In order to get into places where they played pool, Eddie always dressed like a grown man, wearing suits and ties, never having owned a pair of jeans and, to his dying day, was never without perfectly shined shoes. He had a thing about that. Eddie's mother threatened to burn the pool room down if he didn't quit hanging out there but Eddie wouldn't be swayed so when she got him barred from one room he just found another.

By the time Eddie was sixteen, he'd built up a bankroll and hitched his way east to Morristown and played a man named Herman Roddy. Eddie got broke and hitched back home. When his bankroll was built-up again, from playing for anything from fifty cents a game to five dollars, Eddie went to Morristown to play Roddy again. Again, he got broke and went home. The third time he played Roddy, he beat him and in Eddie's own words, "I just kept right on going." When I first met Eddie, around 1960, he was in his prime with a thirty-year champion crushing career already behind him. Later in life when we traveled together, he was never lacking in stories.

"The Knoxville Bear" is what they called Eddie Taylor, a moniker bestowed on him by another Champion, U. J. Puckett, whom Eddie had beaten every time they played. Puckett finally gave up playing him and said, "Trying to beat Eddie Taylor is like trying to wrestle one of those Smokey Mountain bears." The name stuck. How sadly ironic it felt taking the "Bear" to his final resting place in the woods.

There had been a funeral service a few days earlier for Eddie in Shreveport so his friends there could bid him farewell. Enough time had passed that I was over the shock, though the loss was still fresh. Eddie meant so much more to me as a person than he did for being a champion, as he did to so many. He knew the value of sweet words. If anyone, man, woman, or child asked him about pool or showed him their game, Eddie would only sing their praise. In the words of Thomas Shaw, from Pool & Billiard Magazine, "Eddie was just plain likable."

As a young man I watched him play many times but never really knew him, beyond an introduction. But once, at a Johnson City tournament when I was a youngster, Eddie honored me by playing me a game of bank pool "eight or no count, to my eight," for five dollars. This meant I could make my eight banks one or two at a time and add them up, while Eddie, on the other hand, had to run eight banks consecutively or they didn't count. Running eight banks is an almost impossible feat, even for the world's best bank pool player, but Eddie had a trick up his sleeve. As he would make two or three banks often and miss, the balls were re-spotted, lined up behind the spot. When eight balls were lined up, he positioned the cue ball on one side of them and banked the eight in, across the side, with the precision of a Swiss watch. The audience loved his win almost as much as I enjoyed my loss. Naturally, Eddie wouldn't think of taking my five dollars. Instead, he shook my hand and told me "You play pretty good. That's fact." Even if it was more sweetness than fact, just being on the same table with him was one of my finer days to date.

It was later in Eddie's life, after his prime, when we traveled together. I should make note that even out of his prime, my best day couldn't handle his game. I practiced with him last when he was in his 80s and still got my ass paddled. Eddie was the master of the "soft hustle" where he would sweet talk his way in, get the money and get out, without exposing his true game and without angering his victims. The things he showed me about how to deal with people (suckers) and the way he taught me to move around pool rooms helped me win a bit of money and avoid a lot of problems over the years. Eddie taught me how to win people's money without taking their dignity, a practice I find helpful in business today.

At the graveside, the small crowd filled up the three or four lines of folding chairs that had been placed next to Eddie's casket. It looked like about thirty people attended. There were no sports magazine writers, no newspaper reporters or media of any kind, and sadly enough, there wasn't a sign of another pool player. Eddie Taylor was a Hall of Fame champion in a sport hustled by those who live and oftentimes die alone, as was the case this day in Cox Cemetery.

Bossier City, Louisiana - four days prior - September 5, 2005

You laugh between the tears. That's the way grief seems to work. The sweet, caring people from hospice had escorted Eddie home from the hospital so he could say goodbye from his own surroundings. One of them stayed on to assist in his passing. When I arrived at the Taylor home, his wife Doreen met me on the front porch and warned me that Eddie was in his last hours and that I should prepare myself for seeing him in the state he was in. Walking into the house wasn't easy. I could see his bed in the front room just inside the door. Eddie was on his back with a sheet covering his small body. As I moved closer, I was shocked at how a man who had always been so much larger than life to me looked so childlike in his bed. The color was gone from his face, his eyes were closed, and his small arms were moving only slightly. He looked peaceful and Doreen said he had been in no pain. Thank God! Doreen and I each took one of his hands and she said, "Eddie, Alfie's here," and he squeezed my hand and nodded so slightly. My insides were twisting in knots. The others in the room were composed but when the tears rolled down my cheeks, embarrassed or not, I made no effort to stop them.

So this was a death vigil, my first. It's like a greeting committee for the grim reaper. Throughout the night as Eddie's friends came and went, Doreen never left his side. He appeared unconscious but occasional squeezes from his hands when we would speak to him let us know he was still with us. He would occasionally lick his lips to signal for water. The minister who came to visit took us aside and explained that the last sense to go was a person's hearing. He assured us that Eddie was hearing every word we said and probably would be able to until his last breath. Nothing could have pleased me more.

These Bossier City, Louisiana, friends of Eddie's knew him in his later years as a former world champion pocket billiard player and traveling hustler and as Doreen's new husband. All of them had been fascinated by his stories of hustling pool on the road and playing in tournaments. Eddie made no pretences about life's ups and downs. He talked about times of having more money than he could spend and hanging around with famous jazz musicians, and he told what it was like to be broke and sleeping in the parks. He told his stories the way only a Tennessee boy like Eddie could tell them. Doreen, as is typical with pool hustler's wives, had been subjected to these tales repeatedly and knew most of them by heart, but she was a great sport about indulging Eddie his memories. One thing Doreen and I had in common is we could usually fill in the player's names for Eddie's stories at times when he couldn't remember them. Doreen was his angel.

But I had known and traveled with a different Eddie, an Eddie who went balls on into action at the drop of a hat and didn't back down from playing big money pool with any person. I remembered adventures we had together that these people had no idea about, ones that would make us laugh and maybe cry a little. And tonight, I was going to talk about what it was like to hustle the pool highway with the Knoxville Bear. I would play out our stories for Doreen who knew enough about some of them to add her own parts to the tale. I would tell them to his friends who had never heard them, as reminders of happier days in a world champion's life. But mostly, I would think of this night as a last road adventure, recalling stories of great times gone by for my buddy Eddie Taylor.

The majority of serious pocket billiard players in this country would agree that Eddie Taylor was one of the best, if not the best, all-around player who ever picked up a cue. His thirty-five year total dominance of the bank pool world was undisputed. His record of making thirty seven banks in a row will more than likely never be broken. Because of his amazing bank pool ability and his almost perfect touch playing position, Eddie tortured many top players playing One Pocket and one shot shoot out nine-ball as well. In 1993 he was inducted into the BCA Hall of Fame with testimonials from the other greats describing him as "The best of the best." But even more than his world-class pool abilities, Eddie Taylor was a gentleman of the old school and his sweet nature brought out the best in everyone around him. I'm honored that I was able to travel and live with him for a period of my life. Although our same last name was our only real kinship, we were "uncle" and "nephew" to the public. Between the two of us, he said I was more like a son to him and I loved Eddie like a father.

Here's a little background on pool hustlers as I saw them. I break crossroaders down into three basic categories: Gunfighters, Bushwhackers, and Hatchetmen, each effective in their own way. We all moved around the country, constantly looking for action. Our styles of hustling were different but our agenda was the same: Get the money and get away. There were also many equally talented "room players" who either don't want to leave home or didn't have what it takes to handle the road. Room players typically stay in their local pool room and shoot the backs out of the pockets. There was a room player in Texas named Harold Coffey who played so well on his hometown four by eight tables that he would play with four or five people in the game and spot them all three or four balls. Harold won because Harold never missed a ball. I took a good old-time player from Dallas named Sarge McDonald to play Mr. Coffey. We watched him in the multi-handed game for about an hour, then turned around and headed for home. Topnotch road players would eventually wear a guy like this down, but Sarge was past his prime and I would have been tortured in my prime. When Mr. Coffey came to Dallas he was a totally different player, who received a totally different outcome. Room players are the one's a good crossroader will usually avoid or save for last. So much of winning involves talent plus "heart" or a "killer punch" and there are definite lions and lambs in the game. When two players who are equally skilled match up the one with the most heart will prevail. The Chinese have an expression about not letting up: "Shoot the drowning dog."

Gunfighters mostly travel in pairs and usually display a similar modus operandi: they will typically stop at the door or front desk and announce themselves that they are in town to get down. "Are there any twenty or thirty dollar nine ball players around?" they may ask, or something to that effect. They want to get into action quickly or leave. Invariably, Gunfighters only get action from the best players the place has to offer, so to be a Gunfighter you have to have serious pool playing skills. Beating the best local players means you have to win on their home court and trust me, pool tables in the little farm towns don't roll straight like the ones you see on TV. I've seen tables with hundreds of small holes in the cloth from extreme masse (curve shot) attempts. Rarely will you find a table on the road that rolls true and you can't take the time to figure them out. For this reason, a totally different style of pool is necessary. Instead of rolling balls softly like the pros on TV do, you have to shoot more force follow, draw, stun, and kill shots. Sounds like Dirty Harry dialogue but they're pool terms for a firmer style of playing. If you need to follow a ball a few feet for position, when the shot is straight in, you can hit the cue ball dead center using a firmer stroke and more or less force or bounce it where you want it. Draw shots are where you strike low on the cue ball, creating a backspin that reverses its direction after ball contact. A stun shot is similar to the force follow, only used for longer distances. To kill the ball means to use extreme inside English, while cutting in a thin shot, so that the reverse spin hits the cushion and causes the cue ball to stop or slow quickly. Got it? Gonna be a quiz.

A Bushwhacker is usually a little less skilled player who has to exercise more caution in selecting his opponents. He will nose around until he finds the town's weaker players to sneak up on and avoids the better players. A competent Bushwacker will sometime lay down a spread, which means they will lose a large amount of money intentionally to someone who's in on the scam, and then come back later for a kill. Bushwhackers, yours truly, sometimes have different outfits or disguises in order to sneak up on their prey. Because of their naturally cautious nature, Bushwhackers tend to hang on to money better, even if the amounts they win, most of the time, are smaller. The best Bushwhacker of all time was Texas State Champion, Mr. Utley Jim Puckett. He was the master of Bushwhacking disguises and the hardest working road man I ever knew. Traveling the road with Mr. Puckett taught me all I needed to know about Bushwhacking and how to dress for the event. But, that's another character and another story.

Gunfighters have more ups and downs but get to play for higher stakes and more frequently. They usually have little tolerance for Bushwhackers, righteously calling them "locksmiths," or "nut hustlers," scornful terms for players who only take on games they are almost certain they can win.

Lastly, you have a few out there called "Hatchetmen." A Hatchetman is someone like Eddie, who had no trouble trouncing the local champions, but who also wasn't above stalling his game to get lightweight players to play him, or sometimes even talking them into giving him odds. He used to say goofy things like, "I can't shoot good 'less I'm bettin' big money on my stick," or, "I'll shoot you a game for eight dollars and seventy five cents." Talking like a sucker was an art Eddie had perfected many years before our association. After beating the suckers, Eddie would usually dust the local pros. In essence, a Hatchetman gets "all the cheese."

Pool rooms could be the last safeguard against the disappearance of slang and old world or underworld words and expressions. "Railbirds" is the term U. J. Puckett used to refer to the people who come to sweat (watch) the action. For the most part they're a nuisance but they're not totally without purpose. When someone has a tough game they might ask a friend to "sweat them out" which just means watch the game and keep them company, give them confidence or voice their opinion.

"Knockers," on the other hand, are the scourge of the industry. Knockers kill action. They tell people when they have a bad game or that someone is really a good player. Some knockers do it for friends (we've all been guilty of that) and some do it just to show they're in the know. These are the worst. There's a saying in the racket, "If a guy will knock for you, he'll knock on you." I've witnessed more than one knocker get unpleasantly knocked around. In strange towns I would usually only have to talk to the younger kids hanging around the pool room to find out everything I needed to know. For a Pepsi Cola and a "How's it going, buddy?" a kid will spill his insides.

"On the earie" is an expression from the 20s or 30s. It is one of the old time expressions I learned from traveling with Eddie. If you say someone is "on the earie," it means they are trying to listen in on your conversation. In the event you were aware of the intrusion you could feed them information that would benefit you, so the "earie" could work in your favor. If Eddie felt someone was ignoring him, he would say the guy is "playing the ignore." The expressions heard strictly around pool rooms and pool players would fill a book. There's an idea.

There's a certain "hot potato" aspect in traveling any pool hustler's route with Eddie and that was the case on the road in the late 60s and 70s. Almost all of the pool action was in the South, mostly in the smaller farm towns, and Eddie was so well known that if he happened to be recognized by any of the pool room crowd it made the locals leery of any strangers. Actually, they were more terrified than leery. Eddie Taylor was a legend in the South. Generally, when people put up their guard, it's tough to get any play out of them. The trick is to make them relax so they'll go along peacefully. That was Eddie's and my specialty.

I parked my motor home in Eddie's driveway in Fayetteville, North Carolina, and put my son in school, in the first grade. His previous home schooling by his mother had been pretty intense, so after two weeks he was transferred to the second grade. Two weeks later the school released him altogether saying he was so far advanced, school was boring him and that created bad habits; we should start him in the third the following year. Beverly stayed with Eddie's wife, Violet, while Eddie and I tore through the South like Quantrill's raiders. I was a pretty good player and a Bushwhacker who knew a lot about winning, but being Eddie's sidekick was far more exciting to me than my own game. Since hardly anybody knew me, I got to play constantly. Eddie, on the other hand, was known almost everywhere so his role, in most instances, was to be my advisor and to "play the duck." In other words, stay in the car, go to the library, the movies, or somewhere–just duck out of sight while I took care of business. Eddie was a patient man so playing the duck was an easy role for him. He would read a book or newspaper, or stroll around town looking through stores by the hour. You might say he had a Masters in Duckarama. I played the duck only once when we traveled together and nearly went out of my mind.

The previous week I had beaten a guy out of some pretty serious money who owned a bar in Winston Salem. Eddie had stayed in Fayetteville but he was in on the play so we celebrated the victory upon my return. For us, celebrating meant taking our wives to the cafeteria. We really knew how to tear up the town.

The natural thing to do next was to take Eddie to Winston Salem to beat the guy but I was reluctant to get him around bars because of a certain problem he had. After a few days of talking it over in Fayetteville, and both of us promising Violet we'd be extra careful, we packed up our cues and headed north. We arrived in Winston Salem, had an early dinner, and planned our strategy. It was simple; I would wait in Ducksville while Eddie took the guy off, then we'd boogie out of town with the loot. Simple. If my beating the guy gave him any bad dreams, he had no idea of the nightmares Mr. Taylor would furnish him with.

Eddie Taylor was as close to a perfect pool player as you would ever see. His stance was rock solid, with his head directly in line over his cue. His stroke was simple to the eye, yet so unbelievably powerful that someone coined the expression "the stroke of the Bear" as the bar to strive for. Most players will take five, six, or eight warm-up strokes before they shoot and some will drive their opponent mad by taking thirty to forty, which is called "slow playing" your opponent. I remember Eddie watching one of these guys slow playing and saying, "Son, what in the world can they be thinking about down here all that time?" With each shot, Eddie would take three warm up strokes and release his arm in a perfect pendulum motion. His amazing follow through was legendary and when the ball hit the back of the pocket it sounded like "a Mercedes door closing"...someone else's words, but apropos. His motto was "Be true, follow through." Another champion, "Champagne" Eddie Kelly, once said, "When Eddie Taylor stands at the table to shoot, it looks like, if you go in to buy a pool table, he should come with it."

A quick tale about Eddie Kelly and a goofy move by Alfie: Eddie Kelly was a champion player and a close friend of Eddie Taylor's. After Kelly won the Las Vegas Stardust Open nine-ball tournament, he came to Dallas to take a shot at the Cotton Palace group. While he was there he spotted me the seven ball, playing nine-ball. For a champion like Kelly, the seven isn't much of a spot and in retrospect I don't know why I took the game to begin with. To my own surprise, I beat Kelly. It wasn't much money, a couple of hundred. Maybe he let me win. Later he sold me his cue stick that Harry Petros made especially for him. The cue had a mother of pearl name plate on the butt that said Eddie Kelly. The prices on cue sticks today will astound you. There is one cue stick show, put on by a champions cue maker, where the cues sell for $10,000 and up. It is said that Richard Black, a master cue maker from Houston, sold one for more than $100,000. Unaware of what a cue belonging to a player of Eddie Kelly's status would be worth, both in dollars and for posterity, I had the name plate changed to "Alfie Taylor" and voila, it was just another cue. Ego is a strange bedfellow.

Drive time is time for making plans. Eddie Taylor had a nice Cadillac and he preferred that I do all the driving. Those were great times and life was good. We had no pressures and we kept our bankroll healthy at all times. Was I happy? I was on the road with the Knoxville Bear and I was doing most of the playing, what do you think?

I knew our Winston Salem target usually came in around seven and, if he got down playing pool, he was a through ticket. When I beat him, he played until thirty minutes after last call and only quit then because of the law. Eddie wanted to go in like a businessman after work and sluff off a few dollars to the locals before the boss arrived and, hopefully, be losing to someone as the boss came in. The term for that move is "laying down a lemon." As a side note, it always feels better to be a sucker in a pool room than a "smart." Everyone treats the suckers so much nicer. They buy them drinks, laugh at their jokes, and hang close to them in case something falls out or is pulled out of the sucker's pockets. On the other hand, if you have the reputation for being a little bit smart you're far more apt to feel a cold shoulder. Fortunately for me, the advantages of being a sucker came my way even when I was pretending to be one. I've had the same people buying me drinks when I first hit town who felt like kicking my ass by the time I left.

Thanks to some dedicated slipping around in the Carolinas, Eddie and I had a fat bankroll when we hit Winston Salem, North Carolina, so we were prepared to bet high if he got down. The guy had played me for a hundred a game so we wanted to do it right, even if it took a few days. If I knew Eddie, he would like to divide our money into fourths and that would be the bet. When it came to gambling, Eddie liked to get it up out of the dirt.

I parked a half block down the road, on the opposite side, so I could watch the door. It wasn't like I was a high profile duck or anything like that. I was more of a duckling; nevertheless, I had just beaten the guy in front of his patrons, so hiding was the best move, even if not totally necessary. I couldn't stray far from the car. Eddie might not get to play, for one reason or another, and cell phones hadn't been invented. Besides, where would I walk around in Winston Salem at night? I'm a duck. Now what? One magazine (golf) to look through; that killed about five minute. Nothing to do, can't go anywhere. Seven hours 'till closing time and the words "stir crazy" are already in my head. This is just dandy.

The club was on the second floor. There was a long bar table running the length of a plate glass window that stretched across the front of the building. Customers sat on bar stools along the window and either played on one of the four coin-operated three and a half by seven foot pool tables or watched the action. As an option, they could swivel the stool to look at each other or peer down on the street. I knew a lot of these same people had to have been there the night I beat the proprietor, who might himself be there, so walking in the street or even sitting on the car fender was out.

Also, I think I read somewhere in the first edition of The Idiots Guide to Playing the Duck that there was a rule against walking the street. It was in the chapter with no horn honking, interior lights, loud radio playing, or sleeping with your feet out the window. The guide is required reading for crossroaders.

By six o'clock, my cue was buffed cleaner than new, my tip was shaped, my fingers and toes were popped numerous times and, what'd ya know, mosquitoes. God, I love the South. That's when I learned that the little rascals only bite for a couple of hours after sunset. To be precise, they stop at 9:27 p.m. That gave me four or five hours after they quit biting to trap the rest of them in the car and put them to death. Finally something to do.

"Ducktime" is super slow motion to a guy who's used to being in the thick of the fray, but it was evident by the crowd at the window something was happening so I was content. "Come on E. T.," I said, "Put that stroke of the Bear on his ass and let's head to the house." Great! Now I'm talking out loud to someone who isn't here. Realizing Eddie must surely have gotten to play didn't make the night go by any faster but I did relax a little. Nine o'clock, ten—all the way to a little past midnight, when I watched the last of the "last call" crowd stagger out with no sign of my partner. It was a civilized club, so I wasn't concerned. I was wondering if Eddie had the guy stuck so much that they were going to keep playing after hours. Moments later I got my answer. The inimitable Eddie Taylor stepped out onto the stoop at the top of the stairs and executed a beautiful pirouette, complete with his fingers touching over his head. Then he sort of danced down the steps, in Gene Kelly fashion, projecting a mood that looked suspiciously unlike someone who was as used to winning money as Eddie was. By the time he reached the street, I had pulled the car up to meet him and this reason for his dance performance became painfully obvious. Eddie's words to me as he leaned up to my window are etched in my brain so deeply an exact quote is no problem. I only regret you cannot hear the way this sweetheart man was singing them to me. "Got him down, son (which means got him to play). Hundred a game. Got us broke. Let's go home." It seems our host for the evening had been extra generous with his Jack Daniels. And what good Tennessee fellow could turn down "Jack?" The only lesson I got from that night is that being a sidekick may be a kick but playing the duck sucks. Incidentally, I think that was the only loser Eddie ever booked for us.

Money comes and goes but my time spent with Eddie Taylor was priceless. He told me stories about his early days that nobody else knew. Once, in the 40s, when Eddie was living in Knoxville, he had made a four team parlay bet on some football games. The way I heard it was, three of Eddie's teams had won and if the forth team won, the bookie who took the bet would be in terrible financial trouble. Meanwhile, Eddie had been drinking and was passed out on a bench in the pool hall. The bookie woke him up, told him the situation, and offered him a large amount of money to call the bet off before the fourth game began. Drunk or sober, awake or half awake, Eddie had too much play in him to be bought off. They said he lifted his head, smiled, shook his head no and told the bookie, "Let the hide roll with the tallow," then he closed his eyes and went back to sleep. Eddie remembered this expression from his childhood days in Tennessee when they would make candles. The wax was melted in some sort of raised crucible. When the wax was fluid enough, they would remove a small square piece of leather that was blocking the chute to let the wax run into the molds. Sometimes the leather would slip from their fingers and they would just forget it and "let the hide roll with the tallow."

Every pool player I ever met had some crybaby in him for something or another and pool can make you do goofball things. I remember as a kid in Dallas, Tommy Lambert beat me out of forty dollars. Tommy was as close to an archrival as I had. We played each other a lot and our games could go either direction. This time he beat my doggin' ass and laughed at me in front of my friends. It was only a forty dollar loss but I carefully leaned my two-piece cue against the side of the table, put my foot in the middle, and pressed down. Hey! I said it was a two piece cue. Before either piece of my now two pieces of garbage hit the floor, my so called friends were busting apart laughing their asses off at me. I vowed to never do anything so stupid again, but you know how vows in the pool room can go.

Some nights later, I missed an easy payball and blew a game. Taking a more controlled approach to my insanity, I looked around and saw a one piece house cue leaning against the wall. I was so dug in at the Cotton Palace in Dallas that I knew I could get away with breaking any cue that I was willing to pay six or eight dollars to replace. Hell, I could even get away with how I wanted to break it. The tables ran lengthways, in two rows of six tables. I was playing on the second set from the front. Four tables at eight feet each and five feet between them meant it was a little over forty feet to the back wall. I smacked my own cue (a new one, I might add) down on the table in a manner that said something was about to happen. I could tell my friends were wondering what nutty move I was contemplating as they stepped aside. I picked up the "soon to become a javelin" house cue, stepped between the rows of tables and players, waited for a slight clearance of players, and vented my anger by spearing the cue toward the back wall. The throw was worthy of the Olympics, should they ever let maniacs with cue sticks compete. Before it hit, before it dissolved, probably about the time it was passing the fourth set of tables, a voice behind me screamed, and I mean screamed, "Hey man! That's my own cue!" I think he said "cue." The last word was drowned out by the splattering of the cue stick against the wall. Only the strangers in the place were startled. A little groveling, ample dollars, and home court advantage turned my embarrassment and the owner of the cue's anger into a joke.

Eddie traveled with a man in the early days named "Cryin' Sam Crotchner," whom, Eddie said, would cuss himself in the mirror when he missed a shot. Rumor has it that more than once the guy got mad enough to stick his lit cigar in his own face. Eddie told me one time that in the 30s, he and Sam owed three days rent on their hotel room and they didn't have enough money to pay. Eddie said they were on the second floor so he had Sam go outside while he lowered their bags out the window to him. I asked him how much the three day bill came to. Eddie smiled and said, "Six dollars."

Pool players are a breed of their own with their own types of insanity. I saw a guy get beat so badly once in Johnston City that he fell on the floor and started gnawing at the leg of a pool table. True story. Then there was the time I played a guy named Mountain Mullinax who owned a pool room in a little town in North Carolina. Having a baseball background, Mullinax could throw a ball fast and accurately. And owning the pool room meant he could throw as many balls as he wanted, anytime he wanted. He would miss a shot and wop, a pool ball would hit the back wall; another miss, and bam, the coke machine would get it. You didn't need to wonder how often he did it; just count. Each throw left a hole in the dry wall or a huge dent in the machine. Mountain was even known to throw balls at his ceiling and stand under them on their return.

My friend Grady Mathews was playing him when Mountain miss-cued, looked down at his cue and said, "One more time, little baby and that's it for you." Another miss cue and, sure enough, the cue became history. Everybody laughs at bellyachers. There's an expression in the racket that says, "If you're going to be a sucker, be a quiet one." Having almost set the scale with some of my own complaining, I can say everyone who ever drew back a cue in the wrong direction has bitched and moaned about something wrong with their game. Since the arms do the work, most excuses are aimed directly at them. Countless times I've blamed my arm not following through correctly or being just a bit off for that shot. I've heard many others do the same. When Eddie told me about Bricklayer Red, it cured me of that crybaby nonsense forever.

Eddie told me the dates but they escape me now. I think it was in the 40s or early 50s. "Bricklayer Red" was a big man who did for a living just what his name implied. On the side, Red hustled pool and was a good player and smart, as well. As Eddie told it, Red was in a car wreck and his left arm was smashed. The doctor told him it should come off but Red refused. He told the doctor that even if he had to stuff it in his pocket, he wanted to keep his arm. And keep it and stuff it in his pocket is just what Red did.

Some years went by without Eddie seeing Red, until one day Eddie walked into a pool room and saw a crowd of people around a table watching what had to be an important game. He squeezed through, staying out of sight, and lo and behold, there was Red playing nine-ball with one arm. A pool table brush is nine or ten inches long with a flat wooden back and stiff one inch bristles. Red had one of these brushes that he was putting on the table, bristle side up, then lay his cue on it to shoot. Eddie said he watched Red break and run out, break and run out, and break and run out. Now anyone who plays pool knows that running three racks of nine-ball in a row is semi-routine for great players, a notable accomplishment for good players and about as possible as flying to the moon for someone who doesn't play a lot. And Red had just done it with one arm. Eddie went on to say that it wasn't the three racks Red ran so brilliantly that impressed him so much. It wasn't even that it was a one-armed man who ran them. What Eddie said amazed him was the way Red would shoot a ball, then flip his cue up with his hand and catch it under the armpit of his same good arm. Then, with the same hand and only his forearm, he would lean his body over the table or run around the table to grab the brush off of the table before the balls bumped it. And Red did this successfully with every shot, even when the brush was in the center of the table surrounded by balls. So, the next time you feel like crying about a stiff wrist or sore shoulder hurting your play, just think about "Bricklayer Red." Then wipe your eyes, button your lip, and shoot.

Eddie Taylor and Willie Mosconi on the same pool table might be the closest example you'll see of an unstoppable force meeting an immovable object. They were both giants in the sport and are now in the sport's history books. I've talked about Eddie, but Willie, whom I had the honor of meeting only once, played straight pool like he was from another planet. With pool prowess their only connection, these two gentlemen could not have been cut from less similar cloths. Eddie was a backwoods country boy who left Knoxville as a teen and cut a forty year path of drinking, gambling, and partying through the pool world. He hung with everyone from movie stars to music legends. Pool & Billiard Magazine's December 2003 issue has a wonderful story on Eddie written by Thomas C. Shaw.

Willie Mosconi, on the other hand, was Brunswick advisory staff material. He was educated, polished, and he made no bones about his disdain for the hustling world and its occupants. I met him at an exhibition in Dallas and mentioned Eddie. Willie said Eddie was a hustler but still a gentleman. Willie was also known to be a prima donna with a temper he made no attempt to hide. In an interview for a video I produced on the legends of pool, I asked Eddie about Willie. He said, with typical Eddie Taylor diplomacy, "If you were to go to dinner or out to play golf with Willie Mosconi, he was a perfect gentleman. But in a pool room, if things didn't go just his way, he could be a little hard to get along with." Eddie said the last time he saw Willie was when Eddie was living in Florida. A man offered to put up several thousand dollars for the winner if the two would play a match for the public. Eddie called Willie and told him about the offer. He said Mosconi agreed to come with two stipulations. They would only play straight pool and nine-ball and no bank pool or One Pocket. The second stipulation was Mosconi insisted on dividing the money equally, win or lose. Eddie agreed, feeling a little satisfaction that Willie backed away from Eddie's two specialty games, plus the money split offer meant Willie wasn't confident that he could win. The two remained friends all their lives.

Going down the road once, I asked Eddie when and how he met Willie for the first time. He said it was the mid-40s. Eddie had been hustling around the Philadelphia area for a few weeks, beating everybody pretty easily when he went into a beautiful pool room full of antique tables. Willie was sitting at the bar surrounded by his friends and admirers. It was Eddie's first time in the place and Willie didn't hustle around, so he was certain Willie didn't know who he was. Eddie walked up to him, using his full backwoods accent and vocabulary and said, "Excuse me. Aren't you Mr. Willie Mosconi, the world's call shot champion?" ("Call shot" is more of a beginner's term for straight pool.)

"Yes," Willie responded. "I'm the world's straight pool champion," with an arrogant emphasis on the words "straight pool."

Eddie said, "Well, tell me something, Mr. Mosconi. I live back in Mosheim holler and over there, only the kids shoot the balls straight in. The men make 'em hit the railin's first." ("Railin's" are the cushions.) He said Mosconi went into this long speech about how straight pool is the most scientific game in the world, more complicated than chess, blah, blah, blah.

Eddie said, "Well, if you was willin' to make 'em hit the railin's, I'd shoot you a rack for a hundred dollars or two."

Eddie's offer quickly got everyone's attention quickly because a hundred dollars was monstrous money in those days. He said Mosconi jumped off his chair, eager to play but only for one hundred a game. Eddie told me he had his cue in the car but didn't want to leave to get it so he walked over to the cue rack to select a house cue. Eddie was funny about cues. He didn't care what they weighed or even if they were crooked. All he cared about was that the stick had a good tip.

Permit me, if you will, to put Mosconi on hold and inject a story here that shows you that even a good tip isn't a must. Eddie played a guy in Tuscaloosa, Alabama, some One Pocket, giving him these odds: Eddie had to take a house cue that had the tip removed and use it playing jacked up, one-handed. The term "jacked up" means that the cue cannot touch the table rail when shooting, which is infinitely more difficult than resting it on the rail. Eddie's stipulation was that he could dip the end of the cue in water before he shot. I asked him about the ivory ferrule that holds the tip to the cue, and he said after a couple of shots the ferrule was history, leaving only wood. I guess the water made the wooden end less slippery because Eddie said he got where he could spin and even draw the ball pretty good. To add to the story, he was playing for four hundred dollars a game and he won.

But let's get back to Eddie vs. Willie. Everything was in place; Willie at the bar putting his cue together, Eddie looking around the room for a cue, and the kibitzers were gathering around. When Eddie selected his cue from the wall rack and went back to the bar, all Willie said to him, as he was putting his cue back into its case was, "You're a little late, Taylor."

It seems that someone at the bar, who had recognized Eddie, had put their tongue into something besides their glass, namely, Mosconi's ear! The knockers had landed. I was shocked hearing the story. I said, "Eddie, do you mean you walked up to the champion pool player of the world and talked to him like he was a sucker?" Eddie kind of smiled and said, "If he had played me bank pool, that's just what he'd be."

There was the less fun time when Eddie and I drove from Fayetteville to a small South Carolina town to trap this drug dealer who we'd heard would go off real good. We arrived at the pool room where the game was to take place and were told that someone had been sent to get him. We couldn't understand why it was taking a couple of hours to round someone up in a town this small, but then we didn't know that they were flying in a strong player from Charleston, in a private plane. Looking back, I'm honored that I rated so highly. After we had put up five hundred dollars for us to play a ten games ahead set, my opponent who was indeed not the man we had been seeking, said, "Now, Alfie Taylor and Mr. Eddie Taylor, the trapper has become the 'trapee'." In other words, there need be no other words. We had been had.

We played for a long time and at one point I was even five or six games ahead. But eventually he wore me down, broke me down, and took me off (I sound like I'm a set of brake linings). Even though Eddie and I had our own money, we were being staked by Eddie's stakehorse, Charlie Backer... great name for a stakehorse...who told my opponent, "Son, you won yourself a few dollars here on this little table (an eight-footer) but if you'd like to come up to Fayetteville and play Alfie some on a four and a half by nine foot table, I'll give you a chance to turn that little nubbin' into some real money." I was surprised when the guy turned down the offer, but his refusal did allow me a little face saving. He probably would have beaten me in Fayetteville, too.

This episode is burned into my brain because it was the only time I was ever beaten for the cash during the time I traveled with Eddie. The other few times I booked losers during this period were when I was alone and I remember each of them well. While driving back to Fayetteville, fighting back tears (OK, maybe I didn't win every round), I felt I had let Eddie down. It wasn't the money; we'd made plenty of that. And it wasn't even our money that I'd lost. I just hated taking the spanking in front of him. Neither of us spoke much. I could see that he knew how I felt and I remember him saying, "Son, that ain't nothin. Everybody gets beat. I've been beat so many times I can't count 'em. Let's go home to the family."

Not content to blow off my defeat like a man, the next morning when Eddie woke up my motorhome was unplugged and I had hit the road.

Thirsting for revenge and wanting to forget the day before, I headed north on I-95. I stopped in Rocky Mount and went into a black pool room that was attached to a funeral home. Shivers! I got into action immediately with a uniformed policeman, who told me that gambling with him would be no problem. What he failed to tell me was that he was a straight shootin' son-of-a-bitch. I had bet pretty heavily around the rail and played poorly off the bat and my opponent didn't. He was sure he had found himself a sucker so his confidence was soaring and he was proving it by running out real good. Before I knew it I was as broke as the Ten Commandments. There was no doubt in my mind that I could beat him. He was a cop and I was a pool hustler. Do the math.

Pride, being easier to swallow than pork and beans, I called Eddie. "Where in the world did you go, son? Vi's been worried sick," were his first words. I explained my day and he told me to go to Western Union and pick up five hundred dollars he'd have waiting there for me, then "take care of business and come home." It felt so good hearing his voice, I picked up the money and went back to the pool room and beat that flatfoot like he was my private prisoner. And the rail birds who were side betting went down with the constable. It turned out to be a pretty good score, so I asked my opponent if he would walk outside with me until I left. He said he would but that I shouldn't worry; that I won the money fair and square and it was mine. Nicest cop I ever met. I drove all the way back to Fayetteville and split the money up with Eddie that night. His main concern when he saw us was that Violet fix something to eat.

As a side note, a few months later Eddie and I went back into the Rocky Mount pool room and Eddie made his usual "My son wants to play some more pool" speech.

One of the men behind the counter said, "Your son's done been in here. We don't want no more of him. He can shoot the hair off a gnat's nut." Unfortunately for these gentlemen of Rocky Mount, someone said, "But, I'll play you some, old man."

Back in Bossier City, Louisiana, the first indication of time since the vigil began was the morning light coming through the windows. Strange, how a night that had seemed so long at the time, now seems to have gone by in an eye blink. Eddie was showing signs of restlessness and becoming uncomfortable for the first time since I arrived. Doreen held on to his left hand and I his right, the way we had throughout the night, as we both leaned in over him. We knew the time had come and we wanted to be as close to him as we could. I could hear the lack of sincerity in my voice when I was telling him it was OK to let go, and, selfishly, I wanted him to hear my insincerity as well. I didn't want to accept the inevitable any sooner than necessary, but it was obvious that it was necessary now. All at once he let out a small choking sound from his throat and he stretched both arms up, as if to heaven, with a "stroke of the Bear" strength that pulled me from my chair. The next instant Eddie's arms relaxed and I watched the blood pressure gauge by the side of his bed drop to zero, a sight I'll never forget. It was over. The legendary Eddie "The Knoxville Bear" Taylor had left this earth.

Photo: Alf Taylor

TOO LOOSE IN LOUISIANA

In the 1960s, Jack, Pat Dowling and I were traveling and had stopped just outside of Alexandria, Louisiana, at a small cafe on the highway. Stopping for a late night victory sandwich wasn't necessarily a bad idea but straightening and counting stacks of wrinkled money on the table could have used a touch more forethought. I was still pretty wet behind the ears, so I blame my brother Jack for the indiscretion. As usual, when side action is covered on a good score, you wind up with bills of all denominations, usually all crammed together. And as usual, the money smells like it never left the pool room, but hey, so did we. So here we were with stacks of bills amounting to no more than six or seven hundred dollars, but looking like thousands, and the three of us rattling on about the win, like nobody was paying any attention when, in fact, they were.

The cafe was practically deserted, only a table of old timers, the regulars, drinking their bottomless cups of coffee, rolling their own cigarettes, and jawing on and on about the same nothings they discussed the night before. Everything they said contained a complaint about the government, an ailment, or a remark about someone who was no longer around and what it was that "took 'em back to the Lord."

Small cafes in the south are a part of Americana that seem to never change. Typically, the pace of southern cafe hang outers is just below a dawdle, as was this one. I know because I grew up in Dixie. We used to say we liked the Southern girls because they speak so slowly that by the time they tell you they're not that kind of girl, they are.

The front porches of some of these cafes, along with the courthouse lawns throughout the South, are also the last bastion of apple box whittling. This was one of those cafes, evident by the small mounds of wood chips by the rocking chairs on the porch and the variety of hand carved toys for sale by the checkout counter. A box of stick horses, with wheels on the stick bottoms and real horse hair manes, sat by the door. Another box containing those famous wooden dancing minstrels, complete with black faces and white eyes, was on the floor next to it. The minstrel was a flat body-shaped piece of wood about six inches tall and an inch thick, with wooden arms and legs that dangled loosely from small nails driven part way into the body. A one-foot dowel is stuck tightly into their backs. A flat, thin, two-foot long paddle board came with each one. The object was to sit on one end of the paddle with it protruding from between your legs and hold the minstrel by the stick stuck into his back, on the other end of the board. As you tapped on the board between your legs, the minstrel's legs went up and down and tapped on the board while the arms swung up, down, and around. The faster you tapped, the faster he danced. They're a lot of fun.

I had seen toys of these types in the mountain areas of Tennessee and North Carolina, but never this far south, and I'm embarrassed to say that I once attempted to copy and sell them. I saw them at a co-op in Asheville, North Carolina, and tried to purchase some for resale. The people at the co-op told me the toys stayed backordered and it was hard to even get enough to keep the store supplied. Always looking for a niche, I bought a couple to copy and drove to Houston, where wife, Beverly, and I setup two band saws and started slowly cranking them out. I didn't have real horse hair for the stick horses so I used strands of thin rope. A third toy was made with two ten-inch tall, one half inch thick slats, joined in the middle by a three-inch pin. Between the top of the sticks was a wooden trapeze artist dangling from a stretched string. Squeezing your fingers in and out made the man spin both ways, fast.

The toys were quite clever but I must have been out of my mind; they only sold for five dollars apiece and each one took a couple of hours to make; then I had to try to sell them. The mountain people who sit at home have the time to make them. As a matter of fact, time is about all they do have. To top it off, my poor wife and I knew nothing about power saws and we're lucky to come away with all of our digits. This is no success story, folks. It's more a story of being many years ahead of your time. Today, many "green" thinking people are shying away from plastic toys, preferring wooden ones. But, somewhere in a warehouse in Texas sits a couple of boxes of handmade toys, the brainchildren of a very unprofitable idea.

Sitting on each table in the cafe was a small, triangular shaped wooden block, factory made, with holes holding eight or ten golf tees, put there to babysit impatient customers. The object was to remove as many of the tees as you could by jumping one tee over another and taking the jumped one out. On the back was a chart rating your score and giving you a title from "Goof Off" to "Genius." I had seen those things on these same greasy Formica tables many times before, but they never sucked me in. Call it ego or whatever, but I didn't like the thought of a piece of wood labeling me a "Goof Off." I had a perfectly good wife for that.

Our friend Pat grabbed one like it was a free slot machine and by the third try he was feeling like Einstein's sidekick. Pat also loved music and this place had the small jukeboxes at the tables. He always carried pockets full of change and elected to have his own booth next to ours. For the next half hour or so we heard constant flapping from the page switchers so we knew he was in music heaven. Pat was like a baby duck that just wakes up in a new world each day.

Unquestionable proof that we were still in Louisiana lay in the eight or ten kinds of bottled Tabasco and other hot sauces pushed into a big circle around the napkin holder by our elbows. I looked at the names and where each was bottled: "Poppa's Hottest," "Fred's Firebrand," "Volcano Lava." One had just a picture of the devil holding a pitchfork. All of them, except the old standby brands like "Cholula" and "McIlhenny," were bottled within miles of where we sat and some looked like they hadn't been opened since the celebrations at the end of the Civil War, except that we were in the part of the country that didn't do much celebrating. I twisted the tops off just to break the crunching seal, half expecting erupting flames. A couple of them were beyond opening ever again. If it would weld plastic to glass, what does it do to one's innards? After sniffing three or four of them up close, then smelling what I thought was burning nose hair, I gave up the hot sauce inspection.

Next to the cash register sat two huge jars, one of which held the world's pinkest white meat, pickled pigs' feet. It was a brave man who ate the first one of those. Matter of fact, it's a brave man who eats them at all. I saw them in a convenience store in Nashville, where the underprivileged kids would eat them covered with Argo Corn Starch, for cheap filling. The other jar was full of chitterlings (another part of the same creature) which you wouldn't be able to buy without pointing at them unless you pronounced them "chitlins." No problem though; anybody who didn't grow up eating chitterlings wasn't likely to try them. A basket filled with bags of oil-soaked boiled peanuts in their shells was also on the counter, with one bag opened next to a sign that said, "Take one, not two." I wondered how upset they'd get if someone took a handful.

The waitress, who had three pencils piercing her beehive top knot and was rolling what was left of a toothpick on top of her tongue from one side of her mouth to the other, was obviously married to the cook/dishwasher/owner. This was evident from the manner in which they bossed each other around, using married couples' terms of endearment along with light swear words. She began with, "Goddamn it, honey, I said 'well done' on that steak and this one's still bloody. You pull this same crap every day. Why can't you listen?"

Answered by, "That's your ass talking, sweetheart. You didn't write it down and you don't speak up, so don't blame me."

"You want some 'speak up,' smart ass?" she asked, freezing in her tracks and staring over the counter into the kitchen, still holding the bloody steak, as if she was keeping open the option of putting it down or throwing it. A burst of silence erupted from the kitchen. Yes, this was definitely a mom and popper.

An old man with a tennis ball sized purple goiter on the side of his neck was mopping the floors and humming. No tune, just humming, and doing it with his mouth open. Try it. It's not easy. He never spoke and nobody spoke to him. It was like he was there, but really wasn't; like someone who's listening to a Walkman. My guess was that he had never even had his neck looked at and I didn't like looking at it either. I made up my mind to keep my outside eye closed after my food arrived so that I wouldn't see it while I ate. Nothing against the poor guy, he simply wasn't restaurant material.

Jack and I, being jaded to this tempo of excitement, were antsy to eat and leave and couldn't understand why burgers and fries were taking so long. We also didn't know the Louisiana State Police headquarters was about an hour away and that our upcoming visitors were trying to cut the time in half. Our food arrived five minutes ahead of four blue-uniformed gentlemen who were looking to join us.

"Hey, this booth is too small for six. Back off flat foot or deal with a hungry man," is what I would have liked to have said as the four joined our party. Instead I opted for the path of fear (or it opted for me) and I became quieter than Marcel Marceau. "Touch that money copper, and I'll be on you like a dog on a bone," is what I would have liked to have said, as our money was being scooped off the table, but the dummy in me prevailed again.

"It looks like you fellows are 'bout finished eating. Why don't you come with us," one said. Although it was put to us like a suggestion, my gut feeling said it wasn't.

"Hey Barney Fife, I haven't had my dessert, so step off," is what I wanted to answer, but you know my style.

Damn, I thought, these Louisiana cops are hard on pool hustlers. The next move was into their back seat, with the standard hand on the top of my head. Did these people really think that just because I'm being arrested and handcuffed, I can't get into a car without bumping my head? I asked if I could lock our car and was told that it wasn't necessary; it was being seized. Damn, these Louisiana cops are hard on pool hustlers.

Things took a more serious turn when the officer got on his radio and said, "We're coming in; it looks like we got 'em."

What? "Got 'em?" For what–playing pool and counting our money? I could just see the Baton Rouge and New Orleans Newspaper headlines:

"Brother Cafe Money-Stackers Finally Apprehended. Your kids can play outdoors again."

How were we to know that a safe had been cracked in the area, earlier that night, and that an undisclosed amount of cash, in small bills, had been taken? Oh, lucky us!

Earlier that day we had stopped in West Monroe, Louisiana. J. D. Beebe was not only Monroe's best pool player, he was also a guy who would take a shot at playing any road player that he didn't know. That made it easy for Jack to get down with him. Another advantage to playing Beebe was that he typically came in early (by ten o'clock) and early action was hard to find on the road. In Monroe, they like to play six-ball, which is a shorter and easier version of nine-ball, and like nine-ball, the person making the highest numbered ball wins. Beebe and Jack played until early evening. Fans of Beebe came in throughout the day, willing, almost to a man, to donate a few dollars, betting on their local champ. Jack tortured him.

The tables were damp from the humidity and had small pockets, so running out consistently was difficult, even playing six-ball. Jack's smooth stroke and soft touch was perfect for those wet tables. He knew to play all his positions for the following balls with follow shots because draw shots, shots where you make the cue ball backup, are next to impossible when the cloth is damp. Even to this day, at eighty-two years old, Jack still runs out with proficiency. Pool is the only sport where the youngsters don't come in and rule over the older players. As long as you keep your eyesight...they make special glasses for pool today...and keep your hands steady, you can play. Eddie Taylor told me he knew a man who was still on the road at the age of ninety-five. Eddie said it was easy for this old fellow to get action but tough for him to get up out of his chair.

Beebe was a straight shooter but played a country style of pool, meaning that he played less precise cue ball position and ended up with more tough shots. The problem that you face against country players, from time to time, is that they make so many of those tough shots they'll drive you crazy. Their downfall is that country style players too often will make a tough shot only to wind up with their next shot being equally tough or tougher. If a country style player gets stuck a little loser, those tough shots turn into super tough shots, and on a wet table, if a ball is rolling close to the rail on its way to a corner pocket and touches the rail, it just won't go in.

The more Jack ran out, the more Beebe didn't, which is so often the case between players who are gambling. I can usually look at two players' faces and tell who is winning.

We had been on the road for a couple of weeks, with our wives bugging us to come home but Jack insisted that we not go, "Until we get our payday." Jack was in dead stroke and had been going through local room players like Grant through Richmond. Today, Mr. Beebe was no different. He went down for the count. Our bankroll was pretty fat and it looked like, after this score, we would get to enjoy two of God's greatest gifts to man, home cookin' and home lovin'.

At the Louisiana State Police headquarters, Jack explained (lied) to the cops that we were taking a little time off from our jobs to visit Louisiana and "perhaps play a little pool." I could tell by their faces that his story sounded better to us than it did to them. We told them that we had won the money playing pool at West Monroe Billiards, playing J. D. Bebee, and asked them to call him to verify our story.

They did call and Mr. Beebe, who was still sore from his spanking, answered, "I never heard of those guys."

Jailed for a "got ya last," how humiliating. Actually, a guy in my social position doesn't humiliate all that easily. What I felt was more like fright. Into the cell we went, thankfully alone. I knew the home cookin' was out and, being small, I was worried about the other, if we had the wrong company.

Three or four hours into our incarceration two officers and a big bellied sergeant came to our cell and the sergeant asked Jack, "I hear you're a good pool player. Is that right?"

Jack quipped back, "Good enough to land me in here if that's what you call good."

Jack was tough in all aspects, but in verbal bouts, he was unbeatable. Once, in Fort Worth, a guy in a bar stuck a gun in his side and said, "OK Jack Taylor. Give me the money you screwed me out of or I'm going to blow a hole in you." Jack looked him square in the eye and said, "Which one of 'em are you?" The guy got so tickled he bought Jack a drink.

"Come with us, pool hustlers, we got something waiting for you," the sergeant said, and unlocked our cell.

I didn't particularly care for the way he said that and when I saw we were going toward the stairs leading to the basement, I got this sickly feeling. I hoped the chief's wife hadn't run away with a pool hustler. Imagine our delight when, instead of being greeted by rubber hoses, there in the center of the room, surrounded by soft drink and candy machines, a coffee pot under a shelf of cups with names on them, the proverbial doughnut box, and a big screen TV, was a beautiful ten foot antique snooker table. There was a poster on the wall of two cops crouched behind an open police car door, resting very large hand guns on their window sill. The poster said, "Never question authority." I always wanted a game room like this but without the coppers.

Snooker, for those of you who don't know, is a pocket billiard game with smaller balls and smaller pockets, played on a bigger table, usually five foot by ten foot or six by twelve. The game either originated in England or was made popular there. Big money snooker matches are on TV daily in London. A varied number of red balls are used, ranging from six to fifteen. This table had six. There are also six numbered balls, numbered from two to seven, each resting on a designated spot on the table at the beginning of the game. The object of the game is to pocket a red ball, which gives you one point, and then pocket any of the numbered balls, which count the amount of points equal to the number on the ball. The numbered balls are then re-spotted until the red balls are all gone, and then the two through seven numbered balls are pocketed in sequence. Scratching with the cue ball or failing to hit the correct ball results in a seven point penalty. Most hustlers don't care for snooker. The game takes a long time and is slow action compared to nine-ball, where someone can beat you a game and you can get a shot and win it back by the time they get a good swallow of their soft drink. We still didn't know what was going on here, but unless they were planning to beat us with pool cues, things were definitely looking up.

The sergeant told Jack, "If you can run these balls without missing, we're going to release you." What's this? I've heard of Southern cash register justice, but "run out and get out" was one for the books. Running the table playing snooker is almost out of the question, unless you're from England or maybe Canada, and the cues in the place were trash, so their offer wasn't that tasty to begin with.

The sergeant told Jack to, "Bust 'em hard pool hustler, let's see what you got."

Jack did just that, but too hard. The cue ball hit the stack and jumped the table so fast that another big-bellied cop, who was sitting at the head of the table, almost fell out of his chair ducking, bringing the other cops to a howling laughter. Only part of me was glad to see the cop duck.

"Dudent count," said Sarge. "Shoot again," as he handed Jack the cue ball.

No matter how this night turned out, I would never forget this odd police behavior, or the cop dodging that cue ball. If it had hit him, assaulting a police officer might have been added to our safe cracking beef.

For the next twenty or so minutes, Jack's playing was as smooth as a mother's love. One red ball after another dropped into a pocket, each red followed by the numbered ball closest to the pocket. Points were immaterial; all Jack had to do was avoid a miss. It was a larger pocket snooker table and the game room was climate controlled, so the table was dry and dependable. Still, it was snooker, so my hopes were not high.

Jack was running balls like he didn't have a care in the world until every red ball had disappeared. Now he really had my attention. Could freedom be within our grasp? With the red balls gone, he began working on the numbered balls. By this time the basement was packed with uniformed, smiling, whispering spectators. The scene was like something out of The Twilight Zone. The two, three, and four balls are originally spotted in a line close to the head spot, no more than a foot apart. Jack pocketed them all in the two corner pockets closest to them. He had me holding my breath. The five ball is spotted in the dead center of the table, with the six on a spot in the middle of where the red balls are racked before the break. The seven is spotted a few inches off of the end rail, making it the toughest shot. Jack played position on the five, for the side pocket, and dropped it easily, but the cue ball drifted a little too far down the table, giving him an easy enough cut on the six, but leaving himself a bad angle to get down to the seven ball. He had no choice but to pop the six hard enough to send the cue ball three rails around the table to get position on the seven ball. Jack hit the six so firmly that when it barely rubbed against the rail on the way to the pocket, it kind of bobbled back and forth, making a "blub, blub" sound, almost like a bathtub stopper being pulled out, and while the cue ball banked perfectly three rails around the table for straight in position on the seven, the pretty pink six ball stopped, and hung over the lip of the pocket, as though gravity was on holiday. I sank into my chair and looked over at Pat, who looked like he was about to cry.

At first there was dead silence. Then the big sergeant bellowed, "Lock them sum bitches up."

Then he and the whole room broke into cheers and laughter. Cops were patting Jack on his back, shaking his hand, and asking him to show them shots or for tips on using English on the cue ball. This night kept getting weirder by the moment. What we didn't know was that after we were locked up they sent someone to the pool room in Monroe who confirmed that we had won the money. The whole "run out and get out" thing had been a scam. The Louisiana State Police squad had played us like pure suckers. Like anyone else who gets into the game of pocket billiards, these guys were pool crazy and Jack was their new hero. They had never seen shooting like he showed them. Jack had played with such fast and loose confidence, I sometime wonder if he had been in on the joke, leaving only two of us as the suckers. With Jack, you never know. By this time, I was relaxed and thinking of how I could get one of these turkeys to play me some. State workers draw a pretty good paycheck and I would have loved to show them a new form of highway robbery. Nah! Not the best idea.

So it was back on the road, counting our cash one more time (in our laps), feeling good with a hell of a story to talk about and heading for home, this time just looking for a good Louisiana fast food drive-through.

A LITTLE ROCKY IN LITTLE ROCK

In a jail in Little Rock, Arkansas, in the mid-1960s

I asked my brother Jack, "How can we be in here for suspicion of the murder of Pat Dowling when the victim, make that the alleged victim, is in here with us? I enjoy a joke as much as the next potential death row convict, but how about one that's funny for all of us."

From the top bunk, Pat arose from the dead long enough to snicker and say, "At least I'm only being booked for impersonating, make that suspicion of impersonating, Pat Dowling. I should be out years before you guys," followed by his own howling laughter. The remark was both funny and ironic coming from Pat because he wasn't the type to get the last word in or say something funny. He preferred to stay quiet, handle the side action, and drive every mile of our trip.

"Say, twal yea ol', gimme a qwata; I'll show you a trick," hollered a graying old black man, who was sweeping the hall and whistling a non tune, like he was having a good day fishing. Acceptance and contentment were etched in his wrinkled face. He rattled on constantly, jumping from one bull shit tale to another, fully cognizant of his captive audience. The occasional "pipe down" or "shut the blank up" that came from one of the longer term guests down the hall didn't make him drop a syllable. To make things worse, each utterance was followed by his almost idiotic laughter. He had "trustee" embroidered on his shirt and pointed to it constantly, like a badge of honor. Considering where we were and where he was, it did have value. No matter how long the old man had been or would be here, he was pulling what's called "easy time." "Come on, twal yea ol," he prodded, "shake loose wit dat qwata. I gots a trick fo' ya, das gonna bring you back some serious coin." "Twal yea ol" translated to "twelve year old", which is about how old I looked at nineteen.

"Might as well," said Pat. "A quarter's not going to keep a murderer out of the chair." Pat had gotten into his new funny man role. Incarceration was obviously working out for him. I can't remember the tricks, but I shook loose "wit dat qwata," as my new teacher had so eloquently stated, and played the only action around. If we murdered Pat, who would drive?

Pat Dowling was a nice young man whom Jack had met earlier in Houston. Pat had hit an unlucky streak and this particular morning was sleeping in his car outside of the Frat Club, a pool room where Jack hung out. Pat's pool game wasn't very strong but he had two things going for him; a big comfortable Lincoln Continental and a credit card that his mother covered, when necessary. When he offered to buy the gas and food if we would take him on the road with us, he didn't realize he could have used what he had to negotiate himself into a position of CEO. Pat had two stipulations: He had to do all of the driving and he wanted us to call him "Wheels" which was easy enough. So we took our wheel man, along with his big car and little card, and headed into the South. Jack was the only solid road player in the group, but my game was coming together, so by picking my spots, I brought in some money too. Another thing Jack and I had going for us was Pat refused to believe that he couldn't beat me playing nine-ball, a fact that served as his Waterloo more than once. Whenever we needed money he would call his mother for some to "come home." But knowing Pat and knowing he really didn't want to go, I would talk him into playing me some "cheap nine-ball" and by night's end Pat would have lost his turn to carry our bankroll along with his option to go home.

We slept in dumpy motels and lived on sandwiches, canned goods, and bad choices of drinks. Paper plates and plastic ware were the norm and we ate more meals while driving than while standing still. Pat and I watched Jack win peoples' money like they were giving it to him and life, as I remember it, was pretty good. The three of us liked to read pocket novels, mostly mysteries. As we would go down the road we would finish chapters or sections and rip them out for each other to read. It didn't matter which of us had how much money or anything else. All of us (except Mrs. Dowling) shared everything.

In our Little Rock cell home there were no magazines or books other than a scrunched up copy of "Debbie Does Wherever" that was too nasty for any of us to touch. The guests before us left a jailhouse deck of forty some odd playing cards, thick with moisture and age, and so soft they made no noise when they were shuffled. Games like blackjack or poker were still possible but solitaire or gin rummy, forget about it. My favorite two pasttimes in the Little Rock jail were avoiding the open air toilet that sat conspicuously in the center of the room as much as possible and sleeping the time away until Pat came back from his grave and got us through the bars.

The three of us had come to Little Rock, Arkansas, three days earlier and somehow or other met a man named Billy McKim, who told us about a place called Club Hollywood in North Little Rock that had late night pool action. His idea was for the four of us to go in with Jack posing as a lightweight pool player who was a sucker and I as the last heir to the King Ranch in Texas who gives Jack plenty of money to gamble with. The "King Ranch" story was Jack's little touch of color.

The local hustlers knew I would be booted out of the bar for being so young and not wanting to lose their "sucker," they rustled up a girl for me, only half and again my age. It was hard to tell just what she was like under all that makeup but I was in no position to be choosey. She was supposed to take me for a ride and kill as much time as she could, and then, I suppose, she would get a slice of the winnings for her babysitting. She had a nice car and told me we could go anywhere and do anything I wanted. Visions of grandeur raced through my inexperienced mind and body. Billy told our potential marks that with me out of the way they could beat Jack real good. Little did they know, if they messed with my brother playing pool, they were the ones that were going to get "Jacked" good.

Jack was always as capable getting out of tough spots as he was getting into them. One time he was playing in Bisbee, Arizona, a copper mining town who's bragging right was limited to having the world's largest Lavender pit. That's about it for Bisbee. It's not on the way to anywhere and there's zip to do there. Jack was playing the town champ and betting heavily around the side, mostly ten and twenty dollar bets. He was a six or seven-hundred winner when a very large man, still wearing his miner's duds like he just finished his shift and said, "I'll bet you ten." Jack took the bet and won the game. When he went to his new side-better to collect, the man said, "I was betting you on you. Give me my ten dollars." Jack said he was being ridiculous, that nobody bets against themselves. The man kept insisting and Jack kept refusing until the man picked Jack up and draped him over his shoulder and walked toward the door. There was no misconception about what was coming next so Jack asked, with his head still down by the man's butt, "How much did you say you were betting?" The man said "ten dollars" and Jack told him "Well, put me down so I can pay you." Jack returned to the table and started to break the balls when the man asked "Same bet?"

The Club Hollywood plan delighted me. They had the action and I had a real date. Ruby was her name and whatever needs doing in the bar was her game. She wasn't the first person I had been around who lit their cigarettes off of the end of their last one, but she was the first girl and she could do it while she was talking. She would lick her lips and clamp her cigarette down in the left side of her mouth while lighting her new cigarette and speaking semi-coherently, out of the other side of her mouth. And she did this with each new cigarette. A disposable lighter must have lasted her a year. Another thing I remember about Ruby is when my face got too close to hers and I breathed in too deeply (which was automatic, considering my state), her perfume made my eyes water. Was I just impressed by this Goddess or could this be true love? I'm sure our "King Ranch" story weakened a little when I let her pay for the hamburgers. So Ruby drove around Little Rock and I pawed around Ruby. The best part was she kept driving and talking, and didn't resist a bit. She was probably wondering how she would fit in at the ranch. An hour out, and that chick's clothes needed some serious pressing. If time really does fly when you're having fun, she gave me an evening on the Concord. I didn't get a home run from Ruby but I spent enough time on second and third base that I remember her still.

It was after midnight when we pulled into the parking lot of the club and the brightest lights we saw came from the ten or so police cars in the parking lot. Uh oh! Here we go again.

An hour earlier at Club Hollywood, Billy and Jack were spinning their web. Action had not even begun when two guys who weren't involved in the pool scene got into an argument over a woman. Billy, who was friends with one of the men, walked over and politely tried to break it up. The woman pulled a small caliber pistol from her purse and popped it at Billy, who walked over to Jack, unbuttoned the top button of his shirt, and said, "Jack, I think that son of a bitch shot me." Then, without another word, six foot two, two hundred plus pounds Billy McKim, carrying a one half ounce twenty-two caliber slug in his heart, dropped dead on the Club Hollywood floor.

I remember not feeling much, if any, remorse over Billy. It was a shame that it happened but I had just met him and, to my way of thinking, it was just his time. But the dead guy aside, my own heart was wounded to the core because I was pretty sure the romance I had struck up with Ruby was over. I'm sure she was devastated as well.

A day or so later we went to a pool room called Lowber's. Jack wasted no time in beating Mr. Lowber, who was a bit older but a good player, out of a couple of hundred dollars. Without any provocation, other than him losing a little money, Mr. Lowber calmly walked behind the bar and came up with this long barreled pistol that looked like something unearthed at Appomattox. It actually had an ejection rod running under the barrel, like you see in old Westerns. Could it possibly shoot? Who knows? Lowber pointed the relic at Jack and said, "You get out of here right now or you'll get the same thing Billy McKim got."

Good news travels fast; bad news, like lightning. Our participation in the McKim drama must have been on Lowber's mind through the entire evening. I wondered how long the gun had been part of those thoughts. I was already unscrewing Jack's cue and moon walking my ass out the front door, but Jack bellied right up to the old guy and threatened him with shoving his gun where he didn't want it.

Lowber put the gun on the counter, in front of him, and changed his tune to a friendlier, but still firm one, "You guys don't need to be here. Why don't you hustle somewhere else?" as he put his gun back under the bar. It was the perfect no event standoff. We left Lowber, we left Lowber's gun, we left Lowber's Pool Hall, and we left with Lowber's money. What's next in this screwy town anyway? Sorry I asked (I thought) as one set of red lights went on behind us and another pulled in front. Murder? What? Murdered who? I mean whom? Him? Pat?

The officers were talking between themselves like we weren't there but wouldn't discuss any details with us. It was a simple into the cuffs, into the car, and into the cell situation. In actuality, the police knew we were innocent; the same as they knew Pat was Pat. They trumped up the charge to hold us as a favor to Pat's mother, who had tracked us down (Lowber probably called her). Her son was coming home, even if it meant her coming to get him, which she did. I'm sure the fact that Mrs. Dowling was the Head Psychologist for the State of Nevada didn't hamper her request to the men in blue. A couple of days of delicious Arkansas jail food later, Mrs. Dowling arrived and had Pat and "twal yea ol" released. Her same influence got a gambling charge laid on Jack so he could hang around the cell awhile. Any money we had when we were popped was confiscated as evidence. Evidence for what, I didn't know, but I wasn't in too much of a hurry to ask for it back. My guess is it went to some "widows and orphans fund." Mrs. Dowling, though happy to have her son back, was a little upset with all of us. She was nice but didn't have much to say, her quietness being a tool of her profession, no doubt. Everything she felt was justified. Everything she did was kind. My apology to Mrs. Dowling, wherever she is, for being a temporary thorn in her side.

Pat and I slipped off to a pawn shop, hocked a Polaroid camera in his name, and bailed Jack out. Later, we were all cleaning up in Mrs. Dowling's motel room, and Jack, with a totally straight face, asked Mrs. Dowling if she would mind leaving us Pat's credit card so that we would "have identification" to retrieve the camera Pat had pawned in his name. I loved the look of astonishment that Jack's unmitigated gall left on Mrs. Dowling's pretty face. But it's like Jack says, "You can't hit 'em if you don't swing at 'em."

The last thing I remember about our Arkansas trip is that while driving out of town, a carload of college girls pulled up beside us, rolled down their windows, stuck their faces out and yelled, "Soooeee, pigs!" It was years later before I learned that it wasn't an insult at all. It was their Razorback mascot call. I guess part of our adventure in Little Rock will always stick with me a little bit because forty some years later, and to this day, when I look about a hundred and twelve, brother Jack still calls me "Twal yea ol."

A PAINFUL NIGHT IN GEORGIA
(OR, WHY HUSTLING POOL SUCKS)

Atlanta – Early '70s, after midnight

This was the maddest cop I'd ever seen who pulled me over and was yelling at me for driving over a hundred miles per hour down the freeway towards downtown Atlanta. He actually screamed, "What are you, Crazy!?" In a way, I was—crazy with fear of losing my brother. With tears in my eyes, I told him that my little brother Bobby was cut badly and asked if he would help us get to a hospital. When the cop asked Bobby to remove the handful of Kleenex he had pressed up against his cheek, blood streamed down over his neck. I couldn't tell where the cut began or ended. I kept thinking about his throat.

Then I saw Bobby's teeth through the gash in his cheek and my wet eyes turned into sobbing pleas. "Do anything to me when we get to the hospital," I begged, "but please help us."

"Follow me," said the officer, who was concerned now for a different reason. With siren blaring, he led and sped us to the hospital, and then left without a word. "Thank you" to him for his understanding.

Just a short time earlier, we had been at the Chicken Haven. Had the automatic door locks on my Cadillac been up and down switches like you see today, instead of running horizontally on the arm rest, I would have never mixed up the directions. When I started the car to back out of the parking lot and saw the man moving quickly toward the passenger side front door, I hit the lock switch in the wrong direction, and the doors unlocked. The man opened the door, leaned in and said, "Alfie, I need some money."

Bobby was sitting in the passenger's seat. His longtime friend from Pasadena, Texas, Keith Thompson, aka "Pasadena Squirrel," (the youngest player to ever win the Johnston City Tournament) was sitting in the back. The three of us were hustling around Atlanta, which is known to be a hothead pool spot in the first place. I was selling ladies' ready-to-wear in Kentucky and Tennessee for a manufacturer at the time, so an American car with a big trunk was necessary for carrying samples. Hustling a little pool on the side was always fun, almost. This night we had been playing in a "joint," in the truest sense of the word, called The Chicken Haven. We hadn't sensed any trouble as Keith beat the place for us pretty good. He shot down everyone who stepped up to the table, without breaking a sweat. Keith was just a kid who, like other kids, ate a lot of chocolate and read comic books but when it came time to play, he had nerves of steel. The evening had gone pretty smoothly. We had covered a lot of side action, with only a murmur of discontent from the Saturday night crowd, but what were they murmuring?

When the man (assailant) opened the car door and said he needed some money, I thought he just wanted to bum a couple of bucks. He knew my name but I didn't know him. He hadn't even been involved in the evening's action, which many times is the case with trouble.

I said, "Sure! Bobby, give him twenty dollars."

His face flared. He didn't speak, he screamed, "I don't want twenty dollars. I want some money," and with that, he lunged into the car and brought his right hand down onto Bobby's face. In that hand was a hooked roofer's knife. In an instant, what I perceived as a run of the mill bar room panhandle had become a full on needless assault. A threat with his knife would have gotten him our money. His was an amateurish and potentially deadly move for sure.

Bobby punched his attacker and pushed him out of the car with his feet, then screamed, "He hit me with something. A comb, I think." Then Bobby grabbed for a gob of Kleenex from a box on the seat beside us and turned to me. I'll never forget the look on his face or the fear in my mind as everything in front of him, and between us, turned a dark, sticky red.

Gunshot and knife wounds, accident victims, noisy drunks, and abused spouses filled the Atlanta General Hospital's emergency room and spilled over into the halls and out the swinging emergency room doors. One little kid who had swallowed part of a bottle of Clorox was rushed ahead of everyone else. A crying, very angry, very loud woman had her arms wrapped around her pissed off cursing man; the stump from his amputated little finger was wrapped in a bloody handkerchief and the finger conspicuously visible in a plastic baggie on his lap. Ambulances and police cars came and went like taxicabs at an airport. More than one prospective patient was escorted in sporting handcuffs. Nobody waiting spoke in a normal voice or tone. Everyone was either weeping, or mumbling softly to themselves, or screaming for help, or about how they were being overlooked. Only the most critically injured received immediate attention. On his most creative day, Fellini couldn't have conjured up a stranger scene. The nurses and counter staff (God bless them) took it completely in stride as they fended off one irate bleeder after another. To them this was just another Atlanta Saturday night.

When a doctor finally came around to see us, Bobby told him that he was still a young man and asked if he would be very careful sewing him up. I looked at Bobby's face and his long hair, caked with blood and felt nauseated. People do this to steal money? Unbelievable. The cut began on the right side of his forehead, then, luckily, (dare I mention that word) the knife jumped over his eye and down his cheek. Due to the curvature of the knife, the point of the blade went in and cut outward, leaving much of the flesh dangling out. The doctor seemed compassionate and said that he understood. Naturally, I tried to go in while he worked on him and naturally, there was no chance. I knew there was a twenty-four hour window during which time you could re-open a wound and sew it up better, if necessary. I had a doctor in Nashville who would do that for me, but it turned out not to be necessary and to this day, Bobby only has a small scar under his mustache and most likely in his memory.

    I called a friend, Billy Johnson, who was a local champion pool player to see if he knew how to find the person who had cut Bobby. My first thought was to bring in my brother Jack, who knew more about taking care of things like this. Jack would beat this guy to a pulp for sure. My friend told me that I was in over my head and that I had better "leave this one alone." He told us Bobby's assailant was known to have cut a lot of people, at least one of whom didn't recover. He went on to say that the guy was an escapee from jail on a work release program at that very time and said to call Jack only if I wanted Jack killed.

    Tired or not, sleepy or not, discouraged or not, we immediately packed our bags and, like three scared rabbits, pointed that Cadillac north to Nashville. Atlanta, the Chicken Haven, and that money hungry maniac with a knife could kiss our hightailing ass.

THE WEST IS STILL WILD

Superior, Arizona – mid '70s

This is bullshit; I come way out in the middle of the desert to try and win a few dollars and now bullets are flying around the parking lot and I'm sitting in the middle of the freakin' parking lot. Those idiots are making these problems over money. If the love of money really is the root of all evil, these guys must be head over heels.

Off to my left are my two mates for this evening's play, Jackie Wright and his cousin (whose name eludes me), ducking behind a car fender with only a smoking pistol showing. How can anyone expect to duck their head and aim their gun at the same time, proving again an amateur with a gun is more dangerous than a pro with two guns. A few cars away, between a beat-to-death pickup and the front door of the bar, firing toward Jackie, is a very pissed off, very big black man, with a lot less money in his pocket than he had when we met. And who's the Mexican fellow who came busting out of the bar shooting and screaming like an Indian warrior at the same time? What did all of this have to do with him? Later we found out his war hoop came from shooting himself in the foot as he ran out the door. As I said: amateurs. It hadn't occurred to me that anybody had guns and now it looks like everyone, except yours truly, does. But I have something better than a gun, I have a car key.

We were in Scottsdale, Arizona, the previous day and anyone who ever knew Weldon "Junior" Rogers, from Tucson, knew that if he said there was a chance to make some money somewhere, they should listen. Weldon was no stranger to big scores. He was a good pool player on regulation size tables and a killer player on bar tables. Weldon was also a more than capable one-handed player. And Weldon Rogers was, without a doubt, one of the best pool hustlers ever to scoot down the road, which he would do sometimes for months on end without returning home. Weldon also had incredible stamina and liked to play for high stakes. He could play for days on end without tiring and would play anybody, and beat them, if they stipulated that only the loser could quit. He had a lion's heart and could eventually wear anyone down. I watched him in Memphis play another good player, Richard Austin. I was working at a ladies ready-to-wear market at a Memphis motel. At the end of the first day Weldon was twenty or thirty games down when I went back to my room to sleep. The next day after work, I went to the pool room and Weldon, who had played all night was about ten games down. Same thing; I watched the game, slept, went to work and back to the pool room, where the guys had played all night again, more than forty-eight hours without sleep. Richard was collapsed in a chair and Weldon was counting a stack of money a foot high. Did I mention Weldon's stamina? Richard Austin's end was awful. He was convicted of hiring someone to kill a police informer and died in prison after many years on death row. Weldon became a fisherman.

Weldon also wasn't afraid to invest in future plays. Once he took me with him to Indio, California, where he said we were sure to make a good score. That's all he would tell me but that's all I needed to know. Then Mr. Rogers shocked me. We got into town and at the bar about seven. As soon as we walked in a man playing pool yelled for all to hear, "Hey! It's the Yuma kid" which is what Weldon called himself when he was there before. "Come on kid," the guy said, "I'll play you a game of eight ball for a hundred, but you have to use two hands."

I thought I was hearing things. Weldon replied, in an equally loud voice, "No (expletive) way. I only shoot with one. You know me. Two-handed pool can kiss my ass." With that, we sat at the bar and ordered a couple of beers. I never liked beer so I could nurse one bottle through the evening. To correctly identify mine I developed the habit of tearing off the top inch of the label.

Quick side track story: Once, more than twenty years after my divorce from my wife, Beverly, I was visiting Santa Barbara where she lived. I hadn't mentioned my being in town to her. I just arrived. I had a bottle of beer (open container, shame on me) that, out of habit, had the label modified. I stopped at a convenience store and put my half full beer on a newspaper box outside. Moments later I looked up, stunned at seeing Beverly walk in. Even more so when she said, "I was driving by and saw the label on the beer bottle on the paper box and knew it had to be you." Pool widows–sharp to the end.

Back to the bar in Indio. I still thought I was hearing things, but it seems months earlier, Weldon had beaten everyone in the place playing one-handed against their two. He won a lot of money, almost breaking the place, and then convinced everyone that he was a one-handed specialist and just couldn't play with two. He proceeded to back up his story before he left by using two hands to play a couple of people and sluffing off some pretty serious money. Outsiders might call this move "feathering your nest." In the trade it was "keeping a score cool." After more prodding about playing two-handed, Weldon decided the man had accepted enough rope and it was time to let him slip on the noose. He agreed to play using two hands. The outcome was too predictable to discuss. Weldon broke the poor fellow, along with his followers. At the end of this very profitable, two-handed shooting night, we stuck the majority of our loot into the motel closet and headed to Mexico for a night of partying and poking fun at how unbelievably gullible people can be. Weldon is my close friend to this day.

Here's where the problem begins. A lot of us Tucsonans hustled around The Golden Cue, in Phoenix, and Scottsdale Billiards, in nearby Scottsdale. There was good action for us and a two hour road trip to anywhere around the Phoenix area was, for us, like commuting to a day job. Johnny Drain was the local Phoenix area champion and we enjoyed watching him and Weldon go at it. They were Arizona's best players. Sadly, Johnny became a casualty of Viet Nam.

One day at Scottsdale Billiards, Weldon told me about this hustler who was beating these copper miners out of their pay checks at a bar in Superior, Arizona. He said the guy was a black man, big in stature but a lightweight player. He knew the guy played well enough to beat the locals like he owned them, but his talent wasn't a concern. The locals in the town knew Weldon, so he couldn't go. Instead, he suggested I go to play and that his friend Jackie Wright and Jackie's cousin should go along to take off the score. I should have taken it as an omen that the people around Scottsdale didn't call one of my companions "Left, Right Jackie Wright" for his cool demeanor.

The plan was for Jackie to go in first, sit close to the pool table, and be the money man. My cousin and I, dressed in a couple of trailer moving company's uniforms that Jackie had rounded up for us, would come in fifteen or so minutes later. From this point we would play it by ear, but both of my companions were aware of my expertise handling suckers and were willing to follow my lead. The cousin's role was just to watch my back.

The place was constructed from two double-wide mobile homes, but on the inside it was typical western bar. The walls were covered with posters of race cars and beer advertisements. Behind the bar, almost in a place of honor, was a poster of Marilyn Monroe with her dress blowing up. It was the only clean poster in the place. I wanted it. There was a jackalope head, a rabbit's head with antelope horns, hanging over the bar that looked like it hadn't been dusted since the antlers were first glued onto the cottontail's head. Although the jackalopes you'll see around the southwest are no more than a long standing abomination, nobody is sure if they're fact or fiction. European encyclopedias have been mentioning horned hares since the eighteenth century. I didn't want it. Taped to the top of the cash register was a sign displaying the letters "YCJCUAQFTJB" so, when the uninformed asked what it meant, the bartender would say, "It means your curiosity just cost you a quarter for the juke box." The sign, catchy as it was, was either misplaced or outdated because I couldn't see a juke box. Another sign nailed on the wall said, "ONE USED HENWAY – TWENTY FIVE DOLLARS," so when people ask, "What's a Henway?" someone will say, "About six pounds," so everyone can laugh. I fell for it the first time I saw that one, the juke box sign too.

In some western bars (not this one), they have a large jar on the bar with a live rattlesnake in it. The bet from the bartender is, if you put your palm on the side of the jar and keep your eyes open, you pay double or nothing for your drink, depending on whether or not you move your hand when the snake strikes. It is instant terror, however fleeting it may be. I saw a snake jar once in Show Low, Arizona, (a town that was named for the turn of a card) but I didn't have the stones to try it. I'm certain now there must be rules against that to protect the snake, never mind the cardiac arrest.

In bars, a lot of challenge pool is played. You put your quarter on the table rail in line with the other challengers and, when your turn comes up, you play the winner of the previous game. Then, as long as you keep winning, you keep the table. Three or four of the local miners and our mark were challenging a ten dollar nine-ball game on the only table in the place. The mark was the only one with any talent so he was raping the game. The people around the bar were talking about how much money had been bet the previous couple of nights and how the big man had taken all of it. When my quarter came up, my opponent was none other than our target. I asked, very sheepishly, if we could please lower the bet from ten to five dollars. He wouldn't hear of it, so I turned away and peeked into my wallet and agreed to the ten. I lost on purpose, naturally, and handed him two fives that I took out of my wallet. Then I pounded my cue against the floor as I sat at my table, saying to myself, but loudly enough to be heard, "Damn, damn, damn. I shoulda had that one. My bastard ass shootin'."

I had studied suckers so intently that even suckers considered me a sucker. I loved playing the role and I loved this life! When my next turn came up, I beat one of the miners by lucking the nine ball in, and made a production out of taking out my wallet, shaking it in the air like a jerk, and saying in a loud voice, "Yea buddy! That's more like it. Now we're shootin' some stick." Then, very carefully, I replaced the money in my wallet and put it back in my pocket, which I buttoned. Each time I lost or was forced to win a game I repeated the wallet in my pocket move. It's amateurish and irritating as hell to your opponent.

Jackie's role was to act drunk, which he quickly forgot was supposed to be an act, and create some side action with the mark when the time was right. The other challengers got discouraged pretty quickly and left the table for the two of us. Jackie flashed a big wad of bills and started his belligerent, "I want to gamble" role and my opponent went over to talk to him. Cousin slipped over and got the word from Jackie that he had bet the guy fifty on our next game. I lost and when I saw Jackie pay the money, I said quite loudly, "I'm sorry, Mister but I have to quit. Big money gambling makes me too nervous, even if it's not my money." Then I walked over to my table, sat down, and mumbled some more curse words.

Terrified of losing his "sucker," the mark came over and whispered to me, "Listen kid. You keep playing. If you win I'll give you ten and if I win you don't even have to pay me."

I said "Really? I gotta try that. I'm not crazy."

Clearly my opponent was only interested in the big bankroll the side betting drunk was carrying and he had to keep me playing to get it. He walked over to Jackie and had another mumbling session. When I bent down to break the balls, I glanced over at Jackie, who signaled me by barely moving his first two fingers. We were now playing two hundred dollar nine-ball. Oh, boy! I thought. It's time to peek out from under the covers.

The balls rolled in my favor and allowed me to win the next three games without showing much speed. I would win a game and the guy would pay Jackie, then he would race back to the table to get the balls racked for the next game. He insisted I let him put the ten dollar bills he paid me on the cafe table where I was sitting. He wasn't about to tolerate my slow wallet move now that he was losing serious money. He was still in a state of confusion about how some dumb kid could have beaten him three straight games. The hook was set so deep in his gullet you couldn't take it out with needle nose pliers. For the first time since we started playing, I ran a rack from a pretty tough spot, which boggled him. Our mark was pacing around the room while I was shooting, shaking his head and muttering to himself like a bird that flew indoors and couldn't slow down enough to find his way out. And the more I opened up, the more he choked up, until his Adam's apple turned into an Adam's grapefruit. Paralysis set in. In less than thirty minutes, I was six or seven games ahead. I pocketed the nine on one game and my opponent went up to the bar to cash some payroll checks he had won from the miners.

By this time, the bet was three hundred a game. I wanted to wait until the bet on this game was settled before we continued, as anybody in their right mind would do but Jackie, who by now was in a drunken semi-stupor said, "Come on kid. Break the goddamn balls. What the hell's the matter, anyway?" as he pounded the table and spilled beer down the front of his shirt. He was playing his part perfectly, and he wasn't playing.

I complied and broke the balls, and the nine went in on the break, which turned out to be an unlucky luck shot. The nine on the break is a winner and now the mark owed Jackie $600 for the two games. Realizing he had been played, he folded up the money, stuck it in his shirt pocket, said, "Game over," and walked toward the front door. Jackie jumped right up in his face and told him, in a not nice way, "Hey man! You owe me six hundred dollars. Fork it over right now." I'll never forget the man's very deep voiced answer, like Darth Vader in a bad mood, "Don't worry, you're going to get what you got coming." A cryptic message indeed, that I interpreted to mean, "Alfie, head for the car."

So, here I am; motor idling as smoothly as it can with my foot shaking the way it is, trying to see who's who and what fender they're hiding behind and deciding whether to leave their stupid asses squatting in the parking lot. It seems our mark had walked outside and Jackie followed him. Jackie then stuck a .38 revolver in the man's side and said, "Give me my money right now." The man replied with an angry, "Shoot M.F. I ain't givin' you nuthin'."

This presented a bit of a dilemma for Jackie. He was about to have this large guy, who had either thought Jackie was bluffing or who didn't think bullets really hurt, all over him. So Jackie, not up for an ass whipping, took the path of most stupidity and pulled the trigger. Had his revolver not misfired, I would probably be writing this book from a prison library.

Push had definitely come to shove and I was ready to shove off. Jackie and cousin jumped into the car, on a roll, and we went speeding down the highway toward Scottsdale. Jackie was boggled about why his gun had misfired on the first shot. Yeah! Too bad, I thought. We'd have six hundred more dollars and a dead man. He showed us the strike mark on the unspent bullet. To Jackie, the strike mark looked like his gun was defective. To me it looked like a get out of jail free card. There was an inordinate amount of adrenalin bouncing around the car and everyone was talking and laughing at the same time. We were counting money, passing around a joint, and enjoying a little comic relief to help our nerves relax. Everyone was feeling top notch that we had experienced such an ordeal and had made some money and escaped. Escaped?

We rounded a curve and it looked like the Arizona State Fair had set up their midway in the middle of the highway. Headlights, spotlights, and colored lights were accompanied by a sea of bouncing flashlights, all of which were becoming larger and brighter by the second. There were police cars in the middle of the road, on both shoulders, and backed up facing each direction, on each side of the highway. There were shotguns, hand guns, brown dogs, blue uniforms, and black leather jackets, all sported or accompanied by a horde of extremely agitated law enforcement personnel. My first thought was, who was guarding the rest of Arizona? Six or eight well-armed gendarmes swamped our car windows, which we had rolled down quickly, for fumigation purposes. One officer asked if anyone named Grover was in the car. Grover Tappp was an alias I used sometimes, including tonight. I used to tell people "It's 'Tappp' with three Ps" just to watch their expressions.

I said no to the cop, but Jackie said, "Yeah! This is Grover." You might say it didn't take much for Jackie to crack? It wouldn't have mattered what we said at that point. They knew who we were before they asked, we were nabbed cold.

The cop by my window told us to get out and put our hands on the side of the car like we were "trying to push the car over." My guess is it wasn't the first time he'd used that expression. It seems they had received a report on the shooting and were told there was a pool of blood on the front step of the bar that couldn't be accounted for. Our Cisco Kid friend, who had plugged his own foot, had disappeared, his embarrassment probably equaling his foot pain. The way everything else was going tonight, I halfway expected the cops to find him stuffed in our trunk.

So, next came the handcuffs and the "watch your head" spiel, and we rode, God knows for how long, first to one jail, where, for some reason, they didn't want us, then to another. You never really credit seat restraints with their proper importance until you're speeding down the highway handcuffed behind your back. A bite of the dashboard? No thanks. I'm trying to quit.

We walked into the St. John's Jail and, just like out of some B movie, the top cop takes me into a room and hands me this nasty looking, limp and wrinkled striped suit to put on for the night. Looking at it curled my toes, touching it was worse. The thought of wearing it makes me shiver. At the time, the cop and I were alone so I didn't mind my eyes welling up as I handed him back the stripes, and played the "pity card." I explained to him that I used to be on a kiddie television show (the Marshall KGUN Show in Tucson) where I was the Marshall's "Prisoner Alfie." I wore a striped prison suit just like the one he was holding, only clean, and a round striped hat. I rode a unicycle while the kids chased me around the stage and threw stuff at me from their candy sack, that we had given them. I told him putting the stripes on for real would destroy my memories of that part of my life and asked if he would please not make me do it. It wasn't really the kiddie show that produced the eye moisture. Plus, I was paid twenty bucks for each performance. My inner turmoil came from thinking about the suit's last occupant or occupants. He bought my story, with a laugh, and settled for my handing over my belt and shoe strings. With both of us confident that I wasn't going to hang myself over a pool game gone awry, he then escorted me to my suite.

Our "gang" was together in one four-bunk cell and the mark was alone, and steaming, in another cell, directly across from us. Thank God for jailhouse bars. We mostly jawed through the night about what had happened that evening, and, while I avoided looking in the big man's eyes, the guys said he rarely took his off of me.

I tried to add some levity by letting the mark hear the story about how I once helped make and use a "jailhouse telephone." I was sixteen and traveling through Florida with my older brother, Lee. We had a .22 target pistol in the car that we had been using for shooting at cans on the beach. We got pulled over by the police and cited for three offenses: expired plates, Lee had no drivers' license, and I had allowed an unauthorized person to drive my car. It was three times thirty-seven fifty, and we didn't have the hundred and twelve fifty, so it was off to the slammer until mom wired the cash, via Western Union, the next day. The policeman took Lee in his car and told me to follow him into Panama City. I didn't know if the gun under the newspaper beside me was against the law, but it was Florida, so I was taking no chances. I waited until the cop made a sharp right turn so he couldn't see my driver's window, then flung the pistol out the window. Just as it slid to a stop, by the front wheel of a parked, official looking bus, I looked up at a name on a building that said "Bay County Jail." It's all a matter of timing.

An elderly gentleman in our Panama City cell, who seemed to be somewhat of a regular, asked us if we wanted to talk to some girls. Silly question. He took his coffee cup and dipped the water out of the stainless steel, seat-free toilet until it was below the curve. Alexander Bell would be gagging in his grave. Then he went to the sink and, with the heel of his hand, hit the water button three times, causing a loud clanging noise on the pipes with each push. A few minutes passed and a matching three clangs came back. Our cells were on the second floor and the ladies (in a manner of speaking) were on the third. The connection made, we only had to stick our heads down as close to the toilet as we dared and, voila, we had the original cell phone. Only the hard core users didn't hold their nose. The rest of us sounded like we had colds. We talked and flirted for hours and it was the first time I heard a woman sing "Oh baby, you know what I like," from Chantilly Lace, via commode. Sorry, Big Bopper.

Eventually, our bladders cost us the connection, but not before brother Lee and his newly beloved nose throb had gone into the plan making stage of their relationship. She wasn't going to hit the streets for awhile and there was the probation thing but she said she felt the love and wanted to see him and she would let him know her better. Lee explained we would be leaving that morning, so she told him to clang her a signal when we were leaving and come around to the side of the jail by the buses, the same place I had tossed our gun which was nowhere in sight and had obviously made it to the evidence room. She told Lee to look up to the third floor, corner window. (Me too! Me too!) When we got outside, we looked up and she was there. We couldn't tell much about her face but could tell she was smiling. First she waved and threw a couple of kisses then she held up her index finger signaling him to wait and she disappeared for a couple of minutes. She returned and climbed up, squatted in the window, and hung onto the bars, buck naked. She was the first completely nude lady I ever saw and from our angle, not a memory worth hanging on to. I left town thinking, for really stinky phone sex, there's no place like Panama City, Florida.

The St. John, Arizona, jail we were gracing this night was only one story and housed no women, so phone fun was not an option. We talked through the night about nothing but pool, sort of the way we did every night. I wasn't going to put my head on that pillow any more than I would've shared the old man's coffee cup in the Panama City jail. The next morning we were escorted across the street to the courthouse. I told the policeman who was holding my arm so tightly that this was my first experience with a personal crossing guard since kindergarten and that he made me feel extremely safe from traffic. He didn't catch the humor. Of course I was in a good mood; I was out.

The courthouse was an innocent enough building, but in my mind I knew a courthouse is a courthouse, is a courthouse and, when necessary, the smallest one can toss someone the chair. The mark and the Mexican, with his foot still wrapped in a bloody towel, were already in the courtroom, seated across the aisle, in the same row, no more than fifteen feet away from where our "team" was placed. Where were those nice iron bars when I needed them? Better still, where was that easy three hundred dollar nine-ball game?

The judge walked in from behind, cheating us out of the "All rise" announcement, and sat right next to me on the arm of the bench where we were sitting. He draped his black-robed left arm across the back rest behind me and leaned over until I was sufficiently cloaked. I didn't know if he was going to hug me or turn me into a bat. He smiled at me real big and said, in a voice just louder than a whisper, in a room where whispers resound from the walls, "I hear you're a pretty good pool player."

Reveling in the protection of court and cloak, I laughed, leaning forward and looked right at our mark, making certain the black face that was glaring at me could hear, and said, "No, your honor. I'm a real good pool player. That fellow over there is a 'pretty good player'."

At the same time, I pulled out my wallet, put it inches from my nose, peeked in it and grinned. Ahhh! That felt good. I could feel the steam rising from the "pretty good player" and that felt good too. The judge caught the dig and laughed with me, as he asked, "A regular hustler, huh?"

Sensing that his honor and I were now practically homies, I said, "We're all hustlers of one sort or another, even you, judge."

His smile lessened slightly, but enough that he was sure I noticed, as he answered, "I'm getting ready to show you how easy my hustle is." Then he proceeded to prove he was a man of his word by pronouncing the cousin and me guilty of disturbing the peace and Jackie with the same, plus brandishing a weapon. His Honor asked us to count out all of our money and, what do you know? That's just how much our fines amounted to. We didn't stick around to see how much the losers had to pay. I wanted to put some distance between myself and that bloody red towel.

We didn't talk much on the way home, other than cussing the judge. I remember dropping the "wild west gunslingers" off in Scottsdale and driving home to Tucson where I stood in the shower until there wasn't a drop of hot water left. Thinking back about the last twenty-four hours, I swore, right then, that I was going to quit hustling pool forever. But how ya' going to believe a pool hustler? And where is my cue anyway?

THE SPARKLING ADVENTURES OF THE SUN DROP KID

The more believable your cover story, the easier it is to slip in and out of a strange pool hall with the money. Those southern country bumpkins have been hit with every kind of bullshit story imaginable, so fooling them is a challenge, but a fun challenge. Ideally you show up with a legitimate reason to be in town. When I traveled around Tennessee and Kentucky selling ladies ready-to-wear for a manufacturer, my entrée would go something like this: "I'm here to sell some dresses to Mrs. Clark at Mary Lou's Style Shop in the morning and I just wanted to hang out and play some pool tonight. Is that OK?" I even had the country gentleman's attire: black shoes, white socks, and slacks, an inch or so too short. If more convincing was needed, I would bring in my line of ladies' scarves and ask if I could rent a pool table to straighten out my samples. I would spread the colorful scarves end-to-end, covering the table so nobody missed the performance, then I'd take out my clipboard and make notes for awhile. Eventually, everyone was convinced I was harmless. It was like pool hustling foreplay and yes, I followed through.

But nothing works all the time. I was in Russellville, Alabama, and even though that wasn't part of my dress selling territory, I looked up the name of a local dress shop in the phone book and headed to the nearby pool room. I don't know if you've spent any time in this part of the country, but a lot of people's necks have a deep scarlet hue, and a good number of them are drawn to the green felt. I'm not the least bit tough and I cringe at the thought of receiving structural damage on the only me that I have. My timidity worked for me splendidly throughout my pool career. Had I been, or had I thought of myself as being, a bad ass, I know I would have been punched silly more than once. If fighting is your thing, you can usually get accommodated in a pool room. It's about like going around pool rooms hustling cards, the first people you'll get to play are the cheaters.

As soon as I walked into the Russellville pool room I got an eerie feeling. The place was full of people but hardly anyone was speaking. They just stared (make that glared) at me. Nevertheless, I had invested my time in driving here and this was the only room in town so I had to take a shot. There was a spittoon on the floor by the breaking end of each table and one at each end of the long bench running along the wall. One guy sitting on the bench was leaning over one of them with his hands cupped alongside of his head. He never looked up. I couldn't tell if he was getting sick or fascinated with what he was seeing. The house man behind the counter had such a fat bottom the lawn chair he was sitting in stuck to his hips when he stood up and walked a couple of feet to the counter. He made no move to pull it loose and it stayed attached until he sat back down. I told him I was in town to sell some dresses to so and so's dress shop, making certain to say it in a voice to be heard at the tables. The house man grunted something inaudible, spit in a cardboard box at his feet and wiped the dribble off of his stubble chin with his palm, then his palm hit his pants. No part of him was clean. He sat back down and turned his head in a manner that showed he had no interest in me or what I was selling. The clank of his lawn chair hitting and scraping against the concrete was loud and not disguisable and I could tell from the player's lack of reaction the chair on the ass thing was a standard. All of a sudden the house man spun his chair back toward me, scrapping the concrete even louder than before and leaned over the cardboard box. One at a time he placed his forefingers against the sides of his nose and let out a loud blow of gobstuff from each nostril, mostly into the box. I'm not typically squeamish and I've spent enough time on my aunt's farm in Tennessee to recognize, or even pull off, a farmer's blow out in the field, but seeing one inside, down into a cardboard box gave me the willies. Then he raised his head toward me and, using the same flat palm, wiped his face again as he contorted it into a half smile/half sneer, no doubt, dedicated to me. As a finale, he took the same hand, plucked a chaw of tobacco out of an opened container by the register and using his first two fingers, he pushed the plug into the back of his cheek. This was a truly disgusting human being, but I'm so glad I met him.

    A very large country boy, complete with cereal bowl haircut, a couple of front teeth MIA, and a skull and crossbones design imprinted on the top pocket of his one strap bib overalls, was shooting on the opposite side of the first table, facing my way. He stood up and dropped his cue stick on the table with a smack, evocative of a judge's gavel. The place went silent on top of silent and I wished I was elsewhere. "Jethro" then leaned forward with one palm flat on the table and the other wrapped around a seven ball still on the table. A hypnotist couldn't have looked me straighter in the eye and I dared not look away. Emitting a little brown stream of snuffsliva or whatever from the corner of his mouth down to his chin, with no effort to stem the flow, he continued to look at me. I couldn't help watching the liquid as it rounded underneath his chin and into a growing brown bubble, hoping to see it drop on the table when he spoke. The spotted green felt showed it wouldn't be the first time. Then he growled, "We don't need no goddamn girdle salesmen in Lawrence County, boy." Was he serious?

Before I had a chance to react, someone on the table behind him chimed in, without even looking up from his shot, "He's right. Why don't you put on your pink panties and git your girly ass down the road?"

Whoa Nellie! This isn't good. If this is their version of southern hospitality without my winning their money, how would they be treating me if I did? I smiled with the utmost sincerity, and replied, "If you guys think you're running me out of town, you're exactly right." Saying "I'll see you later" seemed inappropriate. No answer could have pleased any of us more so, even sporting no girdles or panties of any color, except for one little gift in my suitcase from my wife, and never knowing if the bubble dropped, down the road I went.

Throughout my thirties I still looked like a kid so I used that as one of my main disguises. I may have looked like a kid but I could get the money as good as a man. Once, in a little North Carolina town, I went into a pool room where four young people were playing ten dollar ring nine-ball on the front table. I made a point of showing them that I was on my bicycle by asking if I could bring it inside. It was definitely the spot for my kid role. I bought a coke, some potato chips, and a couple of candy bars, and then sat on a bench beside the table, tore open my treats and gave them the "Watch y'all playin for?" line.

I flashed a wad and told them I was back to running around on my bicycle because I had just sold my motorcycle. "My mom thought it would kill me for sure," was my closing line. The guys played OK and you could tell this was a regular front table game that people joined into and dropped out of throughout the day, daily. Almost every pool room had a similar situation for regulars but rarely would you find them for ten a man. Joining four lightweights playing "ring ten dollar nine-ball" is a hustler's dream. Winning two or three hundred dollars an hour is no problem.

I bought a round of cokes and jawed with the players for awhile until I didn't need to ask–they invited me to join them. One by one the players in the game went broke and dropped out until only one pretty straight shooting very young player was left to do battle with me. The regular newcomers who dropped by now spotted the game as being more serious and didn't join in. We kicked the bet up to twenty a game and it seemed I was going to leave with all the money. I was still playing the youngster role and by this time a crowd had gathered to see who was breaking their local champ. I leaned over the table to shoot in a game ball when my opponent leaned over from the opposite side of the table, so close up in my face that I couldn't shoot. He kind of screamed out words and laughter at the same time when he said, "Wait a minute. You ain't no kid. You're old. You just actin' like a kid to get in our game. Well, don't that beat all." He wasn't mad, he thought it was funny. I don't embarrass easily, but in this instance I felt my face turning beet red. Not only had he exposed me in front of everyone and quit the game, he (along with Mother Nature) influenced me into putting that particular disguise away permanently.

Once, in Nashville, I met a man named Buzzy who traveled around selling billiard supplies out of his van. He carried house cues, chalk, powder, Kelly pills, some pool felts, and a line of two-piece, custom cues and cue cases. I asked him if I could tag along with him on his rounds through Tennessee and Kentucky. We got action in every room. A bonus for me was that Buzzy was also a lightweight player, with a reputation in the rooms he serviced as being a bit of a sucker. More than once he lost more than he made in his sales so getting action traveling with him was automatic. I would just demonstrate "our latest cues," acting like I knew everything, while scarcely making a ball. A little of that and everyone wanted a piece of me, and I usually gave them a piece they didn't like. The adage "Give a man enough rope and he will hang himself" plays a big role in a crossroader's life.

At one time there were some cue sticks coming in from Korea and Okinawa that had colorfully carved, black hollow butts. The shafts unscrewed and slid up inside of the butts, turning the cues into canes. They were more of a novelty item than anything. For playing pool they were pure crap and as a cane you'd slip on your ass. They had a hollow sound and, to pool players, they were a joke. I had a friend who used to go in and hustle pool rooms with one of these cues. He said getting action was easy because he looked so foolish and after a few games he could switch to a house cue without raising suspicion. Later, someone came up with the idea to create well-made and nicely balanced cue sticks that looked like house cues. They had invisible joints and were initially made so that hustlers could sneak a good cue into a strange place without drawing any notice. Poetically, they were called "Sneaky Petes."

When I was in the service in Wichita Falls, Texas, I had a pretty fair two-piece cue; nothing special except that it played well and I with it. One of my fellow airmen claimed to be an artist, so I painted the whole cue flat white and he painted a black shark, which came out looking cartoonish, on the butt, directly over the grip. This worked great. It was everything–a cue that I could play well with and one that looked fairly stupid as well. Later in life, as my ego started getting the best of me (not to mention having money for better cues), I couldn't do things like that. The cardinal rule for trapping was to look and act a little goofy, no matter how you had to do it.

In the 70s I was hustling around Tulsa and ran into a hustler from New Orleans named Ernie Sellers, whom I knew by reputation to be a very good player. Typically, I avoided playing other hustlers for two reasons. First, it killed any chance for action with the lighter weight players and secondly, and more importantly, I would most likely get my ass paddled. I was with a stakehorse from Dallas named George McGann who insisted that I take a shot at Mr. Sellers playing some fifty dollar nine-ball. You might remember George as one of the killers I described in the chapter on my years at Cotton Bowling Palace. No one resisted when George insisted.

To my own surprise, I played well and prevailed. Instead of being pissed at me, my opponent shook off the defeat and took a liking to me. He was older and wiser about life on the road and gave me the best tip on hustling bar pool I'd ever received, which I'll pass along to you. (These stunts are performed by professionals. Don't try them unsupervised.)

Most of the time bar pool hustling isn't really gambling because your opponent is much more likely to be just a bar hangout rather than a pool player, so winning money is usually more con than shooting. Sellers handed me a pair of dice and taught me this: Most bar players like to play for a buck or two, or sometimes just for drinks and that's if they're interested in pool, at all. You sit next to a potential victim at the bar, talk a little small talk, then pull out your dice and offer to roll him high dice for a drink. Since high dice is a one hundred percent luck bet, everyone has a chance and most everyone will play. A simple "yes" has him in the game and in your hands. A friendly drink bet can easily lead to wagering a couple of dollars or more and before you know it you might be rolling for twenty bucks.

When the bet gets up to where you want it, you just look over at the pool table and say, "How 'bout we play one game of pool for the twenty? I haven't done that in years." The fact that you're willing to roll dice for money removes any suspicion that you might be in there to hustle pool. Before you know it you have a two dollar high dice player, who had hope, now betting twenty on a pool game where he hasn't a prayer. Over the next few years, Mr. Sellers' "high dice for a drink" tip assisted me numerous times.

One of the hustlers I spent a lot of time on the road with was Grady "The Professor" Mathews. Grady was a knowledgeable and competent pool player and a very aggressive hustler. Having a carnival midway background gave him a knack for hustling action and keeping the odds in his favor. Grady was a good sport too, and laughed about everything, almost.

Once, in Birmingham, we needed to check into a room. If we could pay for one and sleep two, that's what we would do (so long as there were two beds). Not terribly original but helpful. This night I was to check in and he would come in about fifteen minutes later, after calling me first to find the room number. The young woman at the front desk was pretty and friendly. I talked with her for a few minutes and told her about a man named Grady Mathews, who might be stopping by. I went on to explain that I was a state counselor for high-risk sex offenders and that Grady was scheduled to come by for a session. I went on to tell her not to worry, that he had been locked away for a number of years, until a few months ago and was now doing much better, other than being a little delusional about being a sports champion. I said he might claim he's a pro golfer, wrestler, you never know. She appreciated the FYI talk and said she would direct him to my room. She bid me a professional good night and a silent good riddance.

Now Grady has always considered himself a ladies' man. Not from his looks, he's smarter than that, but Grady possessed a gift of gab that he used in his hustling, be it for pool or women. Lines such as "Stop that grinnin' and drop that linen" and some even more subtle might flow from his lips. When Grady called me to find out what room I was in, I told him about the pretty girl at the desk and went on to say that I told her a "Mr. Grady Mathews, the world champion pocket billiard player" would be dropping by to pay me a visit and he might stop to find out my room number, only to hear her say how much she would enjoy hearing some pool stories. I told him she was single, she liked to play pool and if he put down his rap, he just might score. Knowing full well how Grady would pursue the opportunity made it difficult for me to talk to him without laughing

Grady said he was at a phone across the street so I gave it about fifteen minutes and strolled down to the lobby, directly into a Kodak moment. Grady was leaning as far over the front desk as he could, without his tip toes leaving the floors. Charm and baloney were flowing from our Romeo at breakneck speed and he was certain he was movin' smooth. He told her he had recently won the world pocket billiards championship and he would like to "show her his trophy" after she got off work. He even used his line, "I'm not particularly pretty or nothin' like that, but it takes me an hour or so to do my thing, if you know what I mean." You couldn't fault Grady for lack of cojones – tact maybe. The poor girl was being sweet but she had her back and head pressed up against the back wall so hard she was squashing the magazines in the mail slots. Her lips were pursed and she looked too terrified to blink and, atypical of most females in my life, she was delighted to see me. It was even more fun later, in the room, as I told Grady what I had done. He still thought she might call.

Another time Grady should have punched me out was when he and I spent a few days hustling at a bar in Hattiesburg, Mississippi, called The

Stoned Toad. One morning I woke up and left the motel early. It was a little mom and pop joint set off on the edge of a park. I took a walk and came across a giant fire ant bed. The fire ant of the south is a strong contender for the title of the world's smallest nightmare. One sting is painful and lasting. Stepping into a nest of them can be downright horrifying. Spotting a long stick within easy reach, I had no choice but to do a little stirring. Instant red madness ensued. You could spot their anger and their eagerness to do battle. If you think about their side of the story, I deserved to get stung. Some of these little demons were still clinging to the stick when I knocked on the back door of the room. Grady, who had just gotten out of the shower, opened the door in his birthday attire. I said, "Grady, look," and shook the stick at him.

Without noticing anything he said, "Alfie, I wish you'd stop messing . . . Ahhhhh!" he screamed, as he doubled over into a fetal position and started rubbing his crotch with both hands. It seems as though one or two of the little red bullies had landed directly on man's worst spot imaginable. I didn't know I needed to run so fast from a guy who had one hand holding a towel. And I had to do it while laughing my ass off. I told him that at least he had the swelling thing going in his favor.

Eventually Grady and I got to Nashville, which is where I was living at the time. There was a pretty good player named Bob Roney, who owned a pool hall in north Nashville. I had beaten him numerous times and even sicced a few of my compatriots on him. He would lose a fair amount and was always a perfect gentleman when he lost. The problem was that so many players had beaten up on Bob until finally he had taken a solemn vow that he "would never play a stranger again" and he stayed true to his word for months. I told Grady that if anyone could sneak up on him and get him down, he could, but we would have to come up with a "hook" of some sort. Driving down the road I spotted a tortoise lying on its back. I slammed on the brakes and told Grady that I had an idea. The little guy was in a bad spot. I could see his legs wiggling, telling us he was alive, but I knew if he didn't get help he wouldn't be that way for long. I scooped him up into a brown paper bag and introduced him to his new dad, Grady.

Grady strolled into Bob's pool room, brown paper bag under his arm, and told Bob that he was Tiweena Slim, from Boggy Bottom, and he wanted to gamble on pool if it was OK to bring in his pet turtle. He said he wanted to leave it behind the desk, under the counter, so that it could get some sleep. Then he brought it out of the bag for a second and told it good night. Bob looked at him like he was insane, but by closing time, Grady had won all of the money Bob had in his pocket, all that was in the register, and some that Bob had borrowed from friends.

I pulled up across the street to pick him up. Grady was just about to get into the car when Bob stepped outside and yelled, "Hey buddy, don't forget your turtle," as the turtle, still housed in the brown bag, came flying through the air, all the way across the street, and sliding to our feet. (No turtles were injured in the making of this pool score.) Grady Mathews still plays and is now involved in the One-Pocket Hall of Fame.

Almost every pool room in the country towns throughout the south seemed to have their own house games or house tricks and, oftentimes, a straight shooting house man. If the idle mind really is the devil's workshop, a lot of his major construction projects are organized in these rooms. "Kelly Pool" or other pill pool games are played using a shaker bottle that contains little plastic balls called pills, numbered the same as the balls on the pool table. Before the game each player shakes one or two pills (depending on house rules) into their hand and hides them from the other players. The balls are broken and various combinations of pill and ball numbers constitute a win. There are as many different ways to win playing "Kelly Pool" as there are pool rooms. Sometimes the rules even let your opponent win for you when they inadvertently pocket your winning ball.

Many rooms in the South have a Keno board on one of their tables that is occupied constantly. A Keno board covers one end of the table about three quarters of the way to the side pockets. The back end slides under the end rail and the sides fit snugly under the side rails. The front is ramped to let the balls roll up onto the board. Beach type, rubber balls are generally stuffed into the four corner pockets on the table to stop balls from going in. The top of the Keno board is covered with pool ball sized holes numbered from one through fifteen, the same as the balls. The object of Keno is to shoot or bank balls onto the board and into the holes. There are variations of games, rules and types of boards. One board is called Amos and Andy, with pictures of those characters by some of the holes and a bonus for landing in them. I never understood the connection or meaning of that, being in the Deep South. What constitutes a win in Keno is pocketing the one ball in the one hole, the two in the two hole, and so on. Just like in Kelly, each room has its own rules for winning. Sometimes Kelly pills are added to the Keno mix, creating even more ways to win. Keno is exciting. The balls spin and drift from one hole to another before stopping. It's actually a lot of fun if you're there for fun.

Although the rules in each place may differ, two things about Kelly and Keno games are consistent. The games are more luck than skill, encouraging everyone to play, and all Kelly and Keno games are designed to end quickly so the house can collect a fee from each player. The insider term for this is "house bust out games" because, eventually, the house winds up with all of the money. It's sales tax: if it is eight percent, then each time money is spent twelve times, the tax masters have all of it and we scrape up more.

One of my hustles was to go into a pool room and announce that I wanted to "gamble on pool." Then I would add, "But, I only want to shoot Kelly or Keno." Right away this would remove any suspicion of my being a hustler, for no crossroader who likes to sleep indoors on a consistent basis would run around hustling luck games. To begin with, I would have the same chance to win in Kelly as the locals or maybe, because of my knowledge of the rails and shooting ability in general, a little better. But invariably, after a short session of Kelly or Keno, win or lose, it was no problem to switch the game to nine-ball or join a nine-ball game in progress. Their guards were let down. Mission accomplished.

In some of the small towns, the pool room hangouts were so eager to gamble they would spend hours on end, every day, "pulling for Cokes." They would each stack quarters, the price of the drinks, in front of them, next to the Coke machine, with the amount they were betting designated beforehand. Most of the time the bet was five dollars per player. On the bottom of Coke bottles you can find the names of the towns where they were bottled. Since there were no local bottlers, the bottles came from all around the country. The players, sometimes as many as eight or ten of them, would take turns buying Cokes. The one who got the bottle with the town the farthest away would take the stakes. There was always a U.S. map on the wall with a nail tied to a string originating from their town, so that the winner could be easily determined. When the machine was empty the house man would refill it with the same drinks, sell the players more quarters, and the game would continue. How's that for profit from a drink machine? And, yes, sometimes I would pull a couple of Cokes myself, but I never won, not once.

The Sun Drop Kid.

In 1971, I accepted a two month market research contract from the Kalil soft drink bottling company in Tucson, Arizona. There was a soft drink called Sun Drop Cola that outsold every other soft drink in one particular part of the country and the Kalil Company, thinking of adding it to their line, wanted to understand the reason for its popularity. When I found out the part of the country that had record sales was North and South Carolina, I jumped on George Kalil's generous offer to research the drink. Sun

Drop was developed in St. Louis, Missouri, and marketed under the names Golden Cola, Golden Girl Cola, and then Sun Drop. Some say Mountain Dew, which has a similar taste copied Sun Drop, other than the real fruit pulp and rinds contained in Sun Drop. Fact or fiction, it matters not.

My assignment was to give away as much Sun Drop as I could to the locals and then talk to them about it. I was traveling in my motorhome at the time, which made it easy to transport the cases of samples that I picked up at the local bottling plants. I would walk straight into the pool rooms, carrying a case or two of the drinks, tell them I was the "Sun Drop Kid" from Arizona, and offer free samples to everyone. As many people would drink them warm as would take them home. I always left the samples I didn't give away with the house man. I would take notes and names and ask people if I could use their opinion in our advertising campaign. They would eat up my malarkey and wash it down with my cola. One thing would lead to another and I rarely had to ask for pool action. It asked for me. It was pure "give and take." I would give them a drink and take their opinion. Then they would give me their money and I would take off. I considered myself to be an entertainer but I'm sure my victims had other, less endearing names for me. Had the expression "Have a nice day" been around in those days it would probably have been followed with "Providing you don't run across Alfie Taylor."

Each week I would file a report back to Kalil in Tucson. The explanation for the record cola sales was obvious. The drink was super sweetened, highly caffeinated, and downright tasty. Because it was marketed to a population of mostly non-label readers, with little-to-no post palate perception, it was a hit. Carpenters and others working in the hot sun would swig down two or three Sun Drops on their breaks and drink as many with lunch. Trust me. I understand the semi-addiction. I got to where I loved the stuff. When I finished the assignment I took a few cases home with me. It's been thirty-odd years and though my taste for soft drinks has waned, I'd drink a Sun Drop in a heartbeat.

Of all the scams pool hustlers have used to sneak up on the Carolinians, Sun drop had to be the sweetest and I'll bet somewhere in those lovely little southern towns where time marches at a snail's pace and the past is used for entertainment, they're still telling stories about "The Sun Drop Kid." Favorable? I think not.

THE OTHER END OF THE BARREL

West Nashville – '70s.

Instead of making a small hole in the glass the way I had seen bullets do so many times in the movies, mine hit the supermarket window almost dead center causing it to shatter. Uncountable pieces of glass rained onto the sidewalk and inside the empty store. Shards splattered around the feet of a very frightened individual who was holding a handful of stolen money, with the biggest piece of glass almost landing on him. I was sorry it didn't.

Maybe it was the Magnum factor of the bullet that made the window give up the ghost so dramatically. The deserted building was trashed to begin with, so other than one more broken window, no real harm was done. The creep who had acted so tough while robbing me just moments earlier jumped forward and ducked down, avoiding the rain of glass as he yelled out something that sounded like a cross between a mad man's violent curse word and a scream for help. Some of the money he was counting, mine, jumped out of his hands and into the street. Hitting him with the shot wasn't my intention, but neither was missing him. I pointed the gun out the window in his direction, more than actually aiming it, willing to let the chips (or in this case, glass pieces) fall where they may.

Admittedly, shooting at someone from a car window isn't the bravest of moves, but neither is hogging someone half your size out of their money. We've always been taught, "Two wrongs don't make a right," but in the words of my brother Jack, "Neither does a wrong and a right." Chew on that.

The touch of satisfaction I felt from terrifying my assailant was short-lived. I no sooner heard the bang when the hammer of my .22 over and under derringer flew by my face and the cheesy little Chinese-made gun turned into multiple small pieces of faux ivory and cast aluminum in my hand. Perhaps Magnum rounds were too potent for this gun after all; but who would think a pawn shop owner would tell you wrong? I loved shooting the Magnum shells in the little gun, which I had done a time or two, because flames actually came out of the end of the two-inch barrel. Showing this guy some flames was my primary intent. The thing's about as accurate as a spit ball so if he got hit, it was just a "wrong place, wrong time" for him situation. I didn't know if shooting toward someone would be construed as shooting at them, under Tennessee law, but I wasn't up for catching a cage to find out. I floored it, which in my wife's Volvo sedan was no wheel screeching event.

Nashville was my home town at the time. My territory for my sales position was Tennessee and Kentucky, and Nashville, being near the center of the area the two states covered, was home to a lot of rag men. I still hustled a little pool on the side, mostly at Broad Street Billiards, around the corner from the original Grand Old Opry and across the street from Earnest Tubbs' Record Shop. There was the typical local contingent who hung around the room, hiding from their wives and looking in all directions for an angle. A couple of lightweight scufflers were always around, diligent to their day jobs of catching a sucker. A regular group of downtown businessmen gathered there on weekdays for long lunches and to play golf. Golf is a game played on a snooker table where each player has their own ball that they pocket around the table, in the six pockets, one pocket at a time. It's a difficult game which requires a good knowledge of the rails and cloth speed, along with a soft touch, in order to leave your ball close to the pocket when you miss. Golf is usually played by the same group of guys daily, typically with four or five older businessmen and one or two local hustlers. The bet is usually small so nobody gets hurt much. For the "straights", hanging out playing Golf at the pool room was their brush with the semi-underworld. They could take off their coats and ties for a few hours, drink some beers, curse out loud, and wind up with something to talk about back at the office. I never saw any trouble, more than a mild argument in the place. All in all, Broad Street Billiards was a nice hangout.

"Bingo" was the only serious player around Broad Street, as well as the best Nashville had to offer, and even though I had a good chance of beating him, I never even discussed playing him. If I won, it would kill too much action for me. If I lost, well that just sucks. I was getting to play a lot of the weaker players simply because they knew I worked for a living. Little did they know, I didn't come to "wheel and deal," I was there to "rob and steal," because that is what pool is. If you're a better player than the other guy, pool is hardly a game of chance. All you have to do is focus on your shots and keep your nerve. Arthur Ashe said, "If you're thinking about the score, you can't think about the game." Of course, if you over bet your bankroll or choke up, a weaker player might prevail. Then see how difficult it is to sleep.

My job kept me on the road throughout the week but weekends usually found me sitting on a bar stool at the Broad Street Billiards, taking it all in. I didn't need to be hustling. My job provided me with everything I needed, but what did the man say? "Money won is twice as sweet as money earned." I liked the victories.

It was around noon on a Saturday, when two young black men came in and wasted no time trying to get into action. One of them belted out, "You got any twenty dollar nine-ball players in this place?" Sensing talent, the house man moved toward the phone to call Bingo, but I gave him "the office" (inside lingo for "don't do it").

I told the man I'd try him a few games and threw in a fake but loud message to the house man, "If my wife calls, tell her I'm not here. I blow my paycheck one more time and it's divorce court for sure." "And, that's a bad thing?" came a voice from the back.

To everyone's surprise, the guy turned out to be a pretty weak player, whose focus was more on how much he could English the cue ball around the table than on running out. He had a powerful stroke so he could really spin the ball and he pocketed the balls OK but he played the game like an imbecile. He didn't know much about playing position and he refused to play a safety. On difficult shots, instead of ducking, he would just blast the balls trying to luck something in. That kind of play is effective on the little seven foot bar tables because so much of the table surface is covered by pockets. It even works a little on eight foot tables, but on regulation nine foot tables the percentages are way against lucking out. More often than not, blasting the balls only leads to giving your opponent an open shot.
I managed to knock the guy off without showing too much speed. I was lucky to have stepped up first. Any of three or four locals in there at the time could have beaten him. As weak as he played, I didn't understand how he could rough hustle a strange room. His friend handled the money until both of them pooled theirs together to pay up for the last game. It was no big score, a little more than two hundred dollars, but the player got a little puffed up and said, "You come over to West Nashville and beat me in my pool room, and you can win all the money in n----rtown." So, he owned his own pool room. That explained his bravado. One time somebody challenged Minnesota Fats to a game if he would play on a certain table. Fats told him "I'll go into your house and bite the corners off your kitchen table to play you." I wasn't about to say this but I thought it. The time for coy behavior was over and three words literally jumped out of my mouth: "I'll follow you."

What was I, crazy? In the few years I lived in Nashville, I had never been in the west part of town or even knew a ghetto like it existed. Every other house had a fenced-in barking dog of the "don't try to pet me" variety. A lot of the dwellings were partly boarded up but obviously not vacant. Trash cans were turned over in the street and someone had dumped a sofa off on the curb that was now home to a family of feral cats. There were no cushions on the sofa and, when I walked by it, two scrawny kittens came crawling out of the springs playing with a torn up mouse carcass. I watched them bat the thing around like it was their regular toy and wondered if the missing part of the critter had earlier served as lunch. There were cars without tires and tires without cars. I saw possibilities in that. I doubt if any of Nashville's country songs were written in or about this place.

My opponent pulled into an alley behind an out of business supermarket which I found out later led to the front and only door of his windowless establishment. (What fire code?) Exhibiting caution, ingrained by years in the racket, I didn't follow him into the parking lot, but pulled on by, turned around, and parked across the street, facing toward my end of town. From getting down to getting out, I covered all angles of hustling pool.

The place was packed, with the jukebox blasting and every table occupied. Two guys on the first table were pulling at each other's clothes, flailing their arms, and screaming the standard, "I'll cut your blah blah," all over what looked like a two dollar bet. There were no blows thrown and it was obvious, by the lack of attention they drew, the problem wasn't going beyond words and wrinkled clothes. The boss, still in a bad mood from the spanking I had given him downtown, ejected the disrupters anyway and picked a table for us to play on, moving the players who were on it to the table he had just emptied. As is typical, the house man had his "pet" table next to the cash register, and I wouldn't have had it any other way. Overall, the table was pretty trashed. There were multiple small holes in the felt cover from players jabbing down on the cue ball to achieve jump or curve shots. Most pool rooms don't allow those shots for this very reason. Some of the rail cloth was dangling loose with the edges pushed up under the rails. Two of the six pockets had broken leather straps and, when more than two balls were in them, they would leak balls onto the floor. I had played on worse equipment, but not often.

Nobody stopped playing when we started our game, but all of the eyeballers drifted our way. I only called a few side bets, two dollars here and five dollars there. I wanted to check out this very scary table, first. That proved to be a good move because for the next thirty or forty minutes my opponent proceeded to shoot me full of holes. After getting beat eight or ten games straight, I was halfway in shock. I couldn't believe this was the same man I had played earlier. He started running out every game. He wasn't playing much position, but difficult shots seemed to mean nothing to him. The big difference, besides his playing on his home court where he knew every tear and funky roll, was that these were eight foot tables and downtown we had been playing on nine footers.

Tennessee is one of the few states where you will find mostly eight foot tables and it's a whole different game, or at least a different thought process. Eight foot tables are considerably easier to run out on than nine foot tables and interestingly enough, they are also easier than their smaller, seven foot bar table counterparts. Reason being, when you break the balls on an eight foot tables they scatter, but the shots are still closer to the pockets than on nine foot tables. When you break the balls on a seven foot bar table, there is so little room on the table that the balls tend to cluster up together more often, making it tougher to run out. Five foot by ten foot tables are scarce, but occasionally you will run across one. The only time I tried to play on one was in Inglewood, California and I was helpless. If you're not used to them, just that one extra foot length down the table can make you feel like you're playing on a golf course.

My opponent's confidence was skyrocketing. He was banking balls in and cutting them in backwards. He was jacking the back of his cue in the air and jumping balls when necessary, paying no attention to the sign on the wall that said "No jump or massé shots allowed!" He also didn't seem to mind how his cue tip was driving little holes, or at least dents, into his cloth. And, the whole time he was drilling me, he was talking trash and struttin' his stuff and I was in a fog. Before I knew it, he had won back what he had lost downtown plus some of mine, so I took a break to compose. I was never very good at stopping between games for anything. Over the years, I had developed an iron bladder from avoiding pool room toilets. I went over to the door and took in some slow breaths of fresh air. Hot, but fresh. Will play resume?

So here I am, sitting on a stool in West Trashville, Tennessee, sweating like a pig (which doesn't really sweat at all) trying to figure out my best move. Do I continue to play or run away to fight another day? Then I remembered what my good friend and very good player Hawaiian Brian once told me. We were in Jacksonville, Florida, so Brian could play another good player, Harley Bryant. They played and Brian won. On another table was a young guy practicing nine-ball (with proficiency) who hustled me to play. Brian told me to play him but I said I'd rather not, that "this guy runs out." Brian said, "Alfie, everyone runs out 'till you play good enough to make them stop running out."

Those were potent words but, at the time, they weren't enough to get me on the table. In the military they teach you there's always one guy shooting and the other guy ducking. As long as you keep shooting, the other guy will keep ducking. It's called, "maintaining superior fire power." At this moment, in Nashville, I was the one ducking, and I didn't like it one bit. With that thought in mind and my slow breathing restored, I got up, told my opponent to break the balls, and in as few words as possible, spent the next two or three hours putting some pool on his ass. Screw the table roll off, I hit the balls with power and precision until the eight foot table was a joke. The more I ran out, the tougher his tough shots became, until he completely fell apart and practically gave me his money. Surprisingly enough, when the session was over and he was both broke and convinced, he was a perfect gentleman and only said, "Good shootin' white boy. Probably won't see you again 'round here anymore. Dig?" I definitely "dug."

A couple of the side betters were a little more disgruntled than my opponent had been, so I made an announcement that I would give someone twenty dollars to walk me to my car. A very large individual said, "Got you covered. Let's go." Little did I know I was summoning the wolf to guard the lamb. We walked outside and around in front of the building.

As I reached into my pocket and pulled out my money to get his twenty, I felt one of his huge hands swallow mine as his other gripped the back of my neck. It was a quick, one round, one-sided hand wrestling match, as he wrenched the majority of my winnings from me and said, "This looks like twenty to me." I wouldn't want to be thought of as over-reactive, but under my collar I could feel fire. Without wasting time on futile resistance to his action, or the even more impossible task of reasoning with him, I briskly walked across the street to my car. As I started the motor I reached under the seat for the little bulging drawstring purple felt sack that held what was soon to become part of a reckoning moment, as well as a handful of junk. And the rest has been told.

I learned three things that day: Stay out of West Nashville, buy a better gun, and, even though gun play in general sucks, there is a definite upside to being at the other end of the barrel.

SIX THOUSAND MILES TO A MURDER

Nashville, Tennessee – Christmas 1972

Pat's scream could be heard in every corner of the funeral home. It wasn't like the sobbing or occasional outbursts of grief we had gone through with her all morning. It was more a mixture of pain and anger, like the crying charge of a wounded animal. I was standing in the front hall by the entrance where I stayed throughout the ordeal, when I heard it. Chills went to my core. So many flowers had passed in front of me that I hadn't noticed the large black wreath that had just been delivered. As if in memory of Alfred Hitchcock, Fred's hit man had sent his victim flowers with a card. The gloat eventually led to his capture but the damage was done. Pat's next scream was to, "Take those goddamn things out back and burn them." In spite of the policeman who had been assigned to stay at the funeral home despite their objections, as well as the funeral home saying they couldn't start a fire on the premises, the burning was carried out immediately by Fred's friends. The black smoke passing by the chapel window only added to the drama. I didn't budge.

Fred Scott was a good looking man, a little younger than I, tall and very distinguished looking with prematurely gray hair. We had matching Cadillacs (same year, different color) and, for a couple of years, we were almost always together in one of them, hustling pool around Tennessee. Fred didn't play pool but he would "bet the farm" on me. In his soft-spoken Tennessee drawl he would say, "We oughta ease on down to Shelbyville (or some other small town) and relieve someone of their money." He always had a good bankroll for me to play on and he didn't think anyone could beat me. Fred also fancied himself a ladies' man which, inadvertently, led to the tragedy we were now dealing with.

Fred had a lot of friends so there was a constant flow of people in and out of the back room of the chapel. Everyone was speaking in a voice just above a mumble. Most of them were shaking their heads and discussing the next step. These guys weren't candyassers. They were a pretty tough lot and there was revenge on their minds. For two years Fred had been my best friend but no amount of coaxing by his wife Pat, or our mutual friends, could make me go into the back room and see him. I didn't see how it was possible to have him in an open casket after his being shot point blank in the face by a shotgun stuffed with nails. I also had a case of the "willies" just thinking about seeing him because, had the day before not been a bank holiday, I would most likely have traveled six thousand miles to be lying in there beside him.

One week earlier we were in Thessaloniki at the Greek/Turkish border. "Motor go chock, chock, chock. Motor go chock, chock, chock," is what the little Iranian jerk who had borrowed our Volkswagen van and neglected to shift it out of second gear was saying as he ran up to us in the restaurant. Any motor going "chock chock" is a bad sign but in a VW engine it usually spells one thing; endgate. The only reason we let him take it to begin with was because he and his friends couldn't legally own it until he got it registered and stamped in his passport at one of the Turkish borders checkpoints. I had the money they paid me for it, but the van license number was stamped in my passport when I came into Turkey and I couldn't get out of the country without it. It was sort of a Turkish standoff. When we towed it to the garage in town the next day and had it opened up, the engine components literally dropped out the bottom. The Turkish mechanic uttered the one word that seems to be used globally . . ."Kaput."

Just three days prior, my family and I were in Athens, Greece. After bumming around Europe for a couple of months, all my wife and son and I wanted to do was get home by Christmas. Sightseeing had lost its glow and we were out of dough. Nobody told me that when you drove a vehicle into Greece, the border guards stamp it in your passport and an act of Congress can't get you out of the country without taking the vehicle with you. We had neither the time nor the resources to drive it back to Amsterdam. My first thought was to find a way to get rid of it in Athens.

The gathering place in Athens for backpacking tourists trying to hook up with rides or traveling companions was the American Express office. The sidewalk in front and on the sides of the office was crowded with travelers lugging backpacks stuffed with dirty clothes, Michelin maps, and half eaten French bread sandwiches. There were also colorfully clad young gypsies from around the world with nothing but time on their hands, laughing, making plans, and exchanging adventures. Some were there to connect with rides, some waiting to receive money from home through American Express and others just longing for company. These were the nomads of our generation; drifters who woke up each day with a new plan or no plan, but knowing adventure was on the menu. There were the haughty Europeans with their long scarves and heavy ethnic jewelry, speaking several languages and looking down their noses at anyone from off continent. There were footloose Americans who listened to the 60s troubadours like Joni Mitchell, Bob Dylan, and Joan Baez, and went searching for memories that only a passport can provide. Tomorrow they could be our doctors, lawyers, and merchants, but today was for play. They traveled by train or by sharing rides and expenses. Many of them arrived in Europe's famous eight-passenger Magic Buses, based out of Amsterdam, with pockets full of drugs to sell.

Very few Orientals traveled around Europe during those days and those who did rarely did it in this slipshod manner. Occasionally we would run across one traveling alone or a couple but, for the most part, they booked their transportation and hotels far in advance and had their itinerary planned to the minute. You hardly ever saw Japanese tourists because the Japanese, as a society, do not like to stray too far from their diet and it's difficult to acquire the foods they need. They mostly prefer to travel with group tours that take certain food staples with them.

Today, I think back on those days. Oh, Lordy! To be young again. But this day, many years ago in Athens, I was on a mission to sell my vehicle and I knew of no better place to begin than the old reliable American Express office. I parked in front and put a "For Sale" sign in the window. The first person to approach me offered to trade me a nice older Mercedes for it, with the stipulation that I drive it to Turkey where I would be met by a man who would buy it for twice the price I was asking for my van. That offer smelled fishier than the San Francisco wharf, so I passed. I could just see getting searched at the border and having the guards find door panels full of something besides window components. Then someone told me Turkey would be an easier place to sell my vehicle. In his words, the Turks were "pretty loose." (I'd like to run across that guy again.) So, I said goodbye to Greece and her lovely islands, loaded up the family and headed to the only city in the world on two continents, Istanbul, Turkey.

We enjoyed our mode of travel. It was comfortable, with a good bed and a two burner cook stove. The best part was it provided us with shelter and gave us the option of stopping anywhere we wished. Coming from Italy to Greece, we traversed the coast of Yugoslavia. We played in the cities of Split and Dubrovnik and camped without any problems on the beaches of the Adriatic.

One night we had an interesting adventure. From our campsite we could see a Russian warship anchored in the harbor. I told my six-year old son we were going to play around with it. We took a flashlight that had a push button on it, went to the water's edge, and started "signaling" the ship. By "signaling" I mean random button pushing. Soon, some authentic signaling was returned, so we fired off a couple more signals and quit. Ten or fifteen minutes later we heard the sound of a motor boat approaching from the ship. Talk about mixed emotions. We were about to have a face-to-face with the same guys who had me ducking under my desk in elementary school. Five or six curious, and not particularly friendly, Soviet sailors had joined our game of mutual curiosity. We didn't feel threatened; we were just tourists horsing around. Knowing that ship food from any navy had to surpass what we had, I told them we didn't mean to cause any trouble and asked if we could visit the ship. When the man who was the obvious leader of the group asked where we were from and I said America, he replied, "Americans," followed by a throaty gagging sound. They left and the adventure was over... or so we thought. A couple of hours later we heard a car stop on the highway above our camp. A Russian officer, possibly the ship's captain, staggered through the trees, singing softly, down to about the same spot where we had played our game. He pulled out a flashlight and signaled the ship. A short time later the same boat showed up and picked him up. It was no more than an incredible coincidence that my son and I had fooled around in the same spot. With our gibberish signaling, the ship's crew must have thought the officer was drunker than he was which to us, seemed pretty drunk.

In Istanbul we made our way to a cafe called the Pudding Shop where travelers gathered to connect with other travelers. I parked across the street in a parking lot and put a "For Sale" sign in the window of the van. That's when we found out Turkey had the same rule for vehicles as Greece, only they were even stricter, mentioning jail as the punishment for attempting to get around it. The Pudding Shop, a cafe which specialized in a variety of puddings, was also where people connected for hashish, as was illustrated in the movie Midnight Express about a drug smuggling event that had taken place in this same cafe the previous year. There were signs everywhere boldly stating that if you get caught with any hashish you will go to jail. In a weak moment I bought a small chunk. In a stronger moment, my wife flushed it down the Pudding Shop's toilet.

Our plan was to circumvent the passport stamp regulation, except it wasn't really a plan, just an idea. "How to go about it was the question. All we knew was our old clunker was complete with cook stove and implements, seats that folded into a bed, and world maps. It was more than a vehicle. It was freedom, and everyone traveling seemed to want it. We bought it in Amsterdam where European travelers buy and sell their vehicles for two reasons. First, selling a vehicle in Holland is as simple as signing the title to the title runners who take care of the paperwork, take your money and walk away. The second and more important reason was that Amsterdam is the perfect party city to spend the money your vehicle brings on your way home. In Amsterdam, permissiveness is a by-word.

The streets of downtown Amsterdam were full of colorful old vans and road clunkers for sale that had been passed back and forth between travelers for years. Most of them were Volkswagens from the 60s. The title runner told us, "People take 'em out on the autobahn and turn them loose. They've done the European circuit so many times they know their own way around."

The first van we bought made it less than a hundred miles to Amersfoort, Holland, before the engine blew up. A nice Dutch family invited us for dinner and to spend the night. A train ride back to Amsterdam the next day, and some serious haggling with the seller, got us all of our money back that the hash cafes and bordellos hadn't drained from him. A few hours back on the streets vehicle shopping the following day landed us in our, now proven through five countries, trusty steed. As reliable as its history proves it to be, I still never feel comfortable hearing the high revs of a VW engine.

The only serious problem we had traveling in the van was one time when the rubber hose from the propane tank that ran to our cook stove came loose at the stove while we were at a campgrounds. Beverly was cooking when the propane instantly sprayed into her hair and ignited. She came busting out of the side door of the van looking like something out of Greek mythology. Actually, the gas ignited and went out so quickly, very little damage was done. Besides, Bev looked good in curls.

The first dark face that approached me at the Pudding Shop about the van looked like it came straight out of central casting. It was very pinched, with a long thin nose that held coke bottle thick glasses. His jet black hair was greased down, with a widow's peak that extended halfway down to his nose. He spoke in a low nasally voice, like he had seen too many Peter Lorre movies. "Come to the Jaguar Leather Shop at eight o'clock, tonight," he said. "We will buy the van and sew a new page into your passport. There will be no problems." Could this guy be for real? I passed on the offer but told him I appreciated the line in case I ever write a foreign intrigue movie. One person even offered to throw in a Swedish passport with a picture that looked frighteningly like a younger, blonder me, with a name I couldn't begin to pronounce. My guess was the Swede probably vanished over a car purchase deal. I would have considered the offer if I wanted to live in Stockholm. Eventually, I was approached by an Iranian gentleman who let me hold enough brand new American one hundred dollar bills to pay for the van. My wife, son, and I were to ride with him and his friend across the Turkey-Greek border at Thessaloniki and make the passport auto stamp exchange. Then he could drive his friends and family to Saudi Arabia for the Mecca celebration and we could make our way north to Luxembourg where we were ticketed home.

We arrived in Thessaloniki around midday without a hitch. The removal of the van stamp from my passport took only a couple of minutes and my family and I danced across the bridge to the beautiful blue and white Greek flag, vehicle free at last. Wherever we were in the world, we were on top of it. We could now take our seven or eight new hundred dollar bills and shop for Christmas presents.

Then, things took a turn and not for the better. Beverly looked back across the bridge and said it appeared the Iranians were having a problem with the officials and "maybe we can help." I said, "Absolutely not. We're out of this and we're staying out." But Beverly had a way turning my "absolutelies" into "maybes" and my "maybes" into "Well OK." It's something she does with her eyes. Anyway, the mother of all henpecked men must have been sitting on her right shoulder when she convinced me to walk back across the bridge, directly into the arms of two very angry Turkish border guards who demonstrated to me that police brutality laws had yet to arrive in Turkey. One held me by the back of my collar while his partner screamed at me, "You do not use our frontier to sell your vehicle," and with that, he stamped it back into my passport so hard I expected to find the imprint on the back cover.

To figure out our next move (since I've never been a wife beater), we all went to a restaurant where one of the Iranians borrowed the van to go buy some fresh bread. It always fascinated me how restaurants throughout Europe and Africa permit patrons to bring in outside food. I have a home in Morocco where many restaurants permit people to bring in full meals that they bought on the street and just buy drinks. In the states you can get flogged for sneaking a Hershey bar into a movie theater. I felt secure loaning the van. I still had the money and title and, until the passport exchange was made, we needed each other. That's when the shiftless, in the literal sense, Iranian came in yelling "Motor go chock chock chock."

The Iranians rounded up some transportation and we were driven to a farmhouse in the country. They escorted us into a cold, dismal bedroom with some sandwiches, fruit, and a promise to "make car good next day." The catch on the bedroom door didn't work, causing the warped door to spring open a foot or so, adding to the drama. There wasn't a chair to hold it closed and our bag was still in the car. The front room lights were off, and none of us were willing to part with any clothing, so the door stayed open. If this is part of a tour, I suggest they leave it out of the brochure. I looked at my sweet wife, whom I knew I had exhausted to the limits, just as the tears began to fall. I was helpless to stop them. An hour or so later I stopped crying and we slept.

The next morning we were served tea and croissants and driven back to the garage. The money for a new engine, which was going to cost twice what they paid for the van, didn't seem to bother the Iranians. They said (through interpreters) that any vehicle someone could get to Mecca was worth a small fortune. It took most of the following day to find a flat bed truck and get the van loaded onto it. They couldn't find any chains so they tied it down with cotton ropes. The Iranians piled into the truck and the Taylors climbed onto the truck and into the van, where we survived a cold, bumpy, curvy night's ride back to Istanbul.

Two days later, with my family tucked into the Hotel Radar (pronounced "Radash") and a new engine installed, the now six Iranians and I began our border search. The Bulgarians wouldn't let us cross, or even explain why not. They were plain nasty. For the next three days, the Iranians (including two very pregnant women) and I drove around Turkey looking for a way out. None of my companions spoke English or paid much attention to me, at all. They stopped every hour or so for coffee and snacks, and spent most of the time when we were driving either singing or chanting their prayers. I couldn't tell the difference. (No disrespect intended.) None of the women ever smoked a cigarette and none of the men ever stopped. Telephones were scarce and I couldn't figure out the ones I did find. I tried, in vain, explaining, "Post, or Post Office" to the other passengers, knowing phones were usually available there, but gave up. For the Iranians it was a combination of "don't understand" and "don't care."

The Iranian men ate inside little open air cafes that had whole skinned animals of unknown origin hanging on hooks out front. They brought greasy food wrapped in greasy butcher paper to their wives in the car. I found bread, cheese, and olives and ate by myself. They all slept in little overnight hovels and I in the van, reveling in my time alone. Stretching is definitely underrated. The many checkpoints we ran across had guards who were less than hospitable and suspicious of the strange mixture of people. All in all, it was a pretty crummy few days.

My wife, who thought I would be gone for an afternoon and hadn't heard from me, later said she had confidence in me but she still worried. A dozen or so postcards that read, "Wish you were here," were scotch taped to the hotel walls. My son, at six years old, had learned his way around Istanbul's Grand Bazaar by himself, which is a feat in itself, and returned each day with souvenir gifts from the Turkish merchants who loved his curly blonde hair. He told me that his mom watched out the window and cried a lot. I get shivers now, thinking about him running around in the bazaar by himself, but at the time it didn't seem so foolish because we were.

Tempers were short in the packed, smoke-filled van. The men constantly passed newspapers around with what seemed to be heated discussions over each article. They kept shoving the papers in front of the driver, keeping him involved and me in prayer. Verbal communication was so difficult we finally quit trying. I was concerned about my family and pretty miserable in general, but we were trapped together and had to see it through. Finally, we took a car ferry from the city of Izmir, Turkey, just a few miles to the Greek island of Khios, where we were able to switch the rolling white elephant from my passport to one of the Iranian's. I was free and, if I scrambled, I would still have time to fetch my family and make our way home for Christmas dinner with the Scott family.

The line between freedom and captivity can be thin and painful. My plan was to take an overnight ferry to Athens and then fly back to Istanbul. I made my way to the Khios Post Office, where there were phones, and called my wife. I told her I was still kicking and caught her up on my plan.

When I walked out of the post office I was greeted by a convoy of Greek military vehicles rolling down the street and soldiers with automatic weapons dropping out the backs of them at each corner. Surely this can't be over the van.

The streets were in chaos. Nobody I approached spoke English or had any time for a tourist's questions. Unlike a typical crisis situation in the movies where everyone runs in the same direction, here everyone was scrambling in different directions like they were hurrying home. As it turns out, they were. A military coup had taken place in Athens that morning. The Greek ruler, Papadopoulos, had been put under house arrest and martial law had been declared. The typically quiet Khios, being situated so close to Turkey, was in pure panic. Commercial transportation permits to and from the island had been halted, other than one for the last ferry to Athens and the ship was filling up faster than a Titanic lifeboat. This vacation was just getting better and better.

A little bribing and a lot of squeezing and shoving, traits I was proficient at, growing up with eleven siblings, found me on board, down in third class. The Iranians and their newly acquired van had made the boat as well, and the men were now celebrating and calling me "Alfie, my brother." The two women sat quietly with their heads bowed and their hands in their laps. They weren't traveling in the van now. They were in public. I wanted no more of any of them.

If you've never traveled third class on a Greek ferry, you don't know what you're missing–or how lucky you are to miss it. There is such a thing as too much local color. Third class is the locals' way of combining island traveling with Greek partying. The cigarette smoke is London fog thick. For those with extra bucks, Ouzo is available, but the drink du jour for the paupers, including yours truly, was Retsina. Retsina tastes like turpentine that has sat around too long and turned. That matters little though, because all you have to do is get past the first mouthful, then there is no more taste. It's as though your taste buds have just died and it feels like it wouldn't take much more to make your body follow. And the bathrooms in third class? I won't punish you with their description, but let your imagination play.

A usual, there was a loophole. I had previously done enough ferry traveling between Athens and Crete to know how to beat the third class sentence. Greek ferries shuttle the islands at night whenever possible, as did this one. Each ship has an open area around midship; I surmised it was for passengers to have a place to throw up over the side. From this area, I located a series of portholes and rope ties that could serve as hand holds to lizard up the side of the ship to a similar opening on the second class deck. My day bag was small and strapped easily to my back. The thought of slipping into the dark Mediterranean Sea next to a churning ship didn't occur to me then, but right now, safely in front of my computer, it's curling my toes. All I knew was that a careful five-minute climb would get me a more comfortable eight or ten hour trip to Athens; the downside being one slip, end of trip. Nobody saw me as I climbed over the railing to second class, worked my way up and around to the back area, and did a squatter's number in a lawn chair type of deck seat. It was the only one available so I figured someone must have just left it. I stretched out and smiled, knowing I was a third class scammer traveling incognito as a second class passenger. With my pack in my lap, I fell asleep watching the lights of Khios slowly disappear into the distance. It was a tough way to save a few bucks on a ticket, but you gotta do what you gotta do.

The following morning the ferry anchored at the Athens Piraeus harbor. Another hitch I hadn't figured into my plan was the fact that Greece and Turkey do not honor each other's currency, even during peaceful times. With the current crisis, they wouldn't even discuss it. I had left the hundred dollar bills with Beverly and credit cards were not part of my pool hustling life. I had only Turkish money and enough American dollars to make it to the Athens airport, where I held up a sign saying, "Lira for Drachmas, please." It worked, and by early afternoon I was back in Istanbul with my wife and boy at the lovely Hotel Radar.

We loaded up with Turkish jewelry and knickknacks for Christmas presents and made our way back to Luxembourg to fly home. The choices our Icelandic Air tickets offered us were to land in New York or Nassau.

Hmmm, let me see, December in New York or the Bahamas? Can I take a minute? Nassau was beautiful, but expensive. Hotels were out of the question, so we found a nice beach and hobo camped for a couple of nights. We were approached a half dozen times by someone saying, "Hey mon. You wanna buy some pot?" "Hey yourself. I'm sleeping with my family on a piece of cardboard, on a beach. Do I strike you as a guy who can afford drugs?"

We only had to figure out how to get to Miami. Bev's mom had sent plane tickets to Los Angeles for her and our son so she could spend Christmas with the family. In retrospect, who could blame her for purchasing them one-way? The best plan I could come up with for myself was to hitchhike the six hundred or so miles from Miami to Fayetteville, North Carolina, pick up our motor home and try to get to Nashville before Rudolph left the rooftops. With no unforeseen problems, I had just enough time to make it. All things considered, ours probably wouldn't go down as a top selling European vacation package.

Airport restrictions were pretty loose in the early 70s, so we were able to hang around the Nassau airport. Having a six-year old boy with us made bumming a ride on a private plane to Miami pretty easy. My family caught their flight to L.A. and I hitched a ride out of Miami to the highway with a couple of painters who had just finished a job and were celebrating by chugalugging one beer after another. Next to me, in the back seat, was a very full, open five-gallon bucket of white paint that sloshed precariously close to the rim with every swerve. I made it to the highway paintless. Three or four rides got me to Fayetteville, where I picked up our motor home and slept and slept. It was Christmas Eve and I had a full day to get to Nashville, which was plenty of time. I knew the Scotts were preparing our Christmas dinner. One week and one fourth of the way around the world, and I was only about ten hours away from home. I couldn't wait.

When I arrived in Fayetteville I picked up my motorhome and headed to Tennessee. A hundred or so miles from Nashville, I stopped at a roadside tavern for a sandwich, where, lo and behold, there were two bar-sized pool tables with celebrating patrons playing five and ten dollar challenge eight-ball on each. I felt Santa coming early as I ordered some food and put my quarter on the rail of the first table. I hadn't played pool in more than a month and the cue sticks in the place were trashed. I had my cue in the motorhome but to leave and come back with it would have spooked them for sure. By this time, I had less than a hundred dollars, so missing Christmas Eve dinner for a chance at some easy action was too good to pass up.

Things went better than I expected and a few hours into the evening found me with plenty of money and playing heads up with the best shooter the place had to offer. The guy shot pretty straight but didn't know much pool. The other challengers dropped out and were content to sit, drink, and watch their hometown hero get his comeuppance. With his cash gone and the bet now being more substantial, my opponent offered to play me a two hundred dollar session if I would take a check. The banks were closed, but he said if I won and waited around until nine o'clock that night, the owner would come in and cash the check. I won the session quickly, bought a lot of beers for my new fan club, watched sports on TV, and waited until the owner came in and gave me the cash. Pool is a great hustle in that you can be short of cash in the morning and pumped up by nightfall for doing something that's fun. I knew it didn't matter that I missed dinner or what time I arrived in Nashville, I would be welcome. I had a pocket full of cash and a good pool story.

It was just after eleven when I got to Fred's house. He was a late nighter and it was Christmas Eve, so I was surprised to find no lights on and no cars in the drive. A young boy came from across the street and asked if I was there "because of what happened to Mr. Scott." At first I thought that by "Mr. Scott" he was talking about Fred's father, but he went on to say that Fred had been killed earlier that day and Mrs. Scott was with the police. I was stunned and without a clue as to what to do next. The boy had no details. I left, found a place to park, and attempted sleep.

The next morning I found the name of the funeral home and went in. Pat ran up and threw her arms around me and cried, "Oh, Alfie, they killed him for no reason. He was so happy fixing dinner and with your coming." She said Fred was cooking outside when he got a call about someone wanting to pay him some money. "He left and the next thing I knew," she cried, "I was seeing him on the six o'clock news, lying dead in the street."

The phone call Fred had received was a ruse for a trap. When Fred pulled into the driveway of the address he was given, a man stepped out from the side of the house and shot him through his car windshield. Fred managed to put the car into reverse, then opened the door and fell out as it backed up. The assailant then put the shotgun against Fred's back and pulled the trigger again. I can't imagine that shell being his last one, any more than I believe a professional hit man would leave a witness, had I been there with Fred. Was that just a guy that I played pool with yesterday who stopped me from being with Fred, or had divine intervention prevailed once again?

The trouble that led up to this nightmare began months earlier when a woman told her husband, who was also Fred's close friend, that she and Fred had been messing around. The man came to Fred's house with a gun and during a tussle Fred pulled his own gun and killed his friend. When the authorities refused to charge Fred, citing self-defense, one of the victim's relatives put out a contract to have Fred killed in this grizzly manner.

Shortly after I arrived at the funeral home, the woman who had accused Fred of the tryst walked in. I remember Pat telling her that because of her two good boys were dead and that she was not welcome there. I never heard of anyone getting bounced from a funeral home. Shortly after that the black wreath arrived.

On Christmas night, Pat and I helped the kids unwrap their presents. For the kids, Christmas calmed the pain. For Pat, it enhanced it. For me, it meant nothing. The following morning we buried Fred. I sat by his grave for a couple of hours after the service, feeling lost and talking to myself and a mound of dirt. My best friend was gone. I had nowhere to go, no family to be with, and nothing more to do in Nashville and leaving was as easy as filling up my tank. I couldn't understand how things had gone so badly and changed so much in the short time that I had been bumming around Europe. Driving out of Nashville, I thought about how hustling pool in Tennessee would always remind me of Fred and I knew I would never be back or ever see the Scott family again.

SEE WHAT A DOLLAR CAN BUY

Washington, D.C. – summer of '71, Chief's Pool Room.

I'm in a tough spot. My back and the back of my head are going to hit the floor first, and hard. I gotta brace my neck in case I hit head first. My heels are raking the shelves under the cash register and trays of colored pool balls are raining down on top of me and rolling around and under me. I look up and my hard landing becomes an afterthought. The long knife stabbing down at me from the end of the long arm on the other side of the not long counter looks like a striking snake. How ironic, trying to serpentine on my back through a sea of pool balls without taking my eyes off of something I don't like seeing in the first place. I'm not even thirty years old and the way this night's panning out, I might never be. I know I gotta go sometime, but not over pride and a buck. Did I really choose to make this happen? Lord! How is this terrible evening going to end?

One year earlier I was in Houston, Texas, running a jewelry store and a gold casting/precious stone setting school. In the late 60s, it was a dream way to make a living so I put my cue aside for awhile, bought into a Feste's Creative Jewelry store, and took a shot at the straight life. The economy was rockin' and free form gold jewelry was the rage. The store was located in a beautiful, European style Houston shopping center called Westbury Square. In the front we had a jewelry store and counters brimming with gold. A plate glass window ran along the back wall of the store to a laboratory where students created their art. Customers could stand at the window and watch the gold being melted into the centrifuge and spun into the molds. On one side of the lab was a long table with a row of stools where students carved and melted their wax designs. On the other side, beside the centrifuges, was a small table with the tools for setting stones. There was something about watching jewelry being created that made people want to buy. Four wax melting ovens lined the back wall. Above the ovens were hundreds of small holes in the drywall made from my throwing and sticking the wax carving tools, which are actually dental tools. The students, who vied for seats out of harm's way, enjoyed my madness and were impressed by my accuracy. No telling what they said when I wasn't around. I spent more time throwing the tools than using them, so I never graduated from my own jewelry design class. Combining the school and store was the brilliant concept of my partner and store owner, Bob Feste. We did all right in the business except that Bob bought treasures from around the world faster than we could sell them. On the side, of course, I hustled a little pool.

After a year of serious retail obligations and the stress that goes along with store life in general, my wife, Beverly, and I decided to leave the business and move into wholesaling, where we thought the big money was. Motorhomes were just coming on the scene and older people (which we were not) were about the only people who drove around in them. We bought a beautiful 24-foot Dodge Sightseer that I talked about earlier, with a plan to travel around the country selling stones. We specialized in opals, emeralds, and rubies, along with our line of original gold mountings. There was good potential for selling our wares to stores in small towns, not to mention small towns were always best for pool action after work. You can take the man out of the pool room but you can't take the pool room out of the man.

To test out our new home away from home, we loaded up our bicycles and swim stuff and took a weekend trip from Houston to Corpus Christi. We played on the beach at Padre Island, parked in the parking lot of a bar that had a reputation for pool action, closed the curtains, and fixed our first gypsy meal. Scrumptious! After dessert, I strolled into the bar, won nine hundred dollars in a couple of hours, and for the next three years, completely forgot about the precious stone business so I could hustle pool full time. Everything became easier with a motorhome. We could go anywhere and present ourselves nicely. We weren't forced to find lodging each night, without knowing if there was action in the town, and we slept on our own sheets. We played tennis at the local parks and rode our bicycles around the little country towns. I always won enough money to pay for our travels and sometimes even got ahead. Everything I wanted in the world was in that motorhome. My pool hustling philosophy was based on the word "beware" which derives from the words "be aware" but, no matter how careful I was, I wound up in and out of some pretty tough jackpots. In retrospect, I should have sold stones.

One of my more successful approaches to slipping into pool rooms without raising suspicion during these years was to drive my motorhome close to the front window of the local pool room, lift the engine bonnet, and rub a little grease on my hands. It was a new vehicle with a clean engine, so eventually I kept a grease soaked rag handy. I made certain to park where I would be easily visible from inside. I would walk up to the house man, holding my greasy hands or rag conspicuously away from my clothes, and ask if there were any mechanics available that time of night. They usually said they had someone they could call until I showed them my vehicle. "Hell boy, you'll have to wait until tomorrow for that thing," was their typical answer.

I would then ask, "Do you mind if I wash my hands and hang out here for awhile?" Naturally, I was welcomed. I was in and I posed no threat. When business was finished, almost miraculously, my motorhome had healed itself.

For me, hustling pool was a talent that I called on to make a living as I moved from one straight business or job, which usually didn't hold my interest long, to another. In 1968 I worked with Senator Barry Goldwater as one of his photographers during his Senatorial race. My brother Jay ran Goldwater's advertising campaign, so he secured a good position for me. Our job was to travel around Arizona shooting pictures of Goldwater in order to re-associate him as an Arizona figure after his devastating presidential defeat. He, along with his seventy-year old co-pilot Ruth, flew us to places like the Grand Canyon, Monument Valley, Roosevelt Lake, and the Navajo reservation, where we photographed Barry visiting with the locals. I was only twenty-five and the Senator much older, but I still remember how difficult it was to keep up with him hiking around the Canyon and the reservation. Barry Goldwater was a man's man for sure.

On Election Day we were given a half-day off to go out and vote. Instead, I went to the pool hall. Two reasons: I had enough inside information to know that Goldwater was a shoo-in, and second, I had ensconced myself in the campaign project completely for months and now that it was over, I craved action. My brother found out I went to the pool room and asked me if they had voting booths set up there.

I went in and out of the pool hustler life more times than I can remember. It was always easier to drop back into than to wiggle out. To be successful at hustling pool involves a combination of ability and wits. The less ability one had, the more one needed to rely on one's wits. I wasn't a great player but I was competent enough to beat most local pool hall champions and I knew most of what I called the "name brand players" well enough to get a good handicap from them or give them a pass. Eddie Taylor, who set the scale for great players, told me he rated my playing at a solid seven. Coming from most people, I wouldn't have thought a seven was much of a compliment, but when said by my traveling partner, Eddie, I was satisfied. He followed up with, "But, son, when it comes to getting the money, you are an eleven."

It's interesting, though, how sometimes your fame can outrun your game. I was at a tournament in Columbus, Ohio, hitting some balls in the practice room, when an old-time great player named Bill Lawson, from Winston Salem, North Carolina, came in. He said, "How ya hittin' 'em, Alfie?" I said, "OK, I guess Bill. But not like you champions."

It was obvious that we were in the room alone but Bill made a big production of looking up and down the room very slowly before he said to me, in his North Carolina drawl, "Alfie, who you trying to shit? I followed you through three states and nobody had any money 'cause the kid on the bicycle got it all. Here's how it works, Alfie; to know how you play, you have to get beat. I never hear of you getting beat."

"Oh no, Bill! I don't like to get beat," I said. "I gave up my youth where I could have been playing sandlot baseball and such to learn this game. I sure don't want to give my money to someone else who did the same." Bill just smiled, like the nice fellow he was.

I didn't run around winning peoples' ranches or cars or really doing any harm beyond making someone catch hell from his wife for blowing his paycheck. When I came into a strange town, I felt I was playing theater in the round. The biggest difference was that in my theater the performers paid the producer instead of the other way around. The plot was simple: I needed to fool everyone in the pool room about my reason for being there, or convince them I couldn't play so they would drop their guard. Then I would proceed to relieve some of them of their bankrolls by performing better on the table than they. Invariably, people either were playing or watching from all sides of the table, so the audience surrounds you. Everyone who wanted to co-star played me or, to get a bit part, would bet me on the side. For the spectators, we relieved their boredom for free. For instance, if I came into a strange pool room, in a little country town and did my thing, the locals wouldn't have to watch the same old Joe Buck play the same old Billy Bob, who went at each other daily. Instead, they got to watch this young (looking) guy ride his bicycle up to the pool room, from God knows where, fool everyone with his rap, and show some pool skills like many of them hadn't seen, to get the money. I earned every dime.

Besides being the best way to move from room to room in the small towns, my bicycle served as an interesting distraction. Immediately, I was pegged as a local or someone visiting a local. Sometimes I would ride right in the front door with my cue stick wrapped in a local newspaper with rubber bands. In the Southern black pool rooms, where no white people ever stuck their heads in, I would just ride through the front door with my son on the handlebars and announce, "Who wants to play this honky a little five or ten dollar six or nine rock while I have to babysit my kid?" and laugh. It usually had a stunning effect but, in a second, they could tell they had met a white man who didn't care one thing about skin color, but just wanted to shoot pool. They never imagined a white man coming on so bold, much less bringing his kid in with him. It showed them I had respect and that earned me theirs. I looked like anything but a hustler and most often they didn't want the oddity to leave, so action was automatic. The black guys had their own vocabularies; they would say things like, "He got that toy on a straing," which translates into, "He puts the cue ball where he wants it." If they wanted a handicap like two balls and the break, they might ask for "two pics and the pop." Or, if they got angry they might say, "I'm finna bus yo mouf," which you didn't want to hear. But trouble only came along once in awhile and, thank God, never around my son. He had the time of his life standing on the table, slapping hands with them, and swapping jive talk. Someone always put their hat on his head. They ate Chris up and I ate them up but I'm glad Child Protective Services never caught our act.

Keep your friends close and your opponent on the opposite side of the table. Once, in Gaffney, South Carolina, where I used to get a lot of action, I was playing twenty dollar six-ball (short rack nine-ball) with a guy so big the locals called him "Big 'un." Six-ball is fast. Greg Stevens, a great player, once told me, "If you get a sucker playing twenty dollar six-ball, you can make more money than a brain surgeon."

Big 'un wasn't a very good player; as a matter of fact, he was downright weak, so even taking it easy on him I would win a game every three or four minutes. I'm sure Gaffney was full of players who could, but wouldn't, beat the man. After an hour or so, Big 'un's emotional state lingered somewhere between livid and out of control. Although he hadn't said anything out of line to me, every slight sound in the pool room ignited him and you could tell he was itching for a reason to turn someone inside out. The place turned into a wax museum lest one of the locals wind up under Big 'un's size thirteen brogans. I said nothing. Years of playing strangers and playing in strange places had taught me to play position so that I could pocket the game ball in a pocket toward where my opponent was standing, whenever possible. This prevented any back attacks at payoff time. This day, I had that skill honed razor sharp. This guy could have picked me up like a twenty ounce cue.

Big 'un kept losing and was on fire, but still said nothing to or about me. I didn't think he was planning to either but there's an expression in the Middle East that says, "Trust in God, but tie up your camel." I shot every game ball right towards Big 'un's crotch. When the game was over and his bankroll looked like a dinosaur had stepped on it, Big 'un threw his cue down on the floor and stormed out of the pool room, furious and glaring at everyone, but still not saying a word to me. Jubilance filled the room. Everyone was laughing and jumping around out of comic relief and I was an instant hero. Not only had they seen someone who was brave (or, in this case, foolish) enough to take Big 'un's money, but Big 'un left without smashing any heads. Still, he was a gentleman to me and, call me crazy, but I'd play him again.

Minutes after he left, another local came in and someone said to him, "Man, you should have been here and seen Big 'un. He was losing his ass and he was mad as a woke up hornet," to which the newcomer replied, "That's nothing, I just saw him kick a bicycle out into the middle of the street."

Someone else yelled, "That bike belongs to Bicycle Willie here." From that time on, those in Gaffney, and a few other people throughout the South (with no lack of encouragement from me), called me Bicycle Willie. I was a pretty smart crossroader and a really good entertainer, but if the audience didn't like the show, I never stuck around for a curtain call. The following story is about one of those performances, in our nation's capital.

I was getting action daily around the South and was in dead stroke when, for some silly reason, I left for a shot at the East. Everyone knows the South is a pool haven but I guess the tourist in me and my wife influenced my decision. We headed to Florida and spent a month or so playing in the pool rooms and on the beaches, down one coast and up the other. In Panama City, we parked close to the beach to play. I swam about fifty yards out to a sand bar where I could stand up. I had wrapped a joint and lighter up in a baggie so that I could experience my swim to the max. Kids stuff from days gone by. Suddenly, just as my buzz was kicking in, a big black fin came out of the water no more than five or six feet from me. I freaked. I ran, as much as a person can run in three feet of water, to the edge of the sand bar, knowing I would have to cross the expanse of deep water to reach safety. I swam and screamed at the same time, "Shark, shark, shark!" all the way out of the water. When I hit the beach and my heart stopped pounding enough for me to regain my composure, I looked around and everyone was laughing their asses off at me. My daytime nightmare had been a dolphin and they were everywhere, playing with the surfers and such. I felt like such a fool. Still, a fin is a fin and I'd probably run again.

Totally embarrassed and beached out, we headed to D.C. for some sightseeing, then up to Baltimore. My friend Billy Stroud, who had been the house champion at the Cotton Palace in Dallas, and his partner Danny Janes were making Joss pool cues there and I knew they would steer me around Baltimore for a small cut. Pool was booming and there was action everywhere. Everyone was buying nice equipment, and these guys were at the top of the cue making industry, so any money they made on my playing was a pittance to them. They were spending more each night hosting my wife and me at the local restaurants than I was putting in their pockets. "How much is that bottle of wine, Billy? Wow! Really?" To them this was all for fun, but I was dead serious.

There was one guy, Al Obsler, who lived in Baltimore, whom I knew from my Dallas days to be a pretty good player but a little bit of a pool sucker. I knew I could win something from him. Al was an aluminum siding salesman, an occupation that seems to breed suckers. I don't know if it's their conscience bothering them from making so many old people sign their savings away on a product they don't need, or if it falls under "easy come, easy go," but most siding salesmen gamble and go off like skyrockets. Just as I had anticipated, Al paid our expenses to, from, and in Maryland.

After a week or so, action slowed for me in the one pool room where Billy and Danny liked to go and I didn't find Baltimore interesting enough to look for another spot. I had never worked the Washington, D.C., area and wanted to give it a try. Billy told me about an action room in D.C. called Chief's but said the place could be "a little rough." By "a little rough," I don't know if they were referring to the time the bartender blasted a guy off the barstool with a shotgun, or the time a group of guys came in and robbed the place and the customers, then moved everyone into a back room where they threw in two hand grenades and bolted the door. The grenades turned out to be dummies but their effectiveness in creating confusion for a getaway cannot be measured in words, except maybe my screams. These could have just been rumors, or maybe not. I didn't care. All I said was "Tell me how to get to Chief's."

As I mentioned, hustling black pool rooms was my specialty. I hit them first throughout the South for two reasons. As I mentioned earlier, hardly any crossroaders ever went in them and secondly, you could get action fast. There was no use trying to sneak around because the white guy thing makes you stand out too much. The biggest upside is you can beat the best player in a black pool room and the second best will say, "I got your game." Third best, the same, and so on. Beat the best player in a white pool room and it's sayonara to any more action.

I wasn't ten feet inside the door when I realized Chief's wasn't like some little black room in Yazoo City, Mississippi, where Whitey was someone they didn't look in the eye on the streets. This was a hard core, X-rated, serious gangster crowd, but I could smell the action. I parked my motorhome in a parking lot a block away, then rode my bike right inside the front door, pulled out a wad of cash and said I was there to, "gamble some money I made selling my motorcycle." I got instant action. In a couple of hours I played two or three black guys some One Pocket and went through them pretty easily. I had been reluctant to ask them to put up stakes for the final game because that would make me look a little smarter than I wanted to appear. As if right on cue, each of my opponents stiffed me for their last game. Naturally, I bit my tongue and didn't let out a peep of protest. These guys had to be better fighters than One Pocket players.

Someone behind me, who seemed like he came out of nowhere, asked, "You up for a little twenty dollar nine-ball?" I turned around to this clean cut, twenty-some year old white boy who was already taking the higher numbered balls off of my table and racking up nine balls. I thought, Hello! This is my table. Step off 'till you're invited, but instead I said, "Flip for the break." When I was beating people I liked to play as many and as much as I could. When I got beat I just wanted to sleep.

I explained to my new opponent that I had gotten stiffed for the last game three times in a row and could we agree not to do that. I said, "If we get broke we'll quit, OK?" He agreed. It was getting pretty late and I was hitting the balls good so I ironed him out of the hundred and something dollars that he had, pretty quickly and, what do ya' know, that prick stiffed me for the last twenty dollars.

This time I had to speak up. I said, "Hey, we agreed, if we got broke we would quit." His answer was catchy but a shade inflammatory. He said "So? I'm broke. I quit."

There was nothing I could do except say to the check out man, in a loud and taunting voice, "Separate checks. I'll pay for mine." Typically the winner pays for the table time and it was only a dollar apiece, but making a point of not paying his share was my only form of retaliation for him stiffing me. I was pissed and he was super pissed and that was a bad formula. He moved toward me and said, "You're going to pay my dollar too or I'm gonna kick your ass."

He was quite a bit bigger than I. Hell, everyone was. He moved up close and I grabbed one of those cafe sugar dispensers, the kind with the screw on metal top, and drew it back. Then he said, "Never mind kicking your ass, I'll just kill you."

With that, he pulled out and opened this long thin knife, in an instant, like a man who had practiced a lot, and pulled it back, not over his head like you see in the movies, but side-armed. I wished I had had the presence of mind to negotiate the situation back to paying the dollar. At that instant, even ass kicking didn't seem so bad. By this time my back was leaning pretty hard against the checkout counter, but enough adrenalin hit these skinny arms of mine to vault me backwards over the counter and into the predicament where this story began.

Damn! So many balls! Such a long knife! This was really getting serious. I felt his knife jab the air in my hair and I knew I couldn't keep up the break-dancing enough to avoid contact. I don't know what the record is for how quickly someone can say, "I'll pay, I'll pay," a half a dozen times, but I'd like to enter my retort in the contest. The blade quit jabbing and I stood up and coughed up the buck. Want a tip? No problem.

More than a bit rattled, it was like I was in shock. I picked my cue off the floor, unscrewed it, and pushed my bike toward the door with my head down. Everyone had heard my pleas for mercy and my fear had switched to embarrassment. Hiding my face seemed like the natural next step. I figured that was enough action for tonight. How about forever, Alfie?

Then my assailant made a near disastrous mistake. He snickered at me as I walked by and ignited a fuse shorter and hotter than he could imagine. Game on, you son-of-a-bitch. I covered the block back to the motorhome at a pace that would make Lance Armstrong drop out and grab a cab. I remember hopping off so fast that I was in a dead run and the bike kept going until it slammed into the side of our dwelling. This was road rage in the bike lane folks. I ran in, got a long-barreled, chrome plated .38 from a cabinet over the fridge and, taking no time to grab my bike, ran back to the room at breakneck speed. I can still hear my wife screaming, "Alfie, come back! Please! Come back!" She reminded me of the movie Shane only her voice was deeper than Brandon DeWilde's. I kicked the door open as loudly as I could, so the one I sought would know I was ready for a little more action, and yelled, "Now where is that Mack the Knife M.F.?"

Actually, screaming the abbreviation wouldn't have packed as much punch. My prey was sitting in a chair on the left, by the first table, close to the door where I had left him. I pointed the gun at his face, not more than ten feet away, and cocked back the hammer. The click was the loudest noise in the joint. Was I a shade out of control or what? I remember the boy going into this sitting fetal position with his arms covering his face and saying, "Oh God, man! Please don't shoot me."

Now who was squirming and begging? I was watching out of the corners of my eyes and could tell I didn't have a lot of worry from the arsenal of weapons in the pockets of the hundred or so toughs in the room. I'm sure they were thinking this guy had it coming for pulling a knife on some innocent kid, especially a kid with a .38. I said to my knife man, who looked much smaller all scrunched up like he was, "Just get into your pocket and get my dollar." Thinking about his knife, I added, "And your hand better not come out holding anything else."

However the night was going to end, this Alfie dog was having his day. I was feeling the power and digging the revenge. My whole world had morphed into a less than a hundred square feet of madness. He just kind of melted out of his chair, directly to a squatting position on the floor, where he placed a dollar bill, then back crawled his way up into the chair without a peep.

As I picked up the bill and started backing away, a man sitting next to him said, "We'll see you again, friend." To which I answered (now that I saw how well this gun thing worked), "You can see more of me right now, if that's what you really want, friend." He lacked a retort of any sort. Now that my bankroll and my craving for retribution were complete again, I backed out the door and started running across the parking lot. I looked around, then realized that only in the movies do they chase the guy who has a gun. Would you want to go after the dollar? Isn't one madman per evening enough?

Later into the night found me calling Eddie Taylor and crying into the phone about how crazy I had gone. I asked him to tell his friend, Chief, that I was sorry and that I was leaving town immediately. I threw two things that night—my gun into a river and my food up. Both reactions let me know the tough guy role didn't suit me. But at least the drama was over, or so I thought.

As I mentioned, I used my pool skills throughout my life as a vehicle to get from one job to another. If I didn't like what I was doing, I could always whip out my cue, gas up my car, and head for some action on the green felt. At this time, around 1973 or 1974, I was writing radio and TV copy for my brother's ad agency in Tucson. I wasn't playing much pool, but occasionally I would drop by the local hang out pool room for a soft drink and conversation. Stuff like, "Don't you remember me? I used to be Alfie Taylor. I could play, really I could."

On this day I was sitting at the bar and listening to the local players talking with a traveling player who had hit town that week and beaten the best Tucson had to offer, "Three Dollar Sam" Bono, who actually played for much more. It was my D.C. friend, although neither of us recognized the other. I still don't understand how he beat Sam when I went through him in D.C. with such ease. In any case, the newcomer had his thumbs thrust further into his armpits than the Governor of Texas, as he spun his tales of conquests across the country. All of a sudden he starts telling about "this kid" who pulled a gun on him three or four years ago in D.C. He instantly had my full attention, other than taking a moment to watch my arm hairs stand up. The "sharpie" spilled the story exactly the way it happened, leaving out only the part where I turned him into a terrified little bitch. (Of course, I wasn't about to mention my crying and throwing up that night, either.)

When he finished, I said, "Excuse me, but can I ask you who was out of line there?" He looked at me for the first time and said, "Well, I guess I was. Why do you ask?" I told him, "Because I'm the guy who almost shot you."

Now you could really hear a piece of chalk drop. I was never particularly proud of the event so I hadn't told anyone about it. It was a startling, but non-threatening moment. Now we were in my room, in my town, with my homies. Plus, he had seen up close that I'm no bargain to do battle with.

He asked, "Are you Alfie Taylor?" I said, "Yes, what do you want to do now?" For a guy who wasn't playing much pool at the time, I really had center stage in the pool room. He said, "I don't know. What do you want to do?" His tone was a mixture of bravado and trepidation.

I told him I'd like for him to come to my house and clear this up for good. He accepted. We had a couple of beers, smoked a joint or two, and talked for hours about his tour across the country and only minutes about our event. My occasional use of discretion stopped me from asking him for the twenty dollars he had stiffed me for in D.C. He told me he had run into my brother Jack down in Florida and, when he told him about our confrontation, Jack told him I should have shot him for "pulling a knife on my brother."

I told my guest this was a big evening for me, that now maybe I would stop dreaming about that night. He said, "You? You don't know how many nights I woke up in cold sweats dreaming about it. I didn't think you were going to shoot me on purpose but the way the gun was shaking, I thought you were going to squeeze one off accidentally." Funny, that had been my concern too.

I asked him if he had a place to stay and said he was welcome to spend the night at my house. He refused, saying he didn't want the dreams to start up again. Now our little drama really was over and I can't even remember the young man's name; and, he stays out of my dreams, completely.

U. J. PUCKETT AND THE FINE ART OF BUSHWHACKING

Killeen, Texas, home of Ft. Hood, mid '60s.

As the old man leaned over the table to shoot, the ends of the medicine soaked gauze bandages covering his face drooped down from where we had pinned them behind his ears several days earlier. The medicine stains were a yucky yellow and brownish blend. Other than holes for the eyes, nose, and a mouth, from which protruded a big cigar that jumped up and down as he spoke, he was wrapped totally from his forehead to his chin. From time to time he would stop shooting, take a long puff from his cigar and slowly shake his head back and forth just enough to make the ends of the bandages dangle. We purposely left a few inches of the gauze loose behind his ears and even pinned one of the bandage press clips to the end of each of them. When he stood straight up they looked like Rastafarian ear rings. It was overdone for sure but that's what the old man wanted. Showman that he was, he adjusted his face covering constantly, even more than was necessary. His overall repulsiveness was testified to by the countless people who grimaced or pushed their plates away when we entered restaurants. He did most of the driving so stopping at red lights and watching the wide-eyed faces in the other cars was a kick.

This night he wore a round, white, wide brim hat, the kind with a loosely attached band for attaching fishing lures. His hulking body wavered (intentionally) as he walked around the table pocketing balls, which he seemed to do just well enough to win almost every game. Other than his enormous left hand out flat on the table, he looked like the invisible man after a car wreck.

We told everyone that he had facial skin cancers and was being treated in nearby Temple, Texas, at the Scott & White Dermatology Clinic and that it was quite serious and all he wanted to do was shoot pool for money, which he had plenty of. He would have been a more pitiable sight had he not been raking in the soldiers' money so mercilessly, while ribbing them the whole time about how they "can't even beat a guy with no face." The worst part for me was waking up in the same hotel room with him for the three or four days we were there and watching him adjust the bandages that, for some reason, he refused to take off, no matter where the eye holes were when he awakened. In actuality, there were no skin cancers at all, and the colored blotches came from various medicines I dumped on the gauze when I mummy wrapped his face. At the time, as a kid, I didn't realize the potency of the fellow I was with. The man under those bandages was none other than the master of pool hustling theatrics and disguises, the personification of a real pool hustler, Utley Jim Puckett.

It was payday at Fort Hood, and Killeen had more than a half dozen pool halls on one main street. We knew the GIs got paid the day before the first of the month and the day before the fifteenth, barring weekend interference, and for Dallas hustlers, myself included, Killeen was a semi-regular, sure action spot. There was a constant rotation of soldiers at the fort so fresh blood was always available. We rationalized that our winning money the soldiers would otherwise have spent on booze was our contribution to the war effort. We didn't rationalize squat. We just robbed them because we could.

Everyone in Texas who played pool either knew or had heard of U. J. Puckett because he was the best player in our state. Killeen was close to his home town of Fort Worth, so if he had gone in without a disguise, someone would most likely have recognized him and it would have killed the action for both of us. Of all the many scams he had put down, beginning thirty years before I ever picked up a cue, this one had to be the wildest. He got this idea when we left Dallas, so as soon as we hit town we checked into a room, I made a drug store run, and we applied his disguise. We spent hours experimenting with the tightness of the wrap and the best places to dump Iodine and the other medicine stuffs. We laughed our asses off at our efforts before we had any idea if this would work.

For this gentleman, trapping Uncle Sam's finest in this manner was a "two bird" situation. First, there was the obvious money thing, but secondly he wanted the world to know and remember what a real pool hustler was like. Boasting of his theatrics and conquests was an important part of Mr. Puckett's life.

Our scam worked splendidly. For three days we got constant, easy action. Playing in service towns was always a little different. The military bond between soldier's turns strangers into brothers, and for these guys, gambling at the pool hall was part of their weekend blowout together. When non-military personnel, such as the two of us play one of them, many of the others feel almost compelled to bet on their brothers. As long as there was beer available, win or lose, they kept the party spirit, they kept playing, and they kept losing.

With our coffers full and the soldiers' weekend over, we headed home. Watching "Igor and his dwarf" ride down the highway, laughing like a couple of hyenas, with a two-foot pile of wrinkled, smelly, government greenbacks between them, would surely have been a Kodak moment. When it was over and we cut up the money, 70/30 percent, as agreed (guess who got the 30), the old man dropped me off in Dallas late at night, leaving me with a pretty fat pocket and a most indelible memory. As he drove away, what I'll never forget is that this icon of American pool history, this bushwhacker of all bushwhackers, this mentor of all mentors for me was still wearing his bandages. Go figure.

"All trappers don't wear fur caps" was an expression coined by and played out through U. J. Puckett's illustrious and most interesting sixty-year pool hustling career. I was fortunate enough to share a small part of that career. Puckett was born in 1910, under impoverished conditions, in Prattsville, Arkansas. With little opportunity or options, he used his cue stick and billiards prowess to escape the apparent fate of his birth. In that respect, he and I had a bond. Over the years, Puckett was a regular opponent of Luther "Wimpy" Lassiter, Joe "The Meatman" Balsis, and Minnesota Fats. His ability and bravado earned him a place of honor in the Texas Billiards Hall of Fame.

I met U. J. in Atlanta, Georgia, when I was about nineteen and just becoming a little bit of an earner on the tables. For me to call him anything but "Mr. Puckett" during the first year of our friendship was simply out of the question. Later he became "U. J." He was a big man who boomed when he spoke, at any volume, commanding respect from everyone within earshot. His mere presence could be intimidating.

At this time there weren't many pool tournaments in the U.S. and everyone was talking about the Gandy Nine-Ball tournament coming up in Macon, Georgia. They said the players were gathering first in Atlanta where there was "a ton of action." I'm not trying to pawn myself off as a tournament player. I was a lighter than light lightweight, but I wanted to sample the action and the Georgia tournament was the next jamboree.

I left Dallas, heading to Macon, via Atlanta, with Vernon Litton and Billy Porter. Shortly after we arrived in Atlanta, an incident came up involving my traveling companions and a considerable amount of money and, I should point out, it wasn't my companions' money. As a junior partner, I wasn't privy to the details, but I heard Vernon and Billy whispering the words, "Philadelphia mob guys," "They're pretty pissed," and "We better hightail it out of town." What I hadn't heard them say was, "Let's leave Alfie here," but they must have said it because I looked up and my road buddies were two dots on the horizon. I was left standing in downtown Atlanta with about eighty dollars in my pocket and my clothes in a grocery bag. Hello cruel world, which way's the pool room?

Actually I couldn't have been happier. I was surrounded by the country's best pool players and life couldn't be any better. I remember walking into the huge, thirty or forty table, old-style pool room in downtown Atlanta, full of champion players, and thinking if I skimped on eating (White Castle burgers were about fifteen cents back then) and found a cheap place to flop, I could use what was left of my bankroll to eke out a little money and make it to Macon by tournament time. I couldn't think about playing the good players but there were a lot of local players around there who were as starry eyed as myself and I could handle their game. I started out playing some five dollar nine-ball and two days later I had a pocket full of money and was playing for twenty. Then my brother Jack showed up so I had someone to share my bankroll with. At the time I couldn't imagine leaving the hustler's life. Today, almost fifty years later and thirty some odd years out of the racket, I find myself having such a good time writing about it that, in a way, I haven't left at all.

At the time of the Macon tournament, nine-ball tournaments, or any kind of pool tournaments, were just taking off. The movie *The Hustler* was hot on the screen and pool rooms were opening around the country in droves. Prize money was minimal and almost irrelevant because stakehorses were plentiful, and big money action was 'round the clock. Today's tournaments are different. Stricter standards of decorum are in place for the players and, other than at the wide open Derby City Classic, which is actually held in Indiana these days, gambling is prohibited. The Derby City Classic is a different story altogether. Big money pool games are played alongside tournament matches and wide open card and crap games are plentiful and you can place a bet on any sporting event anywhere. The tournament should be called The Action City Classic.

At other tournaments there are other ways and places for the players to get together to gamble, but sneaking around to other rooms to play isn't the same. For the top dozen or so players who dominate the game, tournaments pay the bills, but for the rest of the good players and wannabes out there, they are no more than a place to rally and maybe pick up a few bucks outsmarting someone.

One of the problems with today's tournaments is a lack of outside funding. Product sponsors are limited and television coverage is minimal due to the slowness of the game, which I believe is a result of today's safety play rules. When I was out there, nine-ball was played with a "shoot to make the ball" rule or one shot push out, both of which produced great shots and exciting play. Today's rule of "one foul, ball in hand" causes players to take fewer chances on difficult shots. There's nothing exciting about rolling a ball up behind another ball, even if doing so almost assures you of a win. Consequently, television viewers get bored quickly. This new rule (one foul, ball in hand) was put into effect to speed up tournament play, because any player worth his salt can run the table after getting ball in hand.

The best nine-ball I ever saw were the ring nine-ball games at the tournaments in Johnston City, Illinois. Ring games, where more than two players are involved, left no room for safety play. Either you went for and made the tough shot you faced, or you got ready to sit down for what could turn out to be several games. Now I'm starting to sound like every other old guy who says things aren't what they used to be.

For some reason or another, Mr. Puckett, who told me straight away, "And that's heavy on the mister, son," took an instant liking to me when I met him in Atlanta, so I became his little buddy. He let me run around with him and sweat his action. He also helped me get a ride to the tournament in Macon. Puckett was the defending champion of the Macon tournament and I was a pool nut straight out of Hicksville, U.S.A., so I followed him around like a lap dog. I had found my road hustling mentor.

I remember walking down the street with him and passing some other players. They laughed and one of them asked, "That your protégé, Puckett?" Puckett just said, "Yup," and kept walking, barely giving them a glance. I swelled with both pride and curiosity. I was with "the man" and I couldn't wait to look up the definition of "protégé."

There's a funny prank that happened to Mr. Puckett during the Macon tournament. It involved my brother Jack, who was already a seasoned crossroader and Puckett's good friend. Pool hustlers tend to keep their sense of humor throughout their life. They have to. Theirs is a life of uncertainty and alertness, and thoughts of besting someone or tricking them rarely leave their minds. They're never completely off work so most everything they say has a hidden or double meaning. Typically, when they're not in action on the tables, they're swapping stories and those lacking in creativity or humor stay in the listeners' seats. Another thing about crossroaders is that you rarely hear about them fighting with each other. If you're in the racket, you know the score; win some, lose some. It's a small society with a large measure of mutual respect. Most of the trouble we faced came from amateurs; some guy in a bar loses twelve dollars and hits you with a beer bottle or, as some of my stories reveal, some problems were just plain old run of the mill robberies.

But, back to the story about Mr. Puckett and Jack. There was a big cafeteria across the street from the pool room in Macon. Crossroaders rely on cafeterias as a source for vegetables on the road. If they happen to stumble on a smorgasbord where you can eat all you want for one price, they really load up. Fats used to call those places "pitch 'till you win joints." Jack, Puckett, and Bill "Weenie Beanie" Staton were having lunch in this cafeteria. Jack had to excuse himself early so he left, stopping to pay his bill. At the counter he told the cashier, "Be careful, there is a man in the restaurant named Puckett who is a notorious check walker who will try to bluff his way around paying." Jack motioned to where Puckett was sitting then returned to the booth and told Puckett that the manager of the restaurant had recognized him as being the defending champion of the Macon tournament and wanted to comp his bill. Jack said, "Just tell the cashier you're Puckett."

With that information, Puckett opted to hit the serving line while Jack and Beanie left and gathered some of Puckett's cronies to watch the front door from across the street. Puckett, after finishing off multiple entrees and enough deserts to supply a small wedding party, walked by the cashier, already lighting up his victory cigar, and said, in his commanding voice, "I'm Puckett," without missing a step.

Puckett was out the front door and on the sidewalk when he was pounced upon by the cashier, the restaurant manager, and someone in a white kitchen uniform holding a pot in his hand. The staff was incensed and irate, Puckett was startled, rattled, and super ticked off, and his fellow hustlers, watching from across the street, were busting up laughing.

It was years later before my pool game was strong enough to travel with Mr. Puckett. I was living in Dallas, hanging around the Cotton Palace. Puckett would come over from Fort Worth, both in an attempt to catch some sucker and to be admired by all of us shortstops (lightweight players). He had more scams than the Flim-Flam Man, like laying some working stiff a thousand dollars against a hundred and playing ten games ahead. The sucker would have as much chance to swim the Atlantic as he had to get ten games ahead of Puckett.

Another thing Puckett had going for his nine-ball game was his ungodly powerful break. An oversize man to begin with, he had perfected the art of hitting the balls so hard that the cue ball would jump straight up in the air a couple of feet while nine balls raced toward six pockets. The cue ball would then drop down and stop right in the center of the table, giving him the best chance for a clear shot on the one ball. His break was legendary. The easiest time I ever had running out playing nine-ball was when Puckett and I were in Bald Knob, Arkansas. There were two brothers who owned a pool room, both pretty good players, but they knew Puckett and wouldn't mess with him. Puckett talked one of them into spotting me the break, playing fifty dollar nine-ball and letting him break the balls for me. My own break was kind of puny. Remember the song line, "What a difference a day makes?" It's nothing compared to the difference a break makes. To begin with, we were playing on eight foot tables, which are twice as easy as nine foot ones. Puckett would smash the break and so many balls would go in that Mickey Mouse could run the table, and so could I. Eight or ten games of that punishment and my opponent ran like a rat from a burning barn.

Puckett wasn't just big and loud, he was also tough. I guess you have to be if you're going to be as boisterous as he was. Typically, we would go into a pool room and he would boom out, "My name is Jim Sinclair and I have a pocket full of hundred dollar bills that says my son can beat you guys playing pool."

Naturally, the end result he was looking for was for some fool to do the "frying pan into the fire" number and hustle him to play, which, fortunately for us, was often the case. Once, in New Braunfels, Texas, we went into a Mexican pool room and Puckett had his money showing. Sure enough, a young man jumped up quickly and started racking the balls, clearly entertaining the thought of owning those hundred dollar bills. I began playing and Puckett got instant side action with three or four guys hungry for the wad he was flashing. The evening went as planned until Puckett made one too many "My son can do this and my son can do that" speeches. I was taking care of business without letting out a peep, but the man I was playing stopped shooting and said in a loud voice, "Your son better watch out. He might get bloody."

The stillness that instantly blanketed the room was a fitting tribute to the proverbial calm before the storm. I was stunned. I hadn't uttered a syllable. Puckett came pouncing out of his seat, swelled up like a giant on steroids, right into my opponent's face, and said, "Bloody? Why you bunch of wetback, pepper bellied M. F.s, I'll show you bloody if that's what you want. Let's get going."

When you take someone as big and booming as Puckett and add simulated insane anger coupled with properly placed expletives, it will get some attention. The place went still again for a long moment, and then everyone returned to their games. Puckett seemed OK, my opponent and the side betters acted as if nothing had happened, and I was back playing. So why were my hands shaking?

Puckett's toughness turned around and bit him in the ass once in Fort Worth. He was in a bar, flirting with a girl who was with a date who was much smaller than Puckett. This led to an altercation outside and the smaller (martial arts expert) man knocked Puckett out, pulled his body onto the sidewalk, leaving his legs in the street, and stomped both of his knees backwards. Puckett didn't let the wheelchair stop him from hustling. In the following year he learned to play pretty well sitting down.

Puckett had a cigar, either lit or not, in his mouth most of the time. It was as much a part of his persona as it was his habit. He knew cigar smoke caused me instant nausea, so he wouldn't smoke in the car or motel room when I was with him with one exception. We were in St. Louis, on our way to the annual tournament in Johnston City, Illinois. A man named Blackie owned a pool room there and he played well enough to take on any stranger. Blackie beat a lot of crossroaders. I couldn't begin to handle his game, but Puckett wanted some tough, inexpensive action as a warm up for the tournament, so he began playing Blackie twenty dollar nine-ball.

Blackie's was an action joint so I had my pick of customers to choose from. Joe Bowman was a player I knew from Nashville that I had a good chance to beat. It was a mistake to play Joe because there was easier action that I would kill if I beat him. Still, I had beaten him once in Tennessee, so why not here? As luck would have it, Joe was hitting the balls good and beat me four or five games straight, playing twenty dollar One-Pocket, causing me to put down a natural "lemon" (losing to get better action) without even trying. I just failed miserably to take advantage of my lemon.

When I quit, an older man in bib overalls stepped up and said, "I'll play you some, son." Still hot under the collar from the spanking Joe had given me, I popped off and said, "Why should I play you? I can look at you and tell that you ain't got nothin'."

It's hard for me to look back and believe that I would talk that way to another human being, but action in the pool room typically came from people who didn't like you and wanted to beat you, so being obnoxious was part of our M.O. I no sooner gave my smart ass answer than I looked over at Puckett and saw his face scrunch up like he had sat on something hot. Then he put both hands over his face and shook his head like he was crying and saying "No" at the same time. I knew I had blown it, but I didn't know how badly.

As it turned out, the name of the man I had insulted was Sutt and he was known as the best score in the Midwest. Sutt would lose ten or twenty thousand at the drop of a hat and was an extremely weak player. Nobody ever got to play him without spotting him a lot of balls and for him to offer to play a stranger even was unheard of. But Sutt had watched me get hammered by Joe, where I had played terribly, so he figured he had a chance.

When I saw Puckett's reaction, I tried to apologize to Sutt and accept his offer to play. Sutt, still feeling the insult from the little punk, reached into his overall pocket and pulled out a huge stack of hundred dollar bills that he placed on the side rail of the table. Laying his hand flat on the stack, he walked to the other end of the table spreading them out along the way. When the rail could no longer be seen under the Benjamins, he turned to me and asked me firmly not to speak to him again. Later, when we got into the car, Puckett, who had not spoken to me after my screw up, lit up his cigar and puffed it madly in my direction. October nights in Illinois can be super cold, as was this one, so rolling the window down was out. His timing was spot on for as soon as we arrived at our motel, I was able to open the door, right before I hurled. That wasn't enough punishment to please the boss but it was close.

Bushwhacking has a number of elements and rules of thumb. If you're going to sneak up on somebody, you have to come up with a scam they haven't yet been hit with. For example, never make the mistake of walking into a strange room and stopping at the door to look around. While you are watching them, they are watching you. I would always walk in quickly and head directly for the bathroom or Coke machine. This avoided any attention being directed my way. Then I would plop down on a bench or somewhere next to a young kid and act like I was a semi-local. Younger people hanging around a room love to show they're "in the know" and most of them will spill their guts about who plays and for how much, for any willing ear.

Crossroaders almost always travel in pairs so, other than the father and son routine, it's important not to go in together. There are even code words and hand signals. If one partner is in a bad game the other might ask someone if "Tom has been around." "Tom" means bad. On the other hand, "George" means good. If your partner wants in on your action or the game you're getting is good, but can't talk to you, he will lay his open hand on his chest. If he doesn't want any part of it, he will close his fist in the same place.

Then there's the expression "sharking." To shark someone is to intentionally distract them from their focus while they're shooting. It can be something as crude as talking trash or standing in front of them while they shoot or it can be as subtle as a cough or a little squeaking of the chalk on your cue tip. In any case, sharking is amateurish and I found it to be more of a nuisance and not worth the trouble. Besides, someone might get pissed off and bust your pumpkin. I heard Minnesota Fats telling a story about one of his opponents who was crying about being sharked. Fats said, "The guy should play in a wax museum, then if anybody moves, I'd screw out of town."

There are some tricks to the trade that I discovered and didn't tell anybody about. One favorite was my damp ball scam. It doesn't take much to swing a game in your favor if the players are pretty even to begin with. If someone matched up with me where my opponent was the one getting to break, I would keep a damp towel by my chair. After each game, I would wipe my hands with the towel, but not enough for my opponent to notice anything unusual. As we rounded up the balls for the next break, my hands would dampen the balls enough to make them sticky and harder to spread apart on the break. On the other hand, if I was the one getting the break, I would sprinkle my hands with the slightest amount of talcum powder before I handled the balls for racking. Powdered balls will blast apart, roll forever, and race each other to the pockets. The need for this sort of edge doesn't come up often.

There were more hardcore tricks that I didn't use, the hardest being "jarring" someone. This means slipping some kind of drug into your opponent's drink. There are drugs that will relax the muscles to the point that a person who has been "jarred" loses control over their arm muscles, causing their game to suck, yet they cannot figure why things aren't working. I knew someone who put some of this stuff on a stick of gum to jar someone. I was on the receiving end of getting jarred and beaten once in Birmingham. It was awful. I absolutely couldn't get a ball to go near the pocket and didn't know why until the next day when I was told what was put in my drink. If there was someone playing tough guy in a pool room, they might get a "shit mickey." It's a powerful purgative that I heard was used for extreme poison cases. Moments after swallowing it, everything inside you races to the nearest exit without allowing time for undressing, after which you drop to your knees, kitten weak. I used to hang around a bar in Atlanta where it was used regularly on guys who were causing trouble. I was never witness to a shit mickey, but I was told that when the bartender would announce very loudly to a trouble maker, "Mister, I'm going to buy you a drink," his regulars knew what was about to happen. They say it's a comical sight unless you're watching it from your knees.

Puckett loved hustling in his home state and bass fishing, where top fishing lakes were prevalent. For him, a fishing outfit, complete with lures on his hat, was a natural disguise. He could actually play, and play well, wearing his waders. Once we were fishing on Belton Lake in Texas, in a little motorboat, when a storm came up. Puckett was fishing and I was listening to his fishy stories. He told me about a time when he hooked a catfish that was so big that he struggled with it for more than an hour, until it wouldn't budge an inch. Puckett said the fish turned out to be smart as well as big. He claimed it swam into a sunken school bus and then rolled the window up to escape.

I was familiar with ocean waves to the extent of mild body surfing and drowning once, but had never experienced surf on a lake or when my feet weren't in sand. A storm came out of nowhere. The boat began pitching, slightly at first, then without any warning, the water turned violent. The boat was lurching sideways and up and down at the same time, but Puckett wouldn't quit fishing until things got really out of hand. The sky became dark and the rain came hard before he decided we would go in . . . if we could. The little outboard motor barely had the strength to pull us through the chop. When the front was in the air, the motor would push us forward about three feet, then bog down to what sounded like six rpm's. Next, the front would lurch forward and dip down enough to add another gallon or so of lake water to our newly developing indoor pool. Adding sound to the drama, the motor's propeller would clear the water and "zing" like it was on its last two bearings.

I'm not much of a swimmer, we didn't have life jackets, and we weren't close to the shore. I got extremely nervous while Puckett stayed cucumber cool. He kept repeating, "One more minute, one more minute", as he'd cast his line in again and again. Finally, when something came out of my mouth other than words, a portion of which was floating, colorfully, around our feet, he navigated us, fishless, to safety. That was my one and only excursion on the water with U. J. Puckett.

I loved traveling with him. His style of pool was called "hustling the nuts" because he didn't take any game unless he had the best of it. He was a businessman, and winning was his business. I remember him telling me at a young age, "Son, you might not get to play as high and you might not get to play as often, but you have to win every time you play or you're going to spend a lot of time hungry." Nobody wins every time they play but my record was pretty damn good largely because of the big man's advice.

A chapter in pool hustling history closed June 22, 1992, when Utley Jim Puckett died in Fort Worth, Texas. The last time I saw my friend and mentor he was being interviewed on the TV show 60 Minutes, which can be found through Google. It was enjoyable watching him talk of his adventures, some of which I had been a part of or had heard about from the horse's mouth during our travels together. I remember the closing of the 60 Minute segment, when Mr. Reasoner, who once said in an interview, "I loved the guy from the moment we met," asked Puckett if he had any parting words. Puckett answered, "I'd just like to say hello to all those suckers out there who I beat over the years. Hellloo," he drawled out, as he smiled, like it was all a joke, and the scene faded to black.

RUNNING THE TABLE, ALFIE STYLE

South Carolina is about as "deep south" as a person can go—from her moss-covered elms to mint juleps and community fried chicken dinners on court house lawns. There's a gracious quality about South Carolinians and the state's reputation for hospitality is well earned. But, there's a side of this part of the south less well known and far less hospitable, and lucky us, we got to see it up close.

I knew it was a tough ass Greenville pool room even before I walked in. Brother Jack had been beating the place pretty good for a couple of weeks when he called me about coming down. Naturally, he played the "I don't know him" card and to confirm that, he beat me in front of the locals the first night. He even put up some money for a local lightweight to play me, whom I let win fifty or sixty dollars, who then gave Jack half the money. Not a terribly original move in our racket, but almost always effective. I took my faux beating, said a few cuss words and said "I'll be back tomorrow and show you guys some real goddamn money," as I stormed out the door. Back at the motel Jack applauded my performance and assured me, if we took our time and did it right, we were going to do well here. We had plenty of money to play on, the spread we put down came off perfectly, and nobody for miles around had any idea who I was. Jack was right on in his prediction.

The following night when I walked in wearing a coat and tie, the guy who beat me the night before jumped out of his chair and ran to get me before anyone else could. Jack, in his usual theatrical manner, tried to insist to the man that he deserved to take half of his action but the sucker wouldn't hear of it, thus tightening his own noose. This went on for several nights, with Jack sometimes putting money in with people against me in order to get them to the table. I had been out on the road for several months without a break and my game was rock solid so winning wasn't a problem . . . but a problem was waiting in the wings.

A week of trouncing one person after another went by without anyone suspecting what Jack and I were up to, but by this time I wasn't playing the role of a sucker. It was hard core "bring 'em on" time, and the best the place had to offer, offered me little resistance. One night I was playing fifty dollar one-pocket with the house champion on a front table that was reserved for ring games or games worth watching. Jack was sitting on a small set of bleachers next to the table along with a crowd of gawkers. Sitting next to Jack was a very big palooka looking fellow who seemed to be hanging on to Jack's every word. Jack told the guy he needed to leave for awhile and asked him if he would take care of me while he was gone, to which the guy retorted, with aplomb typical in his circle of contemporaries, "uh huh."

Today, I like to think of myself as a considerate person who isn't prone to smart mouthing or insulting anyone, but in those days things were as different, as was I. My opponent fouled the cue ball and I called him on it. He denied the foul but I saw it and he knew it and there was no doubt about the error. In retrospect, I should have let him get away with it, I was winning almost every game anyway but, by this time I was playing the "I won't be pushed around" role and we argued back and forth over the foul. All of a sudden, out of the bleachers comes this loud "I think he's right, kid." It was the big guy. I can't believe I was so bold (foolish) but I said, "Who cares what you think? One look tells me you don't know a cue ball from a grape." The big guy came off the bleachers three, maybe four steps at a time and lunged at me. Everyone moved out of his way so quickly I knew I was in for it. The thing I had going for me is, if running around a pool table ever became an Olympic sport, the U.S. would have their eye on me for sure. I can do that real good. The secret is to hold your cue in your outside hand and use the rails and pockets with the other to round the corners. And this night I wasn't settling for the silver. It was easy to tell that one slip and an ass whipping was on my agenda. Even as big as he was he just couldn't catch me but I still couldn't figure a way out. By this time our audience had moved back far enough to not become collateral damage so my track was totally clear. Mongo, or whatever his name was, would stop or reverse directions and I would follow suit. Suddenly he froze on one side of the table while I did the same on the other. Then, moving like a cobra, he stretched across the table and grabbed my cue. Now he and I both were holding it and I knew one flip of his wrist would disassemble my prize possession permanently. Had he grabbed one of my arms I might have put up a struggle or even chanced a dislocated shoulder . . . but risking an original Billy Stroud Joss cue over a pool game is like hitting someone with a Stradivarius because they didn't like the concert. So I, for lack of better words, groveled my ass off. I told him how sorry I was for smart mouthing him and asked him to please not break my cue or beat me up. I used the same sad eyes I had developed from apologizing to my wife for my worst mistakes and it worked. He released my cue and walked back to his seat as if nothing had happened. An hour or so later Jack came back in and sat next to him. I saw them talking, but it was later that I learned the big guy told Jack "I tried to take care of him like you said, but the little bastard talked his way out of it."

THOUGHTS OF A POOL WIDOW

Beverly, my beloved wife and pool widow, at the time, asked me if she could contribute her thoughts about the lifestyle we led. I never told her "no" in our marriage and I'm not about to start now. Be kind, Bev.

Dear Alfie,

Thank you for the opportunity to write some of my memories of our seven years together. Thank you for plunging me mentally, head-over-heels back to those golden days of many years ago. I think of it as:

"The Other Side of the Road – The other side of the story."

This 60's "good girl" learned to play pool while attending UCLA. In my dormitory we had a couple of bar-sized tables and, the upscale poolroom in town even had a dress code. I loved the game!

I quit school after 1 year to become a stewardess and see the world. At that time, the two most glamorous jobs for young women were modeling or being an airline stewardess. I was too short to model so the second airplane ride I had ever taken carried me to Dallas, Texas, and American Airlines Stewardess School.

I walked into the Cotton Bowling Palace that warm, Dallas night, in high heels, intending to play eight ball by myself. (I played both stripes and solids and didn't care which side won). That night the road of my life took a sharp turn to the right.

Honestly, I really only wanted to practice pool that night, but first there was that kid (Alfie) bothering me and then he insisted that I meet Minnesota Fats. Of course, I'd seen *The Hustler* and I was enchanted by Fat's non-stop banter and trick pool shots. I thought Alfie was about 18, but I was intrigued and somewhat trusting, after Fat's praise of him and his talent. The next day, Alfie and I had one of the longest and most fun dates in history and then at the end of the evening, Alfie kissed me and as they say in the pool world "That was all she wrote." Seven years and one incredible son later I decided to end the marriage. It was time for Christopher David Taylor to start public school and I was very clear that he was not going to live the pillar-to-post, gypsy lifestyle that was the fate of other pool hustlers' children.

But I've never had one moment of regret associated with those golden and exciting years. Alfie taught me how to have fun; he constantly pushed me beyond the comfort zone of my middle-class, city-girl upbringing; and because of him I learned to "be here now." I completely trusted Alfie with my heart, my future, and our son.

I'm the one that proposed marriage to him. I was a "good girl" and we were sleeping together and that's what you did–right? I flew my mother to Dallas with the first, free flight I'd earned from American and when Alfie and I took her back to the airport for her return to Los Angeles we told her of our plans. Bless her heart. She seemed to take it well but told me later that she boarded her plane, headed for the restroom and threw up!

I was a fast learner and soon after we were married in Las Vegas without friends or family, I accepted:

1. That when Alfie went out to play pool I never knew when he'd return, just that he would return and he'd be OK.

2. Alfie was a consummate flirt and any jealousy on my part would be a waste of time and self-destructive.

3. Alfie was not a gambler, he was a pool hustler. And there's a big difference. He might not get to play, but he almost never lost when he did play.

I think of our time together in three parts: The two years before Chris was born; the middle years; and the motor home years. What a ride!

I started out as that pool hustler's wife who has a good job and earns "the nut" (banking was my specialty) but I quickly learned the disfunctionality of a 9-5 wife and a husband who often came in at 3 or 4 am and wanted some lovin'. I quit my job in L.A., we moved to Tucson, and I said, "I'll work when you're working."

Alfie's first job in Tucson was at a TV station and didn't last long, but was a foot into the straight world that he had long avoided. He was a cameraman until he accidentally tipped over an expensive camera. He was a producer aka go-fer, and he was "Prisoner Alfie", riding his unicycle to the delight of the children attending the local, live TV show for preschoolers. He switched from TV producer to copywriter at his brother Tippy's advertising agency. Even then his excellent writing skills were evident. It's not easy making ads funny and entertaining for hardware items like rakes and shovels, but Alfie did!

However, there was always time for pool hustling. In fact, the Friday night that I called the poolroom to tell Alfie it was time for our son to be born, he was just minutes from heading down to Nogales, Tucson's nearby Mexican border town with a couple of buddies. Remember, I'd already decided to never be jealous so I'm sure that even though I was nine-months pregnant, Alfie was planning to drive the 60 minutes south to hustle pool–not senoritas.

Those next, middle years were a jumble of Alfie being an "ad man" (and pool hustler); a "rag man" (and pool hustler); and a jewelry store owner (and pool hustler). I thrived in my role as Alfie's wife and Chris's mother, and pool, to me, was just Alfie's way to bring in more money. We never had one fight in all of those years and we made love every night that Alfie was in town.

About the time that we were closing down the Houston jewelry store we stepped into Tippy's new, little RV and I think we both fell in love with the concept. We closed the store and paid cash for an 8' x 24' Sightseer motor home and became high-toned gypsies for our last couple of years together. The only thing I can say about those years is that you would have to have been there! RVs were fairly new at the time and, armed with our KOA Campground directory, we traversed the south and southeast for two, glorious years. Gasoline was 25 cents a gallon and if we couldn't find a park or campground at the end of the day we'd just crash in a Kmart parking lot.

Alfie remembers pool scores and suckers, guns and jails. I remember waking up each morning with a new backyard. I remember teaching my 4-year-old son how to read using *Dr. Seuss' Cat in the Hat*; I remember taking up photography and developing film in our 5'x 5' bathroom. I remember small-town libraries, cafeterias, and Woolworth dime stores. I remember parks and tennis courts and outdoor adventures. I remember meeting new people daily and making life-long friends. After a few hours in any new town Alfie (always the people-magnet) would have three new friends and a pot dealer. What an amazing life we led!

I learned to "live in the moment" because when Alfie rode away on his bicycle in some little Tennessee town, I had no idea when we would see him again; but I was always certain that he'd return uninjured and with the money. Speaking of the money, I insisted from the very first trip that Alfie give me 10% of his earnings "off the top" and he always did. Little did I know that we were saving for a two-month "hippie trip" through Europe. That trip was the culmination of our travels and, unfortunately, the beginning of the end of our marriage.

The trip was Alfie's idea and it scared me. I tried to get my mother and stepfather to watch Chris (then 5-years-old) while we traveled, but the answer was "No." (Good answer, Mom). During that two-month trek there were too many adventures to recount in this small space, but here are a few highlights:

Chris walking 12 miles (pedometer) the day we arrived with his little

Boy Scout backpack filled with his few toys and books. We spent our first night in the Cologne, Germany, train station sleeping on a wooden bench.

Chris celebrating his 6th birthday in Amsterdam while we stayed in a small hotel on a canal in the middle of the red light district. I wonder what my little angel thought about all those scantily dressed ladies in their little storefront windows with the curtains. When they had a customer, they would just close the curtains.

Chris learning to play chess in the little fishing village of Agia Galini on Crete using a huge, outdoor chessboard and chess pieces that were taller than he was.

I remember Alfie standing behind a stone podium in an underground chamber of the Temple of Kenosis and being certain that he had stood in that exact spot before. I believed him.

And I remember Alfie leaving Istanbul that morning with the new owners of our VW van. He was going to return that evening after getting the vehicle stamp off of his passport at the border. He was still gone three days later! Chris and I explored the city with Chris wearing his signature felt top hat (a bazaar purchase). But mostly I remember staring down at the teeming street below continually searching for that curly head of dark-brown hair. Alfie finally did return unharmed, as usual, but not with the van money because it was in the boots I was wearing.

It was the trip of a lifetime, but I think a little door in my heart closed because of it. I finally realized that Alfie was not going to follow in his "good" brother's footsteps and have a lucrative career in advertising. We were not going to have the big house in Skyline Country Club with a live-in housekeeper. Alfie was a hustler, yes, but even bigger than that was his gypsy soul.

We got divorced in Tucson after our one and only, but really big, fight, and I have told many friends that if Alfie had stayed around and tried to win me back, he probably would have succeeded. I never stopped loving him, just his lifestyle. But almost too soon, a new love entered his heart, one that I had no chance of competing with anyway—Morocco!

NOT TO ME, BUT THROUGH ME

Call it timing, call it luck, or call it faith, but something put me on just the right street corner, at just the right moment, in a city they call The Big Apple.

Manhattan, New York City, the 1980s.

I was playing tourist in New York on my way to Morocco, after giving a successful Moroccan rug show to Calvin Klein and a couple of his designers (name dropper that I am). My pockets were as fat as my duffle bags, which no longer contained my rugs, but were now stuffed with jeans that Mr. Klein graciously gave me to take to the tribal people where the rugs were woven. By this time in my life, Morocco had become my livelihood as well as my passion, and pool was an afterthought. The incredible textiles I found in Morocco took me on a thirty-year "magic carpet ride" from villages in the Atlas Mountains to museum exhibitions around the country, and to my final exhibition at the United Nations, in 1994. But that's another life, and maybe another book.

Spring in New York is the perfect time for walking through Central Park. The 840 acre recreation area is home to more than two hundred species of birds. Flowers bloom in meticulously manicured gardens and blossoms adorn the trees. The smell of magnolias drifts through the air and the purplish hue of the eastern redbud trees show you colors rarely found in nature. Little kids run through pools and play in fountains, oblivious of their soaked clothing or peeved parents. Trikes and Big Wheels skid by in every direction, turning screams, squeals, and laughter into one unpleasant noise. Groups of moms and nannies, pushing colorful strollers and blankets, coo over each others' wards, with real and feigned sincerity. Many carry baby bottles or cans of baby food, which they spoon into gaping mouths, intermittently, for both sustenance and pacification. Each mommy or mommy substitute carries some sort of wiping apparatus in one hand or the other. Some have towels tucked into their clothing or knotted through the handles on the diaper bags. Blue, pink, and multi-colored pacifiers make their rounds from mouths to ground and back to mouth, after receiving a slight brush against an apron, or a quick blow from nanny's lips; a feat usually accomplished without her skipping a word, lest she lose her spot in the conversation. Few organizations meet as frequently or as happily as the baby care club in Central Park.

Dogs of every size and breed, all leashed, greet each other in a manner incomprehensible to most humans, yet the same humans hold still until the last whiff. Businessmen on their lunch breaks, unable to separate themselves from their work, check e-mails and scour the Web with one hand while eating their sandwich with the other. Designated areas are set aside for chess games, where intense players slap the time clocks while the armchair generals walk from table to table, murmuring their ideas for the best next moves. Benches filled mostly with older or better dressed people line the walkways. Musicians, hoping for donations, play beside cups or open guitar cases and couples fawn over each other like they're alone. Nobody bothers the street person sleeping under newspapers until he feels the "move along" tap on his shoe from the park patrol. People of lesser means walk around, openly selling ten dollar bags of pot as if it were legal. The opportunity for strangers to share simple pleasures on common ground is what Central Park gives to New Yorkers, and it's been that way for one hundred and fifty years.

    I left the park this day and was standing on the corner of a busy avenue close by. On the sidewalk, about a foot off the curb was a tree in a big concrete planter. A group of people, me included, was waiting for the light to change. No one seemed to be paying any attention to a woman who was standing on the curb, between the planter and the street, precariously close to the traffic. I watched her, unable to understand her recklessness. I'm a small town boy in a big city so I don't question much about the way things work, but down the street to our left I saw a big flatbed truck barreling toward the light, obviously intent on making it through before it changed. The wooden bed of the truck extended out a couple of feet and the truck's wheels were close to the curb. It was apparent the driver either didn't see the woman standing by the curb or didn't realize how far over he was, and she didn't even look in his direction. She seemed totally unaware of him approaching and it was obvious that, unless the driver made a sharp swerve, the bed of the truck was going to hit her square on. The other people waiting to cross were standing off to the left and didn't notice. I was on the back side of the planter watching this woman, and it looked like she was about to be knocked flat. I felt my body first freeze for a second then jump to life. It's not surprising the first words people tend to utter in crisis situations are, "Oh God!," "Oh no!" or "Oh shit!" I heard myself say one (not sure which) as I reached under the tree limbs with both hands and, without nary a sign of gentleness, grabbed the back of the woman's collar and pulled her body back flat on top of the planter, under the tree. The truck whizzed by with the edge of the bed flying over her prone body. The street corner crowd jumped in unison and I heard a few congratulatory remarks. Then, as is typical of New Yorkers, everyone went on their way as if nothing had happened.

The woman righted herself and turned around to me. Her eyes were solid white like nothing I've seen outside the movies. Chills mingled with pride. This woman, who fate allowed to still be part of our world, didn't see the truck because she couldn't see anything. She straightened herself up, smiled, and said, "Thank you. I'll take all the help I can get," and with cane in hand, she walked across the street.

Little did the woman know her life, or injuries, were not saved by me. I was merely a tool for something so divine it's unexplainable, even as hard as I'm trying.

PLAIN CHEESE, WITH AN ANGEL, PLEASE

Des Moines, Iowa, mid 1990s

"It's a pizza parlor, for crying out loud. Get that gun out of my face, punk, or I'll shove it . . ."

I could think all of that but couldn't say it. As a matter of fact, I couldn't say anything, nor could I move to look up at the rifle barrel that was pointing directly at me, less than fifteen feet away. It was close enough that I could tell it was a smaller caliber gun, but smaller than what–it's a gun. My billed cap hid my eyes from the eyes of the robber, but I could roll them up enough, without lifting my head, to see him without him knowing I could. The weapon was held straight out with one black gloved hand and I could see the bottom of a black ski mask over what was clearly a black man's face. It was time for some Sherlock Holmes caliber deduction; there's no ski lift within hundreds of miles, it was mid-August and he has no skis and one makeshift ski pole. My conclusion was this guy is not here to downhill.

The bandit's left arm was straight out, holding open one of double swinging doors that led to the kitchen. Inside the kitchen, beside the oven, there were three employees lying face down with their hands on their heads. The guy then moved his left foot to hold the door open, never moving his rifle off of me, but now holding it steadier, with two hands, thus lessening the prospect of an accidental discharge. Things are finally starting to go my way.

I was finishing up some paperwork at the time these visions of loveliness crept into my view. I froze my head and kept writing as if I wasn't aware of what was happening. It had nothing to do with me; it was just a straight up, run of the mill, pizza parlor stick up, by a crook who apparently didn't even own a hand gun. Still, when someone is pointing a gun at you, you never know. The pizza parlor was the only place we could find open late and I was just lucky enough to be there, even though I'm not even a big fan of pizza. It reminds me too much of my poorer days. The guy motioned with his gun to the man in the booth in front of me, who was the only other customer in the place, directing him to get into the kitchen. But just as I hoped (and I'm sure a prayer was in there, as well), he thought I didn't notice him because my head never tilted up a fraction of an inch and my pen never stopped writing. Other than the contrived movement of my right hand, I was holding dead still—a bad choice of words but an easy feat when you're scared stiff.

It was obvious the man wanted the loot without having to shoot. My kind of robber, for certain. He was dealing with more factors (and people) than he wanted; consequently, he was happy to exclude one more, yours truly. Even though he and I couldn't see each other's eyes, we saw eye-to-eye on that one.

Action had been good at McCoy's pool room this day. The poor fool had no idea how much cash I had in my pocket or how I would have given it up with a mere suggestion. I thought, isn't this a fine kettle of fish? I made it through hundreds of tough pool rooms and bars for twenty years, unscathed. How humiliating it would be to go down in a cheesy little pizza parlor up here in Niceville, U.S.A. before my book is finished. Technically, I was out of pool hustling by this time and was importing Oriental rugs, but I still picked up extra cash along the way around the pool halls, more for fun than necessity.

Des Moines was my best city for rug business, due to one particular interior designer. For years she and I sold Moroccan rugs to her clients, who consisted of many of the city's most prominent citizens. These people were extremely well traveled and they appreciated ethnic art, so I made frequent trips to Des Moines.

Donny "The Midwest Sleeper" McCoy, who owned the local pool room, was, just as his name implied, a quiet, unassuming Midwestern gentleman who could shoot the spots off the balls. Donny and I had a friendship from years earlier when he traveled the road with my brother. Jack said Donny could do all the things the other champions could do, except that he could do them with less effort. The thing Donny had going against him, as far as beating other champions, was his calm, easy going nature, so typical of Midwesterners. To prevail at that level of competition requires, as they say, "the eye of the tiger."

Donny knew more about my game than any of his customers, but he still let me tax them on a regular basis. He got a kick out of the moves I put on them and he knew I was just having a good time fooling everybody. I befriended a local named Dean Phipps, who steered me around and had a piece of my action. I was doing so much rug business in Des Moines at the time that the few bucks I squeezed out of the locals didn't mean much to me, except for the fun of doing it. None of my victims suffered as much as they were entertained.

"Highway" Paul Baker was another Des Moines resident who had a previous road career, and was a friend who knew how I played, but kept quiet about it. Paul and I had made money together in California in the 60s. He also got a kick out of the way I worked the locals. Paul was the city's other good player.

To the pool players around McCoy's, I wasn't considered a threat simply because they knew I was a guy who worked for a living and came to town a couple of times a year on business. Having a natural entre to be there allowed me to beat them without mercy for years. Then one day, when I was hammering someone on the table in front of the bleachers where everybody sat and kibitzed, someone asked, in a louder than necessary voice, "Listen guys, Alfie Taylor has been gambling in this pool room for years. Has anyone ever seen him lose, even once?" A pregnant pause, a little mumbling and laughing, no sweat, no threat, guards went up and no more easy action in Des Moines. Alas, all good things must end, almost

Still, I would stop and visit Donny and the gang when I was in Des Moines, as I had done earlier this evening. A stranger happened in looking for action and the locals let me have him, and I took him off pretty good. By this time I was no longer perceived as a rug selling, money flashing, potential sucker (who had emptied them out by "luck" for years). I was the mystery guy they quit messing with, who had a game they couldn't figure out. And I was their friend.

But I was not the friend of whomever this was pointing his squirrel gun at me and I was desperately hoping to avoid an introduction. The man from the next booth moved into the kitchen, as directed by the rifle, still without a spoken word from anyone. The ski bum, of a different sort, followed behind him into the kitchen and the door swung shut. Ahhh! Alone at last.

Fight or flight? Nah! "Fight" wasn't even a contestant. The booth I was sitting in was on the back side of a partition that was connected to the front wall. The exit end was by the cash register and in front of the kitchen double doors, each door with the traditional "don't bump the waiter" window. My only exit from the situation, short of fainting, took me right by those door windows. I would have to round the partition at full speed for a straight shot to the front door, all of which could be seen through the kitchen windows should the robber look up. I hoped there was no cheese on the floor at the turn. One more time I found myself with no option except to run towards the fire instead of away. Drats!

I had a young man working for me at the time, named Ken Ben, who was an aspiring musician-singer with a lot of talent. I previously had purchased five or six pieces of John Deere lawn mowing equipment at the factory in Des Moines and taken him and his band to Maui for a month of nighttime concerts and daytime lawn mowing. We opened a business called Discount Lawn Services, where we would answer the phone with "D.L.S.– Mower for less." But, in fact, we could not mow for less than the Filipinos, nor could we squat for hours on end, to garden, the way they could. This was when I found out musicians don't like mowing lawns or working in general, but on stage, Ken and his group could set the girls on fire.

Ken had gone to sit in the van and write music after we finished our pizza, while I stayed inside. He was very tall, young, and no doubt would have made a faster runner, so I would have gladly traded our temporary offices. I remember clutching my papers in my right hand and hauling ass directly toward the kitchen door windows and feeling the buzz that was going through me. As I rounded the partition and headed toward the front door, I realized my earlier feeling was only mild tension compared to what I felt running and not being able to see the kitchen windows behind me. Those little crawly things that can go up the back of your neck were doing the boogie-woogie on mine. When I blasted through the front door into the parking lot and into 100% safety, I felt elated. What had been a serious situation only moments ago was now a fun, high-stepping, parking lot dance. Not only was I still a member of the un-dead, I had captured the gold in "check walking."

I jumped into the van and quickly filled Ken in on my dinner show while we drove to a service station across the street and called the police. I looked down at what I had written while the gun was pointed at me. It was no more than a row of up and down lines, like a heart monitor, apropos. The next day we returned to the pizza parlor for the outcome of the drama and to pay for our meal. The same guy who had been kissing the linoleum the night before was on duty. He thanked me for calling the cops and, naturally, comped our check, but laughed and added, "That was no big deal last night. That shit happens to us all the time."

Whoa! And I thought hustling pool was rough.

MY ANGEL DRIVES A SEMI

March, 2009

Fast forward 35 or so years after my pool hustling era, to the present day (yesterday, to be specific). With my pool career comfortably behind me and my thumbs intact, I find myself in the working world, living a more placid existence. In the Oriental rug business, it isn't often that you sell someone a rug and then have to run out the door, guns a blazing. Consequently, my guardian angel has more time off. But close calls are not limited to the underworld. Last night, while driving a box truck down Interstate 40 outside Gallup, New Mexico, I hit an unbelievable, unseasonal snowstorm that forced me, along with everyone else except for a few big rig drivers, off the road for hours. We ran our heaters and watched the snow plows do their thing.

When I saw the storm let up a little, I rejoined the stream of travelers and headed into a wall of slop. My truck was new and strong so I had no more to worry about than any of my fellow travelers, or so I thought. A touch of irony to the story is that the friends I was going to visit in Santa Fe were named Snow.

I'll pause here and digress to a night when I made a vow never to drive in snow again.

Urich, Missouri, 2006, Interstate 7, the kiss of life.

I was driving from Branson, Missouri, to Kansas City in my Jeep Wrangler in a snowstorm. Fully aware that my vehicle was short wheel based, with poor street traction, I kept my speed to around 20 to 30 mph. I had called home and my wife, Judi, said the weather report indicated the storm had passed and that the highway was clear from Clinton on in to Kansas City. I hadn't wanted to drive home at night in the storm but my little dog, Sadie, was on her last legs and we thought she might not make it another day. It meant turning a three hour drive into five or six hours. I passed Clinton and sure enough, there wasn't a sign of the white stuff, so I kicked it up to sixty, then seventy, for what should have been my last hour's drive.

Passing a small town called Urich, where my sister-in-law lives, I came over an overpass and threw a kiss to her at the off ramp, as my wife and I traditionally did when we made this trip. I didn't see the black ice in front of me and I don't remember flipping over or how or why it happened. All I remember is my vehicle was sliding on the driver's side, over the grassy area between the Interstate lanes real fast. My Jeep had a chrome roof rack and foot step bar, so lying on its side it had become a sled, and one that was now spinning in circles and sliding into who knows where. The lights had gone out leaving me in the dark except for approaching car lights. All I could hear was a whooshing sound from my sliding vehicle and the thumping from the left side of my head bumping along inside the car's canvas top. I remember thinking that I was going to ride this to a stop and would escape unharmed when suddenly I saw a guard rail, not the side of the rail, but the rounded end, and it was coming directly at me. In instances like this, I believe a person's mind speeds up enough to make the event slow down because I remember watching it coming at me for what seemed the longest time and thinking, Oh no! This is really going to hurt!

As the approaching piece of metal grew larger, my confidence about surviving grew smaller. In the last instant, perfect timing from my "perfect companion" caused the big chrome front bumper that extended over the top of my hood, to reach out like a big hand, grab the thirty foot guard rail, rip it off its mounts, and hurl it into the middle of the highway, just before it smashed through my windshield. I know the size of the rail because it was listed on the two thousand dollar invoice I later received from the state of Missouri. The rail did, however, stop me in the middle lane of the freeway, facing the opposite direction, with my Jeep still on its side.

So there I was, dazed and lying on the driver's side, with my seat belt pulled so tightly from my own weight that I was having trouble getting it loose. It was too dark outside to see much, but I could tell cars had pulled over and I heard people yelling, "Run, stop the traffic," "See if he's all right," "Get him out of there," and so on. I squirmed my way into getting the belt loose and crawled out the window. By this time, enough trucks had stopped to block both lanes of the highway, thus ending the possibility of some semi turning me into a hockey puck.

Emergencies invariably bring out the best in people. Everyone was trying to help, asking me if I was OK, saying, "Hold on to me," asking if I was alone in the vehicle, things like that. Someone put a coat around me and a scarf around my neck that smelled of nice perfume. Somebody else put a bottle of water in my hand. A young man offered me use of his cell phone, then asked if he could dial a number for me and he called my home. I remember someone saying we would have to wait for a wrecker to drag my vehicle out of the way, then a woman saying, "No we don't. Come on you bunch of pussies, lift this thing up." Four or five people latched on to the chrome foot rail and in an instant the little Jeep was upright and pushed to the shoulder of the road. My beautiful little, fully styled out car toy was, for lack of a more descriptive word, smushed.

When the policemen arrived and inspected the accident and vehicle for booze or whatever, one of them walked over to me, saw I didn't have a scratch and asked, "Do you believe in God?" Without waiting for an answer, he added, "You should. I don't see how anyone could have gotten out of that thing alive."

Believe in Him? I thought, are you kiddin'? His rep was in there with me.

When the wrecker arrived, the driver started the Jeep's engine and said, "It's runnin' and the wheels still move. I think we can kick the windshield out if you want to drive it to the off ramp and save yourself fifty dollars on the tow."

I remember declining, telling him I had had "quite enough Jeeping for the evening." That's when I decided I also had had enough of snow and vowed never to drive in it again.

Back to I-40 and my present dilemma: So here we are, this long line of 60 mph slush slingers and me breaking the "never drive in snow" vow that I made in Missouri. A short time into the mess, without warning, my wiper fluid ran dry. Almost instantly, I heard a frightening noise from my wiper blades crunching over a brown haze. Even at their fastest speed they simply were not cutting it. The haze got thicker by the moment and my mind was racing for a way out. Within seconds, my windshield turned completely brown except for a one or two-inch space at the bottom. With my chin on the dashboard and cars and trucks whizzing down the dark highway beside, in front, and back of me, I knew I was only seconds away from complete blindness and a certain smash up. All I thought about was my small Lhasa Apso, Dandi, who was on my lap and might die with me tonight. I'm paid for a dozen times over, but she's a baby. My mind jumped to how I had initially left her with a friend, at home in Carefree, before making this trip, only to change my mind and pick her back up at the last moment. Oh! Why?!

Seconds later the bottom of my windshield turned brown and the truck tail lights in front of me disappeared completely. I was driving completely blind. The sound of the other vehicles throwing snow was deafening. In all my pool hustling mishaps I had never felt this kind of fear or helplessness. I-40 had redefined "terror" in my mind.

A scream to God is no more than a loud prayer and, without even realizing it, I screamed, "Oh God! Show me an off ramp," which at this late time would not have done me any good anyway, and in the middle of the New Mexico desert they were practically non-existent.

Trying to stop in my tracks would surely get me smashed from behind. I was out of ideas. The last word barely cleared my throat when I heard an explosion that sounded like a bomb hitting the truck. I jumped straight up. I never heard a louder or more welcome noise. A huge chunk of ice had slid off the trailer of a passing semi and hit flat against my windshield at full force. In a fraction of a second there wasn't a sign of dirt in my view. My windshield looked like I just left a service station, and I was able to drop back from the spray, stop shaking, and begin my prayer of thanks for this icy hand of God. I remember taking in multiple intakes of air before exhaling, the way a child does while sobbing, and I felt every hair on my body stand straight up as if receiving the message, "No off ramp available. Will this do, Alfie?"

It most certainly will, my faithful companion. Welcome back.

I STEPPED OUT TO LOOK UP

Baton Rouge, Louisiana, late 1970s

When I looked over at the other bed in the room and saw the best nine-ball player in the world, I should have felt a sense of pride or power. Here I was, a shortstop pool hustler, traveling with Buddy "The Rifleman" Hall. No one could beat him, at least not playing even. Here was a man who dominated the pool world for more than twenty years, playing nine-ball like nobody had played before, whether it was in tournament play or money games. But this trip Buddy hadn't been able to get any games playing even; to the contrary, he had to give out enormous handicaps and he had been losing. I wasn't getting any action and between the two of us we had maybe four or five hundred dollars.

I remember leaving Shreveport with him a week or so earlier. We stopped by to see Eddie Taylor before we left, who said he hoped we made some money, but mainly "to be careful and stay safe." Eddie said Buddy was the best nine-ball player he had ever seen. He played such close position with just the right angles, that the balls he pocketed each so very carefully, didn't even roll in hard enough to hit the backs of the pockets. He hit almost every ball the same speed and each one dropped slowly over the edge; he could do it without faltering for hours on end. Once, in Shreveport, Buddy practiced me out of a hundred dollars at five dollars a game, spotting me the six ball, playing nine-ball. At that time I was hardcore road hustling, playing pretty well, and the six is a tremendous handicap, but Mr. Hall never missed one ball in two hours. He paralyzed my arm and my heart. Mine was like a hundred dollar admission to witness pool perfection up close.

Maybe I should have been feeling proud or powerful that morning in Baton Rouge, but I didn't. I felt discouraged and empty. Not so with Buddy; he couldn't have been a nicer guy to roam with. His Kentucky upbringing produced a pretty laid back man. My glum was more about my life. This was where my twenty years of dealing out small doses of misery in pool rooms around the country had landed me: out of money, out of sync with the world, and running out of time to change. The worst part of the "no future" life is you can't see it happening while it's happening.

It was after one o'clock when I got up and walked outside where I was immediately drenched by the muggy Louisiana summer humidity. I looked around at the cheesy, Indian-owned motel with its trashy parking lot full of trashy cars. It was just another of hundreds like it that had served as my home for a couple of decades. Then I looked at the car we were running around in, with our clothes hanging in the back window and magazines scattered on the back window shelf. I thought about the Waffle House breakfast, with their butter-soaked everything, which we would be facing when Buddy finally woke up, and how we'd have to find some action soon, before we were broke. Depression paid me a visit as I sat on a curb with my eyes as wet as my shirt and swore, right then, that my life as a pool hustler was over. Something shifted within me and I knew that no matter what I had to hustle to feed myself, it was no longer going to be pool. Later, when Buddy woke up, I asked him to take me to the bus station so I could get to Houston, and that was the end of Bicycle Willie . . . forever.

The Plaza Hotel, 1995.

As the receiving line passed in front of King Hassan II of Morocco, he shook hands with a nod or a smile and passed his guests on to meet the Princesses standing next to him. Everywhere I looked there were serious looking security men in business suits, some American, some Moroccan, all sporting earphones. The FBI had interviewed or given an extended hello to each of the guests as they entered the ballroom, which was understandable considering King Hassan was one of the most important statesmen in the world. He was the primary communicator among the Arab nations and maintained friendly dialogue with Israel as well. The treaty of friendship between his country and the U. S. is America's longest unbroken treaty and extends back to 1786, when President George Washington appealed to and received military assistance from Morocco. In short, King Hassan was the real deal.

The Americans were shaking his hand and the Moroccans were kissing it or shaking it, then kissing their own hand. Using a joy buzzer on him would probably stir things up, but not in a good way. The guest list was long so people were rushed quickly through the receiving line. I looked ahead into the dining area at the gold plate holders and special eating utensils that had been brought in from the palace in Rabat for the dinner. The wait staff was standing, almost at attention, in a row behind the far tables, as if waiting for an inspection or a whistle to blow. Their white outfits gleamed. Five or six very black-skinned Moroccans, wearing traditional Moroccan djellabas and red Fez hats, were off to the side. I knew these people to be his Majesty's personal security from having seen them around the palace in Rabat. They were comprised of people from the south of Morocco, from one tribe or family, who had been guarding the royal family of Morocco for much of the Alaouite dynasty's four-hundred year reign.

Their loyalty to the throne was impenetrable. Flowers and crystal decorated every table and a copy of my book *A Treasure Hunter's Guide to Morocco*, was placed at each setting. The book's gold stamped glossy covers were gleaming and, best of all, my name was right there on the cover. Someone once said, "If you want to look good, write a book about yourself." With my treasure hunter's guide, I had done just that. The book shows what a warm and gracious country Morocco is for tourists and what a treasure trove of shopping awaits you there.

The Moroccan Ambassador asked me to step out of the line and said that His Majesty would talk to me after the line had passed. I had met the king briefly at a party for him in Washington, D. C., a couple of nights before. I was invited to his party so that I might bring his guests copies of the book I had written to honor the thirtieth anniversary of his ascension to the throne. I was one of many in the receiving line in D. C. and the king didn't know me as the author, so we only shook hands and said hello.

I flew home to Aspen after the Washington party only to receive a call the next morning from the Ambassador saying that His Majesty had read my book and liked it very much. The king was also pleased with what I had contributed to his party in Washington and asked if I would come to New York and attend his party at the Plaza Hotel the following night with my books. It's not good to say no to a king, especially one from a country where I have a home and one I might be addressing shortly. So I FedEx'd four hundred copies of my book and hopped on a plane to New York and the Plaza Hotel. Hang the expense. I'm going to a royal party at the Plaza.

My first stop in the Big Apple was the lobby bathroom of the Plaza, fresh off the plane, changing from my old jeans into a suit, for my upcoming audience. No matter how brief our meeting might be, in my mind it would be an audience. My tie had been pre-knotted, just right, at home, and my suit survived in my carry on quite nicely, so I walked out of the bathroom looking like I might actually be a guest in the hotel. Little did they know I was only a guest of their men's room.

The Ambassador introduced me to His Majesty as "the author of the book." King Hassan took my hand and thanked me for being "such a good friend to my country." Then he said I would always be welcome in Morocco. I wasn't certain how long I was supposed to hold the handshake but he seemed in no hurry and there was no way I was going to let go first. I thought about asking him about his golf game but held back, thinking he might ask me if I played. I don't, but I had worked on a couple of his tournaments in Rabat, as a photographer and guide for the golfers and foreign press, so I knew he loved the game. (Payne Stewart won the tournament both years I attended.) Instead, I hung onto each word he had to say, thrilled to be in the presence of royalty. Maybe he plays pool I thought to myself; nothing serious, just a little thousand dollar nine-ball. He was, after all, one of the world's ten richest men.

The ambassador told the king, "Your Majesty, Mr. Taylor's passport may be American but his heart is Moroccan." The king smiled.

For one brief minute my mind jumped from the Plaza, back twenty-odd years, to a moment outside a motel in Baton Rouge; the moment when I looked up or my angel looked down and the direction of my life changed dramatically. It was a defining moment, to say the least. Then I asked myself, had all that really happened? That pool thing?

GLOSSARY

action: To be "in action" is to be involved in a bet or wager of some sort. "Big action" indicates that the gambling is for high stakes. An "action joint" is a place where gambling is common. "There's no action in this dump, let's hit the road."

backer: A person who provides financial backing or support for a pool player. He usually pays all expenses and puts up the money for matches in return for a percentage of the winnings. The backer commonly takes 50% of the net winnings, giving the player the other 50%, but just about any method of splitting the winnings may be negotiated. See also stakehorse.

bite artist: A person who frequently asks for a loan, usually with little or no intention of repaying the loan. "Watch out, Fred just came in and you know he's the world's worst bite artist."

dog: A domesticated form of the wolf member of the Canidae family of the order Carnivora. Whoops! Wrong dog! In the pool world, to "dog" a shot is to miss the shot because of nerves or anxiety. Minnesota Fats might have said, "I never dogged a ball in my life!"

dumping: Intentionally losing a game or match so that the two players end up dividing up a backer's money. A player known for this might be called a "dump artist." "Don't bet on that match. Sam is known for dumping his backers."

English: To put spin on the ball.

fun players: These are players who play the game strictly for enjoyment and who do not gamble on the game. Fun players are usually held in low regard by those who gamble on the game.

heads up: To play "heads up" is to play even, with no handicap involved. "He asked me for the seven ball because he knows he can't beat me heads up."

jarring: To drug your opponent in some manner such as by slipping a drug into his drink. "The only reason I lost that match was that I got jarred."

lemon: To "lay down a lemon" is to intentionally exhibit less than ones true level of skill or ability in order to fool a prospective opponent. "That guy doesn't look like he can play a lick, but he might be on the lemon."

lock or mortal lock: A game or proposition that cannot be lost. A player may have a "lock" because of the poor skill level of his opponent, because of an insurmountable handicap, or because of other factors. "I'm telling you, there's no way I lose to Kenny. I've got a moral lock!"

locksmith: A person who is known for playing only when they have a lock or certainty of winning. "Man, that Andy will never match up unless he has the nuts, he's a real locksmith."

match up: To "match up" is to negotiate the terms of a match, often with some form of handicap involved. As two players try to negotiate a game, they are said to be in the process of matching up. "I offered him the called 8, but he just didn't want to match up with me."

mooch: A person who is always trying to borrow money or put the bite on someone.

nit: A person who refuses to gamble for high stakes or who refuses to gamble unless they have a sure win. They'll squeeze a dollar until George's eyes pop out of the paper. "He's such a nit he wouldn't bet a nickel that water's wet." (But on the other hand, a shrewd road player once said, "If they call you a nit, you must be doing something right.")

proposition bet: A bet made on an outcome or proposition. For example, I might bet you that I can do 100 pushups or that I can throw a golf ball 100 yards through the air. Also included would be bets such as which of two birds will fly away first or whether the next phone call will be a male or female. Without a doubt, the greatest proposition bettor of all time was Titanic Thompson and many of his famous proposition bets have been recounted in books and articles.

railbird: A spectator watching a money game. Also referred to as a sweater.

score: To "score" is to win a bet or come out ahead in a gambling session. "He took off a good score when he played Tommy."

shortstop: A strong player who can only be beaten by a top player or strong road player. A shortstop would be expected to beat any fun player or recreational player.

side bet: Usually a bet between one of the players (or his backer) and one or more of the railbirds or sweators. "I was only playing for $20 a game, but I had a $100 side bet with one of the railbirds."

stakehorse: A person who provides financial backing or support for a pool player. He usually pays all expenses and puts up the money for matches in return for a percentage of the winnings. The backer commonly takes 50% of the net winnings, giving the player the other 50%, but just about any method of splitting the winnings may be negotiated. "OK, I'll play you heads up nine-ball, race to 10, for $1,000. Just let me get the OK from my backer." See also backer.

stalling: Playing below your true skill level in order to keep your opponent in the game or to induce him to raise the bet. This may involve occasionally losing a game on purpose or simply missing shots or position on purpose. See also lemon.

sweator: A person watching a money game. Such a person might be said to be "sweating the action." See also railbird.

Grady "The Professor" Mathews, a good player and sly as a fox

THE PLAYERS AND CHARACTERS, YESTERDAY AND TODAY

Rudolph Walter "Minnesota Fats" Wanderone

Luther "Wimpy" Lassiter and Eddie "The Knoxville Bear" Taylor
1967 Las Vegas Stardust Open champions

Bill "Weenie Beanie" Staton, the class of the sport.

The undefeatable Eddie Taylor. At nineteen, he would play anyone in the world bank pool, one-pocket or one shot shootout nine ball.

SIMPLY THE BEST

Billiard Congress of America Hall of Fame Champions
Allison Fisher and Eddie Taylor.

13 times World Straight Pool Champion Willie Mosconi.
Record high run – 526 balls

"Cowboy" Jimmy Moore, Alf Taylor, Eddie Taylor
Moore's BCA Hall of Fame induction, 1994

Utley Jim Puckett, "Champagne" Eddie Kelly, Ronnie Allen

WPBA champions Gerda Hofstatter and Allison Fisher, along with Alfie Taylor, salute their countries' flags. Iao Valley, Maui, HI

Eddie Taylor with Judi Taylor at his Hall of Fame induction. Kansas City, 1993

Judi Taylor, Minnesota Fats, Theresa Wanderone, Alf Taylor

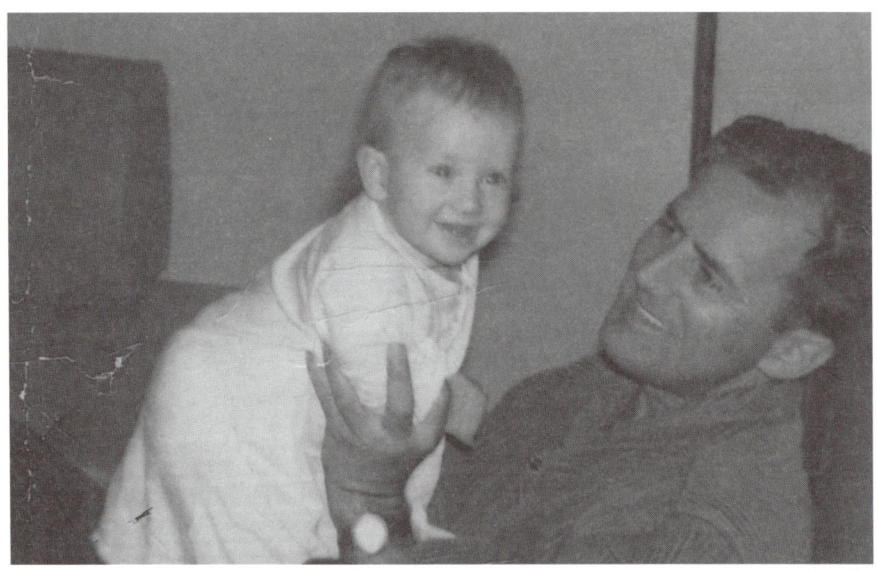

Jack Taylor with daughter Lisa Gem

"Titanic" Thompson with wife Jeanette

WPBA super star Allison Fisher and Nova Sue Mills

Alf Taylor, H.O.F. champion Ewa "the Striking Viking" Laurance, Weenie Beanie, Jack Ta

"Handsome Danny" Jones and Eddie Taylor

Richie "Little Bulldog" Florence

THOSE SCARY HUSTLERS

Alfie "Bicycle Willie" Taylor and son Christopher

Chris the magician

IN THE MOTORHOME

Beverly "the Pool Widow" Taylor with son Chris

Alfie and Bev

THE TAYLORS AND STATONS, WORLD TRAVELING COMPANIONS

Bill and Norma, Alf and Judi, Princess Islands, Turkey

Bill and Alf at the Golden Temple, Kyoto, Japan

My pal, Eddie. Not only did he let me ride his coattail, he let me wear his coat, a Billiard Congress of America Hall of Fame blazer.

Professor William Porter. Contributing author and one-pocket specialist.

Allison "The Duchess of Doom" Fisher and Johnny "The Scorpion" Archer, 1997 W.P.A. World 9 Ball champions.

Eddie Taylor, Doug "The Terrell Kid" Taylor, back off the road.

"San Jose Dick" McMorran...World class one-pocket player.

MY BRIEF STINT IN POLITICS...
PHOTOGRAPHER FOR SENATOR BARRY GOLDWATER 1968

Roosevelt Lake, Arizona

Grand Canyon, Arizona

Front: Eddie, Alf, Fats, Red "Mr. Pool" Jones.
Back: "Machine Gun" Lou Butera and unknown.

The Taylors: Alf, Bev, Chris, Violet and Eddie take on Disneyworld 1971.

Judi and Alf Taylor with Ambassador Joseph Verner Reed.
United Nations Moroccan Exhibition – 1994

Alf and Joseph
Ambassador Reed's home, Greenwich, CT.